W9-ADM-557

Microsoft®
Excel 2000
QuickTorial®

 Patricia Murphy
St. Thomas Aquinas College
Sparkill, New York

VISIT US ON THE INTERNET
www.swep.com

South-Western Educational Publishing
an International Thomson Publishing company I(T)P®
www.thomson.com

Cincinnati • Albany, NY • Belmont, CA • Bonn • Boston • Detroit • Johannesburg • London • Madrid
Melbourne • Mexico City • New York • Paris • Singapore • Tokyo • Toronto • Washington

Managing Editor: Carol Volz
Project Manager: Dave Lafferty
Marketing Manager: Larry Qualls
Design Coordinator: Mike Broussard
Development and Production: Thompson Steele Production Services, Inc.

Copyright © 2000
by SOUTH-WESTERN EDUCATIONAL PUBLISHING
Cincinnati, Ohio
ALL RIGHTS RESERVED

ISBN: 0-538-68856-4, soft cover student book
ISBN: 0-538-68855-6, soft cover student book/Data CD-ROM pkg.
ISBN: 0-538-68853-X, spiral cover student book

1 2 3 4 5 6 7 8 DR 03 02 01 00 99

Printed in the United States of America

I(T)P®

South-Western Educational Publishing is a division of International Thomson Publishing, Inc. The ITP logo
is a registered trademark used herein under license by South-Western Educational Publishing.

The names of all commercially available software and other products mentioned herein are used for
identification purposes only and may be either trademarks, registered trademarks, and/or copyrights of
their respective owners. South-Western Education Publishing disclaims any affiliations, associations,
or connection with or sponsorship or endorsement by such owners.

Microsoft® and Windows® are registered trademarks of Microsoft Corporation.

Microsoft and the Office logo are either registered trademarks or trademarks of Microsoft Corporation in the
United States and/or other countries. South-Western Educational Publishing is an independent entity from
Microsoft Corporation and not affiliated with Microsoft Corporation in any manner. This text may be used
in assisting students to prepare for a Microsoft Office User Specialist exam (MOUS). Neither Microsoft
Corporation, its designated review company, nor South-Western Educational Publishing warrants that use
of this publication will ensure passing the relevant MOUS exam.

Open a Window to the Future!

With these (exciting new products) from South-Western!

Our exciting new **Microsoft Office 2000 QuickTorial®** books will provide everything needed to master this software. Other books include:

 NEW! **Microsoft® Word 2000 for Windows® QuickTorial** by Murphy
15+ hours of instruction for beginning through intermediate features
0-538-68849-1	Text, Soft Spiral Bound
0-538-68850-5	Text, Perfect Bound, packaged with Data CD-ROM
0-538-68851-3	Electronic Instructor Package (Manual and CD-ROM)
0-538-68939-0	Testing CD-ROM Package

 NEW! **Microsoft® Excel 2000 for Windows® QuickTorial** by Murphy
15+ hours of instruction for beginning through intermediate features
0-538-68853-X	Text, Soft Spiral Bound
0-538-68855-6	Text, Perfect Bound, packaged with Data CD-ROM
0-538-68854-8	Electronic Instructor Package (Manual and CD-ROM)
0-538-68939-0	Testing CD-ROM Package

 NEW! **Microsoft® Access 2000 for Windows® QuickTorial** by Murphy
15+ hours of instruction for beginning through intermediate features
0-538-68857-2	Text, Soft Spiral Bound
0-538-68858-0	Text, Perfect Bound, packaged with Data CD-ROM
0-538-68859-9	Electronic Instructor Package (Manual and CD-ROM)
0-538-68939-0	Testing CD-ROM Package

 NEW! **Microsoft® PowerPoint 2000 for Windows® QuickTorial** by Murphy
15+ hours of instruction for beginning through intermediate features
0-538-68861-0	Text, Soft Spiral Bound
0-538-68862-9	Text, Perfect Bound, packaged with Data CD-ROM
0-538-68863-7	Electronic Instructor Package (Manual and CD-ROM)
0-538-68939-0	Testing CD-ROM Package

 NEW! **Microsoft® Office 2000 for Windows®, Introductory Course** by Pasewark & Pasewark
75+ hours of instruction for beginning through intermediate features
0-538-68824-6	Text, Hard Spiral Bound

 NEW! **Microsoft® Office 2000 for Windows®, Advanced Course** by Cable, Morrison, & Skintik
75+ hours of instruction for intermediate through advanced features
0-538-68828-9	Text, Hard Spiral Bound

A new feature available for these products is the **Electronic Instructor**, which includes a printed Instructor's manual and a CD-ROM. The CD-ROM contains tests, lesson plans, all data and solutions files, SCANS correlations, portfolio analysis, scheduling, and more!

South-Western
Educational Publishing

Join Us On the Internet **http://www.swep.com**

APPROVED COURSEWARE

What Is Certification?

The logo on the cover of this book indicates that these materials are officially certified by Microsoft Corporation at the **Core** User Skill Level for Excel 2000. This certification is part of the **Microsoft Office User Specialist (MOUS)** program which validates your skills as knowledgeable of Microsoft Excel.

Why Is Getting Certified Important?

Upon completing the lessons in this book, you will be prepared to take a test that could qualify you a a **core** user of Microsoft Excel—which can benefit you in many areas. For example, you can show an employer that you have received certified training in Microsoft Excel 2000 or you can advance further in education or in your organization. Getting this certification makes you more competitive with the knowledge and skills that you possess. It is also personally satisfying to know that you have reached a skill level that is validates by Microsoft Corporation to help meet your personal and professional goals.

You can also be certified as an **expert** user of Microsoft Excel. The difference between expert and core users is the level of competency. Proficient users can perform a wide ranges or basic tasks. core users can do all those same tasks, plus more advanced tasks, such as special formatting and features.

Where Does Testing Take Place?

To be certified, you will need to take an exam from a third-party testing company called an **Authorization Certification Testing Center.** Call **800-933-4493** to find the location of the testing center nearest you. Learn more about the criteria for testing and what is involved. Tests are conducted at different dates throughout the calendar year.

South-Western Educational Publishing has developed an entire line of training materials suitable for Microsoft Office certification. To learn more, contact your South-Western Representative or call **800-824-5179**. Also, visit our web site at **www.swep.com**.

WHAT'S NEW IN EXCEL 2000

Microsoft Excel 2000 includes the following new features:

■ Microsoft has improved the installation process in Excel 2000 so you get the program you need when you need it. The Detect and Repair command on the Help menu will reinstall files that are missing or corrupted. Your system administrator can configure your user profile to travel with you to make logging on and working from remote locations easy.

■ New basic features include improved File Open and File Save dialog boxes, the Office Clipboard, See-Through View, and the Euro currency symbol. There are new features that help you get Excel up and running. Four digit date formats are available, and the List AutoFill feature lets you automatically extend formatting and formulas in lists.

■ The new PivotChart report adds the power available in PivotTable reports to your charts. You can also make axis text shorter by changing the display unit when you chart values containing large numbers.

■ Web improvements include the ability to create and run queries to retrieve data on the Web, fast and easy ways of creating and customizing Web pages in Excel, the use of the Pivot Table list component for Web pages, improved management of files and their companion files, international text encoding, and new online collaboration features.

■ New PivotTable features let you lay out reports, directly on worksheets, use new indented formats, use AutoFormats, and hide or display items in fields.

■ In addition the improved Office Assistant uses less space on the screen, provides great *and often entertaining* help, and will take you to the Web for help it cannot provide.

START-UP CHECKLIST

HARDWARE

Minimum Configuration

✓ PC using 486 processor operating at 25 MHz 8 Mb RAM

✓ Hard disk with at least 30 Mb free disk space

✓ VGA monitor with graphics adaptor

✓ Mouse or tablet, and Printer

Recommended Configuration

✓ PC using 486 or Pentium processor operating at 66 MHz and 16 Mb RAM

✓ Hard disk with at least 91 Mb free disk space

✓ CD-ROM drive, 2x or faster

✓ VGA monitor with graphics adaptor

✓ Mouse or tablet, and Printer

SOFTWARE

✓ Microsoft Windows 95 or 98

✓ Microsoft Office 2000 or Microsoft Excel 2000

PREFACE

To the Learner

Excel 2000 is a database program and a component of the Microsoft Office 2000 suite. This book assumes that you have already learned to use your computer and that you have learned to use Windows, Microsoft's operating system for the personal computer. This book also assumes that Excel is installed on your computer and is set to work with your printer.

It is very important that you watch your screen carefully as you go through the exercises in this book. If you click press keys without understanding what is happening, you will miss a great deal. It is also important that you work through this book in the order presented. Each lesson builds on what you learned in previous lessons, so you may find yourself missing a lot if you skip through a lesson.

Every effort is made throughout this book to use Microsoft Excel terminology when working with the program to help you to access Help files. Once you work through this book, you will be able to use many of Excel's features to create professional-looking database objects quickly and easily. The first few times you use a feature, you may have to use this book or the Help system to refresh your memory about the steps involved. For features you seldom use, you might always need to use Help.

You can do as many or as few of the exercises at the end of the lesson as you like or are assigned in class. The exercises concentrate on the main points covered in the lesson and provide good practice.

Conventions Used in This Book

Each topic includes brief explanatory text on using the particular Excel feature and includes screen captures to help learners understand what should happen on their screens. Whenever a toolbar button is mentioned for the first time, the term is in boldface type and often the button is displayed nearby. Information useful to the learner but not appropriate in the explanatory text is entered in a Hot Tips, Important, Concepts Builder, Did You Know?, Teamwork, Extra Challenges, Note and Internet boxes. Terms that appear in the Glossary are shown in boldface type in the text.

The Step-by-Step exercise that follows each small group of topics allows the learner to use the features just covered. The numbered steps in the exercises begin by telling the learner what is to be accomplished in that step.

Menus, commands, file names, and toolbar buttons the learner is to click during the exercises, and short entries the learner is to type are shown in boldface type.

When more than one key is to be pressed at one time, the learner will be asked to hold one key and press the second.

The word *mouse* is used to refer to any pointing device learners may be using (IntelliMouse, trackball, pen, etc.). You will use the mouse rather than keystrokes whenever possible to accomplish tasks. You should know the following mouse definitions:

- *Point* means to move the mouse until the pointer is in the appropriate position on the screen.

- *Click* means to press the left mouse button with a quick motion. Always click the left mouse button unless you are directed to click another button.

- *Double-click* means to click twice without hesitating between clicks.

- *Drag* means to hold down the mouse button while you are moving the mouse.

About the Author

Pat Murphy has been teaching computer applications in corporate and educational environments since 1980. Pat was teaching at The Berkeley College in New Jersey when she founded Abbott Institute in 1982. She was president until she sold Abbott in 1994. Pat has been developing, licensing, and delivering end-user computer training for major corporations and colleges for all those years. She has often been a featured speaker at national and regional conferences. South-Western Educational Publishing Company has now published 22 of her books.

Acknowledgments

Thanks to Dave Lafferty and Carol Volz at South-Western for their support throughout the Office project. Thanks to Elinor Stapleton and Thompson Steele Production Services for their editorial input and for the book's production.

Once again, I must thank my husband, Mike, my children, Michael, Patti and Mark Schuette, and Kathleen, my mother, Lily Hough, my sister, Mary O'Callaghan, and many other relatives and friends who have been supportive throughout. A big thank you to the community that is St. Thomas Aquinas College for making so much of what I'm doing possible. Thanks also to Larry Luing and The Berkeley College where I was teaching when first introduced to computers.

The biggest thank you of all, however, goes to Abbott Institute's corporate clients—at among others, Exxon, Warner-Lambert, RJR Nabisco, Morgan Bank, and Olsten Services—whose insistence on top-quality end-user training shaped my ability to develop instructional materials for computer applications.

Patricia Murphy
St. Thomas Aquinas College, Sparkill, New York

How to Use this Book

What makes a good applications text? Sound instruction and the most current, complete materials. That is what you will find in *Microsoft Excel 2000, Quicktorial.* Not only will you find a colorful, inviting layout, but also many features to enhance learning.

Microsoft Office Certification– This icon is shown wherever a criteria for Microsoft Office User Specialist (MOUS) certification is covered in the lesson. A correlation table with page numbers is provided in the Electronic Instructor.

SCANS– (Secretary's Commission on Achieving Necessary Skills)– The U.S. Department of Labor has identified the school-to-careers competencies. The five workplace competencies and foundation skills are identified in the exercises throughout the text.

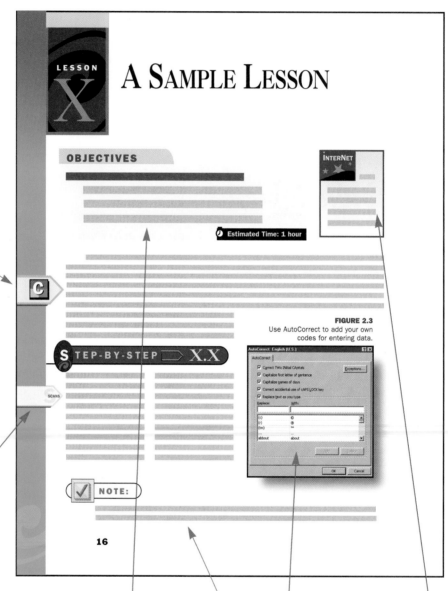

LESSON X

A SAMPLE LESSON

OBJECTIVES

Estimated Time: 1 hour

INTERNET

FIGURE 2.3
Use AutoCorrect to add your own codes for entering data.

STEP-BY-STEP X.X

NOTE:

16

Objectives– Objectives are listed at the beginning of each lesson, along with a suggested time for completion of the lesson. This allows you to look ahead to what you will be learning and to pace your work.

Notes– These boxes provide necessary information to assist you in completing the exercises.

Enhanced Screen Shots– Screen shots now come to life on each page with color and depth.

Internet– Internet terminology and useful Internet information is provided in these boxes located throughout the text.

How to Use this Book

Important– These boxes provide important information about Excel.

Marginal boxes– These boxes provide additional information for Hot Tips, fun facts (Did You Know?), Concept Builders, interesting Web sites, Extra Challenges activities, and Teamwork ideas.

Tables– These may appear in a lesson to help clarify and/or summarize key ideas and application functions.

Summary– At the end of each lesson you will find a summary to prepare you to complete the end-of-lesson activities.

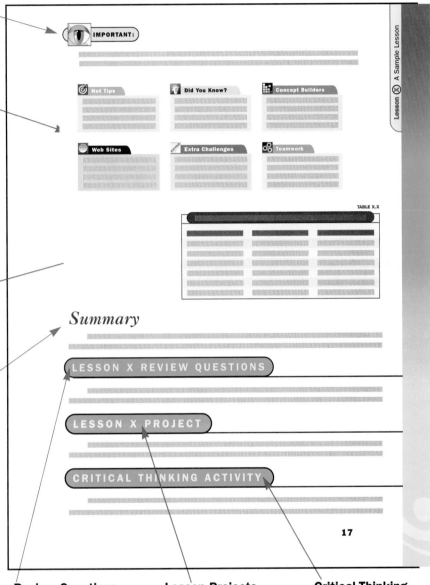

IMPORTANT:

Hot Tips

Did You Know?

Concept Builders

Web Sites

Extra Challenges

Teamwork

TABLE X.X

Summary

LESSON X REVIEW QUESTIONS

LESSON X PROJECT

CRITICAL THINKING ACTIVITY

17

Review Questions– Review material at the end of each lesson enables you to prepare for assessment of the content presented.

Lesson Projects– End-of-lesson hands-on application of what has been learned in the lesson allows you to actually apply the techniques covered.

Critical Thinking Activity– Each lesson gives you an opportunity to apply creative analysis to situations presented.

TABLE OF CONTENTS

GETTING STARTED WITH EXCEL

LESSON 1   UNDERSTANDING WORKBOOK BASICS

LESSON 2   USING FORMULAS AND FUNCTIONS

LESSON 3   CREATING, PRINTING, AND DISTRIBUTING WORKSHEETS

EXPLORING EXCEL'S DATA ANALYSIS AND OTHER TOOLS

LESSON 9

GETTING STARTED WITH EXCEL

Introduction

Excel 2000 is a spreadsheet application that you can use with the Windows 95 or later operating system or Windows NT 3.51 Service Pack 5 or later. You can use Excel 2000 on its own or as part of the Microsoft Office 2000 suite of applications.

A **spreadsheet** is a grid in which you can enter, calculate, and manage data. In the past, spreadsheets were created by entering data by hand on ledger paper. When calculators came along, calculating was easier but results were still entered by hand.

Today, however, advanced spreadsheet programs like Excel make it easy to manage numeric information, to create charts, and to maintain data lists. If you are using Excel with other Microsoft Office applications, you can use information or graphics from Word (word processing), PowerPoint (presentation package), and Access database files as well as from non-Microsoft applications in your Excel workbook. You can use the hyperlink feature to create links to other files.

In this lesson you will reset your Excel software to match the default settings used in this book and learn the basics to get started using spreadsheet features.

Starting Excel

The large area you see when you start Windows is the **desktop.** To start Excel, use the Start button on the Windows taskbar, choose Programs, and then choose Microsoft Excel on the Programs submenu (see Figure GS.1). If you are using Excel as part of the Microsoft Office 2000 suite, you can also use the Microsoft Excel button on the Office Shortcut bar (see Figure GS.1).

Hot Tips

There are many other ways of opening new or existing Excel documents, but we will work with the two mentioned.

FIGURE GS.1
Click on one of the areas marked Microsoft Excel to start Excel.

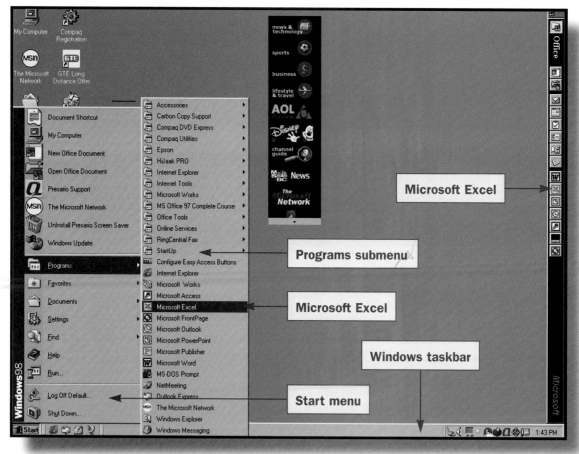

Identifying the Parts of the Excel Screen

An Excel spreadsheet is referred to as a **worksheet,** and an Excel file is called a **workbook.** A workbook can contain many worksheets.

When you open a new Excel workbook, you see a screen similar to Figure GS.2. If you've used any Windows application, you'll notice that the Excel screen has many of the same components you see in other Windows applications. There are many common elements in Windows programs that make it easy for users to learn new applications.

FIGURE GS.2
Parts of the Excel screen.

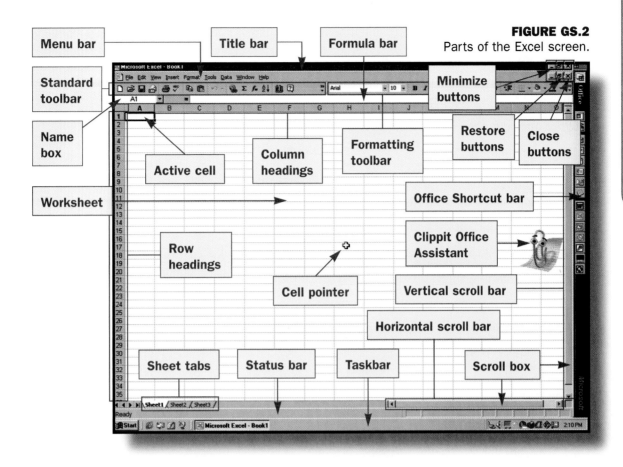

- *Title bar*—shows the name of the application and the workbook in use.

- *Maximize button*—use to enlarge the window to fill the screen.

- *Minimize button*—use to reduce the window to a button on the taskbar.

- *Restore button*—use to return a maximized window to its previous size.

- *Close button*—closes the window.

- *Mouse pointer*—changes according to what you are doing at the moment. You click the cell pointer in Figure GS.2 to activate a cell. You control movement of the mouse pointer with the mouse.

- *Menu bar*—shows the names of drop-down menus.

- *Scroll bars*—let you click above or below or to the left or right of the scroll box to move a full screen up, down, left, or right.

- *Scroll boxes*—let you move to a position by dragging the scroll box until Excel displays the part of the worksheet you want to see.

- *Status bar*—displays information about current settings.

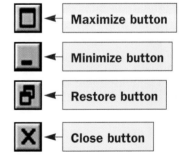

Hot Tips

Notice you sometimes have size/close controls for both the application and the open document.

3

- *Standard toolbar*—contains shortcut buttons for commonly used menu commands.

- *Formatting toolbar*—contains shortcut buttons for commonly used formatting commands.

- *Taskbar*—displays the Start button and buttons representing open applications and files so you can easily access other applications.

- *Office Shortcut bar*—lets you quickly switch between Office applications.

- *Office Assistant*—offers tips and lets you ask questions about using Excel features.

- *Worksheet*—where you enter and edit data.

- *Active cell*—cell with a dark border that is ready for data to be entered or edited.

- *Name box*—identifies the name of the active cell.

- *Formula bar*—displays the data or the formula entered in a cell.

- *Column headings*—letters that identify each of the 256 columns on the worksheet.

- *Row headings*—numbers that identify each of the 65,536 rows on the worksheet.

- *Sheet tabs*—display the names of the sheets in the workbook.

NOTE:

You will learn later in this lesson how to remove the Office Assistant from the display.

Exiting from Excel

You can exit from and close the Excel application by clicking the Close button on the title bar or by choosing the Exit command on the File menu.

When you exit from the Excel program, Excel prompts you to save any unsaved changes in workbooks and closes open workbooks. You will learn to save workbooks later in this lesson.

IMPORTANT:

You should always exit from open applications before using the Shut Down command on the Windows Start menu to turn off your computer.

STEP-BY-STEP ⟹ GS.1

1. To start Excel, click the **Start** button, click **Programs,** and click **Microsoft Excel** on the submenu.

2. To familiarize yourself with the names of various parts of the Excel window, carefully look over your screen and Figure GS.2 with the parts of the Excel window identified.

Your Excel window may not look exactly like the one shown in Figure GS.2.

3. To exit from Excel, click the application **Close** button on the title bar.

4. To start Excel again, click the **Start** button, click **Programs,** and click **Microsoft Excel.**

Working with Menus and Dialog Boxes

You use menu commands and dialog boxes to let Excel know how you would like to work with the program.

Using Menus

Drop-down **menus** display commands (see Figure GS.3). You click the menu name on the menu bar to see its commands.

Excel displays collapsed forms of menus when you first click the menu (see Figure GS.3). After a short delay, or by clicking the Expand button at the bottom of the menu or double-clicking the menu, the entire menu appears (see Figure GS.4). Only the most often or recently used commands appear initially.

When there is no possibility of using a command, the command is not available and Excel dims it. In Figure GS.4, for example, Excel knows that nothing has been cut or copied that can be pasted as a hyperlink, so the Paste as Hyperlink command is dimmed.

You can close a menu without selecting a command by clicking on a blank part of the workbook window or by pressing the Esc (escape) key twice.

FIGURE GS.4
Menus contain related groups of commands and Excel adjusts them to coincide with the work you do.

FIGURE GS.3

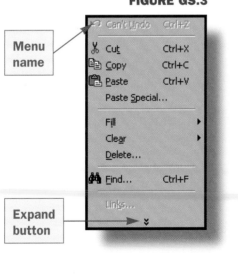

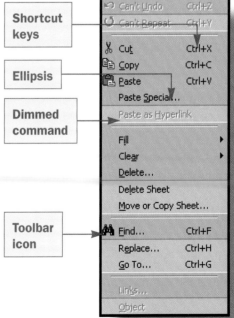

5

Some menu commands have **shortcut keys** displayed to the right of the command name. They are keystrokes you can use instead of opening the menu with the mouse (see Figure GS.4). If you find you often use a command and would prefer to use keystrokes, check the menu to see if the command has shortcut keys. You will not use them in this book.

Some commands such as Find (see Figure GS.4) display icons to the left of the command. These icons may also appear on buttons on the toolbars. You will use toolbar buttons whenever possible in the exercises in this book.

If a menu command has a right-pointing arrow to its right, Excel will display a **submenu** with additional choices when you choose the command. (See the Toolbars command in Figure GS.5.) To select a command from a submenu, just click the command.

Some menu commands display check marks to the left of the command (see Figure GS.5). If the check mark is displayed, these commands are turned on. You can toggle them on or off by clicking them or sometimes by making another selection.

When you select a command that has an **ellipsis** (…) after it (see Figure GS.5), you will see a dialog box. The Print dialog box (see Figure GS.6), is where you enter additional information that's needed to carry out the command.

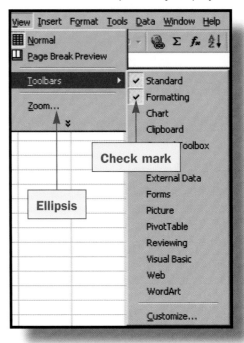

Using Dialog Boxes

Excel displays a **dialog box** when it needs more information to carry out a command. Table GS.1 describes how to work with various parts of dialog boxes.

Dialog boxes also contain **command buttons** (see Figure GS.6). The command buttons you will see most often are used to carry out choices you make in the dialog boxes, and Close or Cancel to close a dialog box without making changes.

TABLE GS.1

SELECTING OPTIONS IN DIALOG BOXES	
TO SELECT	**CLICK**
A tab in a dialog box	Tab name
Or clear options in round option buttons or in check boxes	The button or the box
A number in a spin box	The up or down arrow until the number you want appears
An item in a drop-down list	The down arrow to display the list and click the item you want
An icon option	The icon

6

When you want to see a brief explanation for a part of a dialog box, click the Help button (your mouse pointer will have a ?) and click on the item to display a ScreenTip. ScreenTips are available for commands, various parts of dialog boxes, and other screen areas (see Figure GS.7).

Many frequently used commands are also available on **shortcut menus** such as the one shown in Figure GS.8. Shortcut menus are function-specific. That is, the shortcut menu displays commands that are frequently used at the location where you access them. To display a shortcut menu, simply point at the area with which you want to work and click the *right* mouse button.

FIGURE GS.6

Excel displays a dialog box when it needs more information. The Print dialog box appears when you choose the Print command.

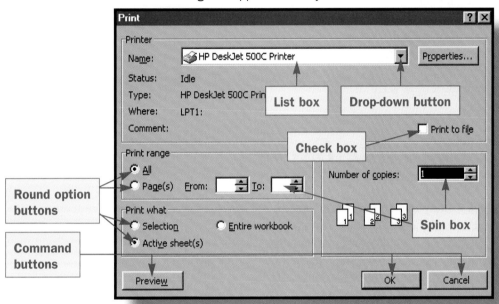

FIGURE GS.7

You can see a ScreenTip explaining an option in a dialog box.

FIGURE GS.8

A shortcut menu appears when you right-click in the active cell in a blank workbook.

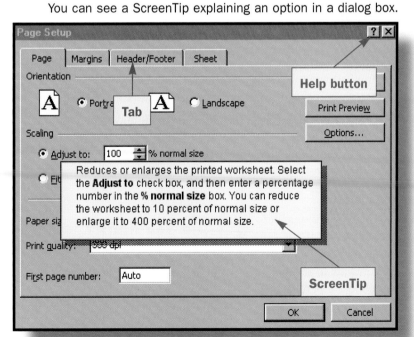

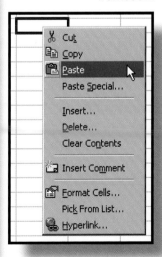

7

1. To open the File menu, click **File** on the menu bar.

2. To close the menu without making a selection, click a blank cell in the worksheet. When you click on a cell, you activate that cell and a black border appears around it.

3. To display a dialog box, click the **File** menu and then click **Print**.

4. To display information about the **Properties** button area, click the **Help** button at the top right of the dialog box and then click on the **Properties** button.

5. To close the ScreenTip and the dialog box, click the **Cancel** command button.

Customizing Excel

Because Excel makes it easy to set up the program to suit your own needs, your screens may not look exactly like the ones shown in this book. Whenever you start Excel, it opens with the settings that were used during the last session.

If others are using your computer, you may have to change these settings each time you start a lesson so that your display matches the one used in this book. Even if your screen display matches, you should go through the exercises that follow so you become familiar with the various options and commands available to you.

Using the Full Screen Command

If the last user turned on the Full Screen command on the View menu, you may not see the title bar, toolbars, scroll bars, or status bar on your screen. The Full Screen command lets you display as much as possible of your worksheet without the other parts of the window that are usually displayed.

If you do not see anything but your workbook and a Close Full Screen button, you can click the Close Full Screen button to return to the previous view.

Maximizing Your Windows

When you start Excel the first time, the Excel window does not fill the screen. Also, if Excel used less than the full screen to display workbooks during the last session, you may have to click the Maximize button for both the application and workbook windows. When a window is already maximized, Excel displays the Restore button.

Using the Zoom Command

You can use the Zoom command on the View menu to open the Zoom dialog box (see Figure GS.9) to set greater or lesser degrees of magnification on your screen. Choose 75% rather than 100% when you want to see more of your worksheet data on the screen; choose a percentage higher than 100% to "zoom in" on a portion of the work-sheet. The Fit selection option resizes the selected cells to

 Did You Know?

Your Windows Screen area setting can also affect how much of the worksheet your screen displays.

fit within the current window. The Custom option lets you enter a specific degree of magnification.

If the last user changed the Zoom settings and did not return to the 100% view, your workbook may appear to be smaller or larger than those in the figures in this book.

Using the View Menu

When you start Excel for the first time, the formula bar and the status bar are turned on. If they are not displayed, use the Formula bar and status bar commands on the expanded View menu to toggle them on.

Using the Toolbars

As you already learned, you can click a toolbar button to use a menu command without having to open the menu. Toolbars contain buttons for commonly used commands. When you position the mouse pointer on a toolbar button, a ScreenTip appears that identifies the button.

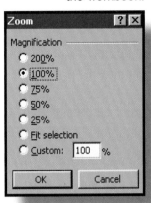

FIGURE GS.9
The Zoom dialog box displays magnification options for viewing the workbook.

By default, the Standard and Formatting toolbars are displayed when you start Excel. Those toolbars contain buttons for the commands used most often in Excel. They may be docked side-by-side on the toolbar.

When you click on the More Buttons drop-down arrow at the right of each docked toolbar, the Add or Remove Buttons command appears and displays other buttons and lets you add or remove buttons. Each button that appears on the toolbar is checked on the Add or Remove Buttons submenu. To add or remove a button, check or uncheck the button's name.

To move any toolbar, point to the vertical bar on the left or top side of the toolbar and drag when the move pointer appears. To create a floating toolbar, drag the toolbar to a position other than at an edge of the program window.

You saw earlier in the lesson the Toolbars command's list of toolbars available to you. You will sometimes see other toolbars on your screen because Excel displays toolbars appropriate for the Excel features with which you are working.

Use the Toolbars command on the View menu to display the list of Excel's toolbars (see Figure GS.10). The Standard and Formatting toolbars should have check marks on the submenu. A check mark beside a toolbar indicates that it is currently displayed. To turn off a toolbar that is displayed, open the toolbar submenu and click the toolbar name.

You will learn to use the various buttons and toolbars throughout this course.

FIGURE GS.10
Use the Toolbars submenu to turn toolbars on or off.

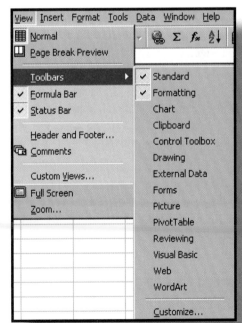

NOTE:

You can right-click on the menu bar to display the toolbar submenu.

You can customize toolbars to display buttons for commands you most often need.

Using the Customize Command

You can use the Customize command on the Tools menu to customize toolbars and menus. If you find your toolbars are different from the ones used in this book, you may be able to return to the original settings with the Reset button.

Hot Tips

You can even assign a hyperlink to a toolbar button or a menu command. You will learn more about hyperlinks later in this lesson.

STEP-BY-STEP ⟹ GS.3

C

1. To return to a different view if your screen is in Full Screen view, click the **Close Full Screen** button in the center of the worksheet.

2. To maximize your display if your Excel window and workbook do not fill the entire screen, look for any Maximize buttons and click them.

3. To check the settings in the Zoom dialog box, click the **View** menu and click **Zoom.** If 100% is not selected, select it. Then click the **OK** command button. If 100% is selected when the Zoom dialog box opens, you can click **OK** or **Cancel.**

4. To display the formula bar if it is not already displayed, click the **View** menu, click the **Expand** button if needed, and click **Formula**

Bar. Remember, if the Formula Bar command is checked, it is turned on. If you click it again, you will turn it off. Click on a blank cell in the worksheet instead to close the menu.

5. To display the status bar if it is not already displayed, click the **View** menu and click **status bar.**

6. To display the **Standard** and **Formatting** toolbars, click the **View** menu and point to **Toolbars.** If you do not see check marks next to both Standard and Formatting, click the one that does not have a check mark. You may have to click the **View** menu again, point to **Toolbars,** and click the second one if both were turned off. If you see check marks next to any other toolbar names, repeat the procedure to turn them off.

Using the Options Command

The Options command on the Tools menu lets you change the default settings for many of Excel's features.

You will use the Options command to match your system's setup to the default one used in this book. Many of the selections in the Options dialog boxes will be covered in later lessons.

In the following exercise you will look at each of the tabs in the Options dialog box to be sure the settings match those in Figures GS.11 through GS.18.

STEP-BY-STEP ▷ GS.4

1. To display the Options dialog box, click the **Tools** menu and click **Options.**

2. To check the settings on the **View** tab, compare them to those in Figure GS.11 and make any necessary changes. Do not click **OK,** yet.

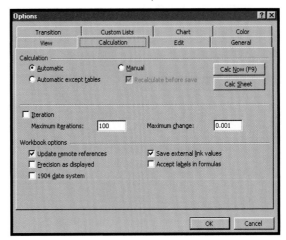

FIGURE GS.11
View options affect how Excel displays your workbook.

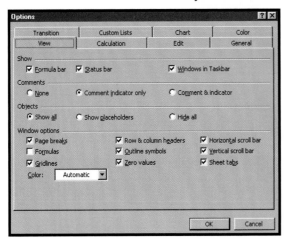

3. To check the settings on the Calculation tab, click the **Calculation** tab, compare the settings to those in Figure GS.12 and make any necessary changes.

4. To check the settings on the Edit tab, click the **Edit** tab, compare the settings to those in Figure GS.13, and make any necessary changes. If you find you are accidentally moving cells when **Allow cell drag and drop** is turned on, you can turn it off.

 **Hot Tips**

Change the Direction drop-down option to Right on the Edit tab if you find you want to move right most often.

FIGURE GS.13
Edit options affect how you enter and edit data.

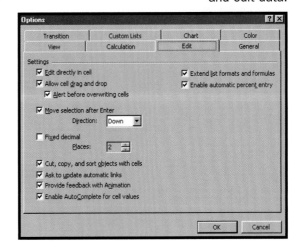

5. To check the settings on the General tab, click the **General** tab, compare the settings to those in Figure GS.14, and make any necessary changes. If your instructor followed the directions for using this book, your files should be in a folder with your name. Otherwise, check with your instructor for the proper file location and User name.

(continued on next page)

FIGURE GS.14

General options cover miscellaneous settings.

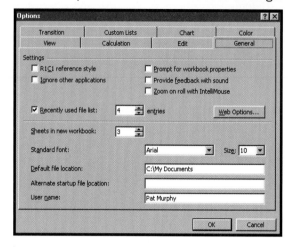

7. To check the settings on the Custom Lists tab, click the **Custom Lists** tab, compare the settings to those in Figure GS.16. If there are other lists in the box, someone else may have added them, and you should not change them.

FIGURE GS.16

Custom Lists options aid in entering repetitive data.

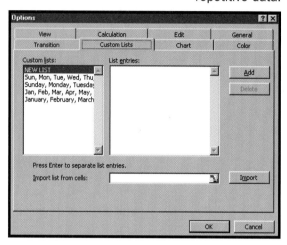

Hot Tips

Do not use drive A to work on Excel files. Workbook files must be on a hard drive.

6. To check the settings on the Transition tab, click the **Transition** tab, compare the settings to those in Figure GS.15, and make any necessary changes.

FIGURE GS.15

Transition options let you specify the file format for your files.

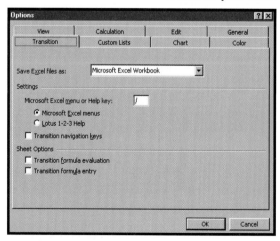

8. To check the settings on the Chart tab, click the **Chart** tab, compare the settings to those in Figure GS.17 and make any necessary changes.

FIGURE GS.17

Chart options control some chart settings.

9. To check the settings on the Color tab, click the **Color** tab, compare the settings to those in Figure GS.18. You should not attempt to make changes here.

10. To carry out any changes you made and close the dialog box, click **OK**.

Getting Help with Excel

There are several different ways you can use Excel's Help system to get information about working with any of the Excel features or dialog boxes.

The Office Assistant

The Microsoft Excel **Office Assistant** can answer questions and provide tips on easier or quicker ways of accomplishing tasks (see Figure GS.19). The Assistant displays suggested help for tasks you are performing and sometimes a yellow light bulb to let you know there is a tip for using the features or shortcuts effectively. Click the yellow light bulb to see a tip.

By default, the Clippit Office Assistant is turned on when you begin to use Excel. To turn off the Assistant, click the Office Assistant to display the dialog balloon, click the Options button in the Assistant's balloon and remove the check mark from Use the Office Assistant on the Options tab, then click OK (see Figure GS.20). You can turn the Assistant on again by clicking the Help menu and clicking Show the Office Assistant.

NOTE:

We will turn the Office Assistant off for the exercises in this book so you will have one fewer of us competing for your attention. When you are working in Excel on your own, however, the Office Assistant can be very useful.

You can display the Gallery tab (see Figure GS.21) in the same Office Assistant dialog box. Then use the Back and Next buttons to scroll through the different assistants available for you.

What would you like to do?

- Change the way data is plotted
- Check spelling or automatically correct spelling errors
- Default sort orders
- Sort a list
- Troubleshoot correcting spelling and typing errors

▼ See more...

Type your question here, and then click Search.

Options   Search

NOTE:

The Office Assistant is shared by all Microsoft Office programs. If you change any Assistant options in one program, you may affect the Assistant throughout all the Office applications.

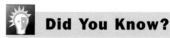

Did You Know?

The Office Assistant can be quite entertaining. Watch its antics.

FIGURE GS.20

The Options tab allows users to turn off the Use the Office Assistant feature.

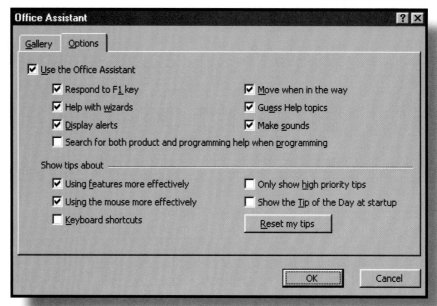

FIGURE GS.21

The Dot is another of the Assistants you can designate.

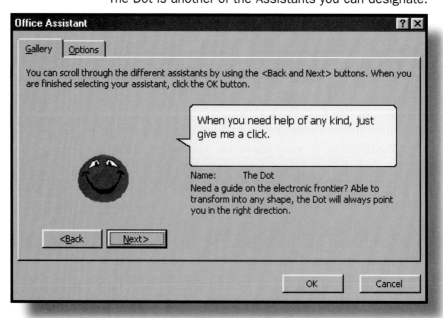

Using Hyperlinks

A **hyperlink** is a shortcut to a document that can be stored on your hard drive, a network server, or the Internet. To follow a hyperlink to its document, point to the hyperlink. When your mouse pointer changes to a hand, click it.

Hyperlinks are underlined. By default, those that have not been clicked are blue and those that have been clicked and followed are purple.

Hot Tips

Graphics can also be used for hyperlinks.

The Help Menu

Microsoft Excel's Help menu contains the following commands (remember to use the Expand button if needed):

■ *Microsoft Excel Help* displays the Office Assistant and its balloon if the Assistant is turned on but not displayed. If the Assistant is already displayed, clicking the command displays the Assistant's balloon. If the Assistant is turned off, Excel displays the Help window (see Figure GS.22).

Use the Contents tab (shown in Figure GS.22) on the Help window to display topics organized by category. To see a list of topics in a category, click the expand indicator (+) beside the folder icon. To see information about a topic, click it. To collapse the expanded category, click the collapse indicator (–).

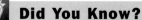

Did You Know?

If your Contents display shows only the letters A through Z, click the expand indicator to display topics.

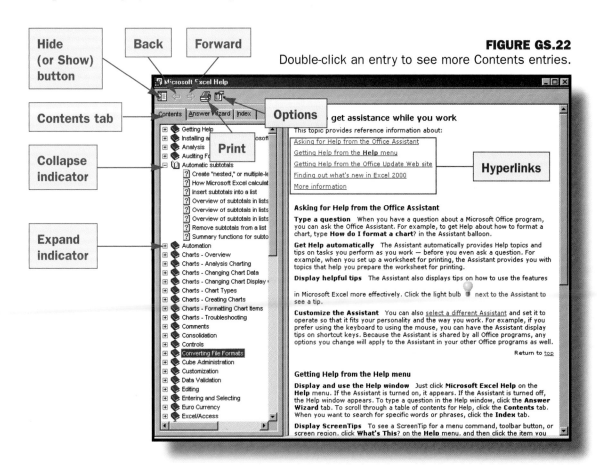

Hide (or Show) button
Back
Forward
Contents tab
Collapse indicator
Expand indicator
Print
Options
Hyperlinks

FIGURE GS.22
Double-click an entry to see more Contents entries.

NOTE:

To determine precisely when you want the Office Assistant to appear, use the Options tab in the Office Assistant window and select what kinds of tasks you want the Office Assistant to help you with.

Use the Index tab (see Figure GS.23) to type a topic you want to find or to scroll through the list of key words. To display information about an entry you typed, click the Search button. To display information about a keyword in the keyword list, click the keyword. Then click a topic in the bottom box to display information about it in the right pane.

Hot Tips

If the Contents, Answer Wizard, and Index tabs are not displayed, click the Show button (see Figure GS.22).

FIGURE GS.23
The Index tab is displayed.

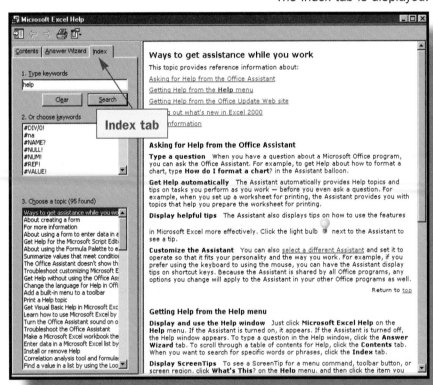

Use the Answer Wizard tab to pose a question (see Figure GS.24).

Concept Builders

On most Help screens, you can click the Print button to print a copy of the information.

FIGURE GS.24

The Answer Wizard tab is displayed.

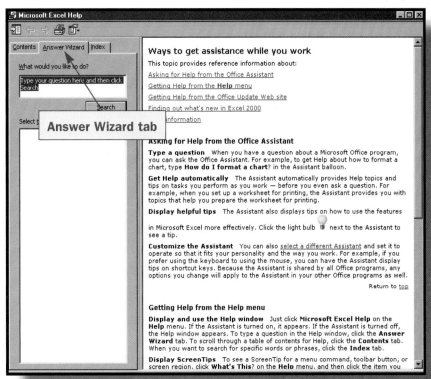

- *Show (or Hide) the Office Assistant* displays or removes the Office Assistant from the Window. This menu command does not turn off the Office Assistant. You must use the Options button in the Assistant's balloon to turn off the Assistant.

- *What's This?* adds a question mark to your mouse pointer. Then when you click something in the Excel window that you want help with, you will see a ScreenTip, a box that explains the item you clicked. To use the What's This? feature in a dialog box, click the Help button at the top right of the dialog box and then click an option you would like explained. A ScreenTip appears. To display a ScreenTip for a button on a toolbar, slide the mouse pointer across the button until a ScreenTip appears.

- *Office on the Web* takes you directly to the World Wide Web. You will learn more about the Web later in this lesson.

- *Detect and Repair* will find and fix errors in the application. You may need your Excel installation software (see Figure GS.25).

- *About Microsoft Excel* displays information about the license agreement for the Excel program, system information, and information about getting technical support.

INTERNET If the Assistant does not answer your question, you can click None of the above, look for more help on the Web to see suggestions on how to phrase a question or to narrow a search. You can even let Microsoft know the information you need to help them improve future versions of the software.

FIGURE GS.25
Excel displays this dialog box when you use
the Detect and Repair command.

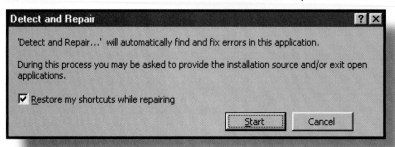

STEP-BY-STEP ⟹ **GS.5**

1. If you do not see the Office Assistant window on your display, click the **Help** menu and then click **Show the Office Assistant.**

2. To find out how to get help while your work, type **How can I get help while I work** in the bubble's text box and then click the bubble's **Search** button.

3. To display the **Ways to get assistance while you work** topic, click its blue button. Notice the hyperlinks (underlined) topics at the top of the window.

4. To move to the **Finding out what's new in Excel** topic without scrolling down through the other information, point to the hyperlink and when the hand appears click the hyperlink. Notice the list of hyperlinks in the **What's New in Microsoft Excel 2000** help screen.

5. To follow the hyperlink to the Basic features, click the *Basic features* hyperlink. Notice the list of new basic features.

6. To return to the previous screen, click the **Back** button at the top of the Help window.

Hot Tips

Remember to slide your mouse pointer across buttons to see a ScreenTip if you are not sure which one to use.

7. To display the Contents, Answer Wizard, and Index tabs, click the **Show** button at the top of the Help window.

8. To display the Excel Help topics in table of contents format, click the **Contents** tab.

9. To display subtopics on the Getting Help topic, click the (+) expand indicator to the left of **Getting Help.**

10. To get help with printing a Help topic, click *Print a Help topic.* Notice the information in the pane to the right.

Did You Know?

To see more of a Topic's text, you can move the pointer to the divider between the left and right panes until the pointer turns to a double-headed arrow and then drag the divider left to resize the pane.

11. To print the topic, click the **Print** button at the top of the window.

12. To display the Index tab, click the **Index** tab.

13. To enter a keyword for a search for getting help, type **help,** click the **Search** button. Notice the list of topics at the bottom of the pane, and click *Ways to get assistance while you work.*

14. To close Microsoft Excel Help, click its **Close** button.

15. To find out what the button that looks like a scissors represents, click the **Help** menu. Click **What's This?**. Notice the question mark attached to the mouse pointer. Click the **scissors** button and read the information in the ScreenTip.

16. To remove the ScreenTip, click anywhere in blank space.

17. To turn off the Office Assistant, click it, click **Options,** click the **Use the Office Assistant** check box, and click **OK.**

Using the Internet and the World Wide Web

Excel 2000 has many features you can use to take advantage of the Internet and the World Wide Web. The **Internet** is a global network of computers that use a common language to communicate. The **World Wide Web** provides a graphical, easy-to-use interface for looking at documents on the Internet.

NOTE:

You must have a connection through a modem or server to an Internet service provider (ISP) to reach the Internet.

Simply put, the Web is like a library on the Internet. Web sites are like books in the library, and pages are like specific pages in a book. The starting page for a Web site—the equivalent of a table of contents—is called a **home page.**

Each page on the Web has an address called a **Universal Resource Locator (URL).** The home-page address for Microsoft, for instance, is http://www.microsoft.com.

You can click URL hyperlinks to jump from one page to another. Hyperlinks have Web addresses embedded in them. You can easily identify a hyperlink because its text is a different color from the rest of the text in the site. Hyperlinks may also be underlined or bordered to stand out. Graphics can also be used for hyperlinks. You will usually be asked to click on a graphic to move to another Web page.

When you follow hyperlinks to access different Web pages, you are *surfing* the Web.

When you finish working on the Internet through an ISP, be sure to close the application and disconnect from the service provider. Remember you are paying service provider charges and may also be paying long-distance

Concept Builders

Remember the Web is changing by the minute, and Web pages must change to keep up with the latest needs. You will very often find new and different information at a particular site.

telephone charges. You may also be preventing others from accessing the Internet if you leave your connection open when you are not using it.

In the next exercise, you will use the Office on the Web command on the Microsoft on the Web Help command to see how easily you can access and move around on the Web. You will continue learning about and working on the Web throughout this book.

STEP-BY-STEP ⟹ GS.6

SCANS

1. To use the Microsoft on the Web command to learn some Web fundamentals, click the **Help** menu, click **Office on the Web,** and if necessary enter a user ID and password to connect to the Internet.

2. To familiarize yourself with the Web site, click some hyperlinks to follow items of interest.

3. To print a page, click the **Print** button on the Web browser toolbar.

4. To exit from the Web, click the **Close** button. If you see a dialog box asking whether you want to disconnect, respond that you do.

Managing Documents and Files

Before you can effectively work with Excel, you must know how to create, open, save, and close workbooks. Workbooks are also referred to as documents or files.

Creating Workbooks

You have already seen that when you start Excel, you see a new workbook on the screen. The new workbook is the equivalent of a blank pad of ledger paper where you can begin entering your data. Each workbook you create has by default three worksheets. You can add many more sheets to the workbook and will learn more about that later in the book.

The first workbook of any Excel session is called Book1. Each new workbook you open during a session will have a consecutive number. You can have as many workbooks open at one time as the memory in your system allows. That means you can work with more than one workbook at a time. Each open workbook will have its own button on the Windows taskbar so you can easily move from one to another.

To create a new workbook during an Excel session, you can either use the New button on the toolbar or open the File menu and choose the New command.

New button

✓ NOTE:

To create a workbook based on one of Excel's templates, use the New command on the File menu and display the Spreadsheet Solutions tab.

Opening Existing Workbooks

Use the Open button or the Open command on the File menu to display the Open dialog box (see Figure GS.26). You can use the Open dialog box to open existing workbooks on your hard disk, on a floppy drive, on a network drive to which you are connected, on your company's intranet, or on the Internet.

Open button

FIGURE GS.26
Manage files in the Open dialog box.

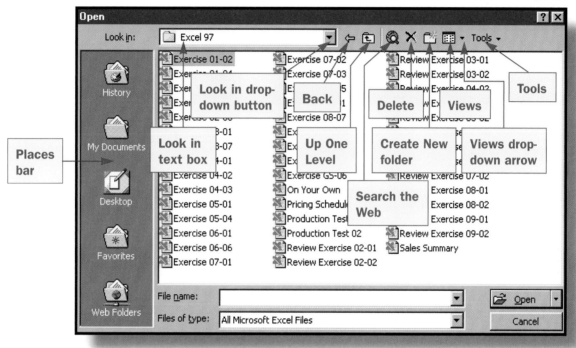

You can use the Open dialog box to manage your files. Use the Places bar (see Figure GS.26) to quickly display the folders and locations you use most often.

NOTE:

The names of the last four workbooks opened appear at the bottom of the File menu.

History button displays the last 20 to 50 Excel workbooks or folders with which you've worked.

My Documents button displays all files and folders in the My Documents folder which is the default folder for storing Excel files.

Desktop button displays files and folders on the Windows desktop.

Favorites button contains shortcuts to workbooks you use frequently. The actual file remains in its original folder, but you can open it quickly without having to remember where it is located.

Concept Builders

Deleted files stay in the Recycle Bin until you empty it. To empty the Recycle Bin, double-click its icon on the desktop, open the File menu and choose Empty Recycle Bin.

Web Folders button displays shortcuts to files and folders located on Web servers. You must have access to a Web server to use this feature. See your system administrator to see if there is a Web server to which you can connect.

The Open button's (lower right of Open dialog box) drop-down list lets you open a file for:

- All uses (Open)

- Read-Only (no changes can be saved)

- Open As Copy

- Open in Browser (see how your worksheet will look on the Web or on your intranet).

Hot Tips

Open a copy of a file when you want to keep the original file intact. Revise the copy.

Saving Workbooks

To save a workbook for the first time, use the Save button on the Standard toolbar or the Save or Save As command on the File menu. The Save As dialog box then appears (see Figure GS.27).

Save button

FIGURE GS.27
The Save As dialog box is where you make decisions about how Excel saves a document.

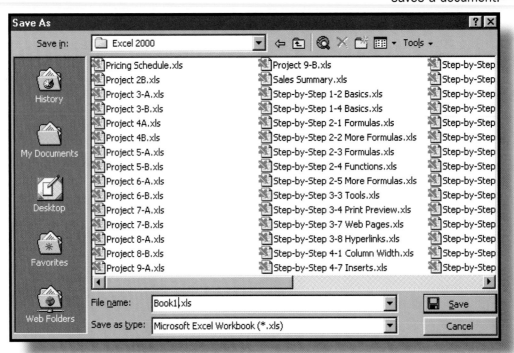

TABLE GS.2

You can see the purpose of each of the toolbar buttons at the top of the Open dialog box.

O P E N   D I A L O G   B O X   T O O L B A R

NAME	WHAT IT DOES
Look In Box	Text box contains the folder Excel is currently looking at
Back	Displays the name of the folder that was previously in the Look In box
Up One Level	Moves you one folder level higher in the folder hierarchy
Search the Web	Displays the sign-in dialog box or connects you to the World Wide Web
Delete	Deletes the selected file and sends it to the Recycle Bin
Create New Folder	Creates a subfolder in the current folder
Views	Drop-down button lets you display the names of files in large icon style; with additional information such as date last saved and file size; properties such as title and author for the selected file; a preview of the selected file
Tools	Contains additional commands for procedures such as printing or finding files

To save a new workbook, display the folder in which you want to place the document, type a file name in the File name box. Once you have saved the file, you can use the Save button or the Save command on the File menu to update it with your changes.

The Save as type drop-down list box lets you save a workbook in another format. The commands on the Tools button's drop-down menu on the Save As dialog box let you delete, rename, print, and add files to the Favorites folder. You can also set Web options and add passwords.

Concept Builders

You can create a new subfolder in the folder Excel is looking at in either the Open or Save As dialog box.

Closing Workbooks

To close a workbook, you can use its Close button or choose Exit on the File menu. Excel prompts you to save your work if any changes were made since the last save.

IMPORTANT:

It is wise to close workbooks as soon as you finish using them because they use memory when left open. Think of it as keeping the desktop neat.

2 3

Working with Multiple Workbooks

The Window menu lists all open Excel workbooks (Figure GS.28). A check mark signals the **active workbook**—the workbook on top. Select a workbook name on the Window menu to make that workbook active, or click the workbook's button on the windows taskbar.

The New Window command creates a second window in which you can see the active workbook. This feature lets you look at two or more parts of the same workbook at the same time. You will work with this feature later in the book.

You can use the Arrange command on the Window menu to display all of your open workbooks (see Figure GS.29). The workbook with the colored title bar is the active workbook. Any commands you select or data you enter will affect the active workbook. If you want to return to a window that displays only the active workbook, click on that workbook's Maximize button.

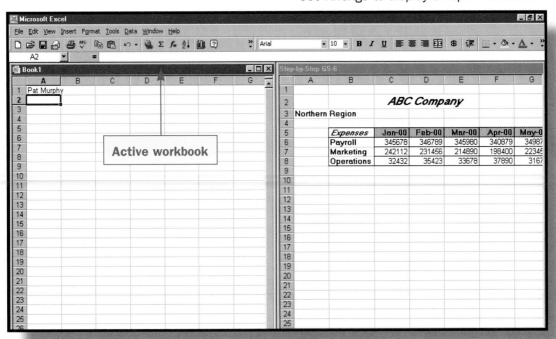

NOTE:

To arrange the windows of just the active workbook, not all open workbooks, first use the New Window command on the Window menu. Then use the Arrange command to choose how to display the windows, and be sure to put a check mark in the *Windows of active workbook* box.

Did You Know?

To save and close all open workbooks in one operation, hold the Shift key while clicking the File menu. Excel displays the Close All command. Then respond that you want to save changes to all workbooks.

S TEP-BY-STEP ▷ GS.7

1. To enter some text in the workbook on your screen, click any cell to make it the active cell, type *your name,* and press the **Enter** key.

2. To display the Open dialog box, click the **Open** button on the toolbar.

3. To display the files for this book, be sure the folder containing the files is the one displayed in the Look in box. If it is not the correct folder, click the buttons on the Places bar or the drop-down button in the Look in box, click the correct drive, and then double-click the correct folder.

4. To see the size and type of files and when they were last modified, click the Views button's drop-down button and click **Details.**

5. To see a preview of the Step-by-Step GS-7 file, click that file name, click the Views button's drop-down button, and then click **Preview.**

6. To return the display to list view, click the Views drop-down button and then click **List.**

7. To display the Favorites folder, click the **Favorites** button on the Places bar.

8. To return to the folder containing the files for this book, click the **Back** button.

9. To open the **Step-by-Step GS-7** file, double-click it.

10. To display the original workbook Excel created when you started the program, click the **Window** menu and click **Book1.**

11. To see both workbooks on the screen, click the **Window** menu, click **Arrange,** click **Tiled,** and click **OK.**

12. To see the properties information for the active file, click the **File** menu and click **Properties** (click the **Expand** button if needed). Click each of the tabs to see the kind of information available. Click **Cancel.**

13. To save Book1, click somewhere in that workbook to be sure it is active, click the **Save** button on the Standard toolbar, type **your initials** and **First,** be sure the Look in box contains the name of your folder for this book, and click the **Save** command button in the dialog box.

14. To close the document, be sure to click the **Close** button at the top right of its window.

15. To fill the screen with the Step-by-Step GS-7 window, click its **Maximize** button.

16. To close Excel and **Step-by-Step GS-7** without saving any changes, click Excel's **Close** button and click **No** if asked to save changes.

Summary

Y̲ou have now learned how to start Excel, customize the program to work with this book, work with the Excel window, use Excel's Help system, access the World Wide Web, open, save, and close workbooks, work with multiple workbooks, and exit from Excel.

Try the exercises on the following pages to test how well you remember what you learned. Don't be afraid to go back and look up the answers, because that will help to reinforce what you learned.

TRUE / FALSE

Circle the T if the statement is true. Circle the F if it is false.

T F 1. You can open only one Excel workbook at a time.

T F 2. You should leave workbooks open when you know you will not use them again during the Excel session.

T F 3. It is faster to use menu commands than to use toolbar buttons.

T F 4. The shortcut keys for many commands are listed on the menus.

T F 5. Excel opens with the settings used in the previous session.

T F 6. There is a Help button in most dialog boxes.

T F 7. You need a connection to a service provider to access the World Wide Web.

T F 8. The Office Assistant lets you type specific questions about tasks or features.

T F 9. More than one workbook can be active on your screen at the same time.

T F 10. You can print most of the Help topics that you access.

COMPLETION

Complete the following sentences by writing the correct word or words in the blanks provided.

1. You click the _____ button to close an application or a workbook.

2. You can use the _____ button to make your workbook fill the screen.

3. You can open the _____ menu to see a list of files that are open.

4. You open the _____ menu to choose the Exit command.

5. You can use the _____ command on the Window menu to display all of your open workbooks.

6. The part of a window that shows a workbook's name is the _____.

7. You can use the _____ at the bottom of the screen to switch from one open application or workbook to another.

8. Use the Look in box in the _____ dialog box to specify where to find a file.

9. Use the _____ dialog box to see a preview of a file.

10. To close a dialog box without selecting any of its options, click _____.

GETTING STARTED PROJECTS

PROJECT GS-A

Use the list below to identify each of the features of the Excel screen shown in Figure GS.30. Write the letter of the feature next to the number that identifies it on the figure.

____ 1.   a. Close button   ____ 8.   h. Restore button

____ 2.   b. scroll bars   ____ 9.   i. Taskbar

____ 3.   c. Standard toolbar   ____ 10.   j. worksheet

____ 4.   d. Office Shortcut bar   ____ 11.   k. Menu bar

____ 5.   e. Minimize button   ____ 12.   l. scroll box

____ 6.   f. Title bar   ____ 13.   m. Office Assistant

____ 7.   g. Status bar   ____ 14.   n. Formatting toolbar

FIGURE GS.30
Identify the various parts of the Excel window.

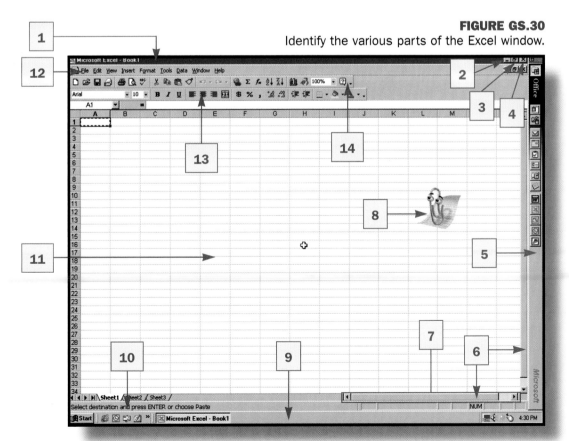

SCANS

Find out what Excel users most often want to know about Excel from Microsoft online. Use Excel's **Help** menu, the **Office on the Web** command, and then look for the **Frequently Asked Questions** option to access the information. Check out some of the FAQs. Have they answered any questions you might have had or is it too soon for you to have questions? Remember to disconnect when you finish.

Extra Challenges

Use Help to get information about closing a workbook. Print a copy of the information you find.

CRITICAL THINKING ACTIVITY

SCANS

Discuss with your classmates the information you looked at on the Help Web site and what you think of the idea of having more information about the application on a Web site.

UNDERSTANDING WORKBOOK BASICS

LESSON

1

OBJECTIVES

When you complete this lesson, you will be able to:

- Distinguish between a workbook and a worksheet.

- Move around in workbooks and worksheets.

- Select cells.

- Enter and edit text and numbers.

- Use the Fill features.

- Use the Undo and Redo commands.

🕐 **Estimated Time: 1½ hours**

Introduction

This lesson introduces you to basic Excel workbook features. You will identify the components of a workbook and learn how to move around in a workbook. You will enter different types of data and learn how to edit data. You also will discover Excel's power to calculate data quickly and easily.

Workbook and Worksheet Basics

An Excel document is called a **workbook.** When you start Excel, it automatically opens a new workbook file (see Figure 1.1). The grid where you enter data is called a **worksheet.** Each workbook can have as many as 255 worksheets. By default, a new workbook displays only three sheets that are named Sheet1, Sheet2, and Sheet3. You can rename the sheets to better identify the data they contain.

Each worksheet is independent of the others. However, the values in different sheets can be combined to let you work in three dimensions. For example, you might use different sheets to separate financial information by month and then consolidate the individual months. Budgets prepared for various sections of a company can easily be combined to produce a companywide budget. You will see in Lesson 5 how useful the workbook feature is when you work with multiple worksheets to consolidate values.

FIGURE 1.1
Parts of the Excel window are identified.

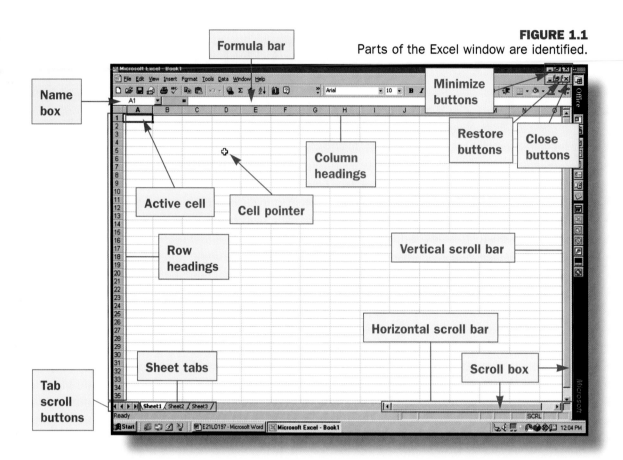

The name of the workbook appears on the title bar. The sheet names appear on tabs at the bottom of the workbook window. The name of the active sheet—the sheet you are looking at—is always in boldface type. You can click on the sheet tabs to move from sheet to sheet.

A worksheet consists of a grid of columns and rows. Each Excel worksheet contains 256 columns and 65,536 rows. Columns are labeled from left to right beginning with A through Z, then AA through AZ, then BA through BZ; the last column is IV. Rows are labeled down the left side of the worksheet with the numbers 1 through 65,536.

The rectangle where a column and row intersect is called a cell. Each cell is identified by an address that is the column letter followed by the row number. You can see the Name Box showing the name of the **active cell,** A1, in Figure 1.1. The column letter and row number of the active cell are shown in bold type on the column heading and row heading.

The cell pointer looks like a thick cross when the pointer is over a cell. You use the pointer to select or activate a cell. There is always at least one active cell.

A range is a group of cells. It can be a column, a row, or any group of cells that forms a rectangle and is identified with the address of the first cell, a colon, and the address of the last cell.

Moving Around a Workbook

You can move from worksheet to worksheet by clicking the worksheet tabs or the tab scroll buttons at the bottom of the screen (see Figure 1.1). When there are more than three worksheets, the tab scroll buttons make different worksheet tabs visible. You must click on a sheet tab to make the worksheet active. When you move

Hot Tips

Right-click on the tab scroll buttons to display a shortcut menu which contains the names of all sheets.

to a different sheet, there is always an active cell(s) in that worksheet.

- To select a worksheet, click its tab.

- To display the first tab in the workbook, click the leftmost tab scroll button.

- To display the last tab in the workbook, click the rightmost tab scroll button.

- To display tabs to the right or left by one tab, click either the right or left scroll button.

Concept Builders

You can also hold the Ctrl key and press the Page Up key to move to the previous worksheet, and hold the Ctrl key and press the Page Down key to move to the next worksheet.

Moving Around a Worksheet

A worksheet can and often does contain more data than what you can see on the screen. You can use the horizontal and vertical scroll bars and scroll boxes to move through a worksheet and display different parts of it.

- To scroll up or down one row, click the up or down arrow buttons in the vertical scroll bar (see Figure 1.1).

- To scroll up or down one screen, click the scroll bar area above or below the scroll box on the vertical scroll bar.

- To scroll any distance up or down, drag the scroll box on the vertical scroll box up or down. You will see the row number location in the ScreenTip to the left of the scroll box.

Hot Tips

Microsoft's IntelliMouse makes scrolling through Windows documents much easier.

- To scroll left or right by one column, click the left or right arrow buttons on the horizontal scroll bar.

- To scroll left or right by one screen, click the scroll bar area to the left or right of the scroll box on the horizontal scroll box.

- To scroll any distance left or right, drag the scroll box on the horizontal scroll box left or right. You will see the column letter location in the ScreenTip that appears as you drag the scroll box.

When you use the scroll bars to move within a sheet, the active cell does not move to the area you display. You must click a cell with the cell pointer to activate it.

You can also use the Go To command on the Edit menu to move to a particular location in the workbook. Select Go To and the Go To dialog box opens, as shown in Figure 1.2. Simply enter the cell name or range name in the Reference text box and click OK.

FIGURE 1.2
Use the Go To command to move quickly to a designated area.

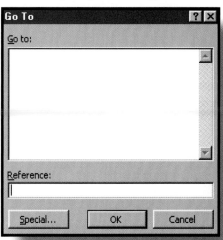

To access some commands on a menu you may have to click the menu Expand button or wait a few seconds for the menu to expand.

You can also use the Find command on the Edit menu to search for text or a formula in your worksheet and move to it (see Figure 1.3).

FIGURE 1.3
Use the Find dialog box to search for and move to data.

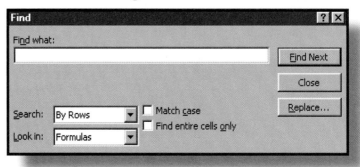

The keystrokes in Table 1.1 also help you to move around the worksheet. When you use these keystrokes, you change the active cell unless you press the Scroll Lock key (usually to the right of the Function keys on the keyboard). When Scroll Lock is turned on, you can use these keystrokes to move to another part of the worksheet without changing the active cell.

You can move to another Excel workbook, to another Windows file, to a file on your network, or to a Web page, by clicking a hyperlink on your worksheet. You will learn about adding hyperlinks to your worksheets in Lesson 7.

TABLE 1.1

KEYSTROKE COMMANDS

PRESS	TO MOVE
↑ ↓ ← →	Up, down, left, or right one cell
Page Up or **Page Down**	Up or down one window
Home	To the first cell of a row
Ctrl + Home	To cell A1 at the beginning of the worksheet
Ctrl + End	To the last cell containing data
Ctrl + Backspace	To the active cell when it is not displayed on the screen

STEP-BY-STEP ▷ 1.1

1. To start Excel, click the **Start** button, click **Programs,** and click **Microsoft Excel.**

2. To activate cell D4 on Sheet1, be sure **Sheet1** is displayed in bold on its worksheet tab, and click the cell pointer on cell **D4.** The active cell has the bold border.

3. To activate cell **D3,** press the **up arrow** key.

4. To move to and activate cell A1, hold the **Ctrl** key and press the **Home** key.

5. To move the display down one row on the worksheet, click the down arrow on the vertical scroll bar. You see the next row, and row 1 is no longer displayed. You also do not see the active cell.

6. To move the display down one window on the worksheet, click the vertical scroll bar below the scroll box. You do not see the active cell.

7. To return to the active cell, hold the **Ctrl** key and press the **Backspace** key.

8. To move the display one window to the right, click the horizontal scroll bar to the right of the scroll box.

9. To move back one window to the left, click the horizontal scroll bar to the left of the scroll box.

10. To move the display one column to the right, click the right arrow on the horizontal scroll bar. You see the next column, and column A is no longer visible.

11. To make cell N5 the active cell, position the cell pointer on **N5** and click.

12. To display Sheet2, click the **Sheet2** tab. A1 is the active cell.

13. To return to Sheet1, click the **Sheet1** tab. Cell N5 is still the active cell on Sheet1.

14. To display and activate cell **Z36,** click the **Edit** menu and click **Go To.** Type **Z36** in the Reference text box and click **OK.**

15. To enter your initials in cell Z36, type *your initials* and press the **Enter** key.

16. To return the display to the beginning of the worksheet, drag the scroll box on the vertical scroll bar to the top of the scroll bar. Then drag the scroll box on the horizontal scroll bar to the left of the scroll bar. Again, you do not see the active cell, which is Z37.

 Did You Know?

If a dialog box hides data on the worksheet, you can move the box by clicking on its title bar and then dragging it to a different location.

17. To make A6 the active cell, click the cell pointer on **A6.**

18. To move to the cell with your initials, click the **Edit** menu and then click **Find.** Type *your initials* and click **Find Next.** Click **Close.**

19. To return the display and the active cell to the home position, A1, hold the **Ctrl** key and press the **Home** key.

20. To close the workbook, click its **Close Window** button. When asked if you want to save changes, click **No.**

Selecting Cells

Before you can enter data or use Excel commands, a cell or range must be selected.

A range is a group of cells. It can be a column, a row, or a group of cells forming a rectangle. A range is identified by the name of the cell in the upper left corner of the range and the cell in the lower right corner separated with a colon (:). For example, a range that includes all the cells between cells A1 and C5 is identified as A1:C5.

Excel lets you select nonadjacent cells or ranges (see Figure 1.4).

Excel identifies a selected range by using a different background color for the cells included in the range. However, the first cell you select in the most recently selected range is the active cell (see Figure 1.4) and does not change color. Table 1.2 contains instructions for selecting cells.

FIGURE 1.4
An Excel window displays nonadjacent selected ranges.

	Step-by-Step 1-2 Basics							
	A	**B**	**C**	**D**	**E**	**F**	**G**	**H**
1								
2	Select All button		WILLIAMSON MANUFACTURING					
3			COMPANY					
4				Range	*TOTAL*		*GRAND*	*SHIPPING*
5	**STOCK**	**ITEM**	*QTY*	*COST*	*PRICE*	*TAX*	*TOTAL*	*CHARGE*
6	2810A	Wall Cabinet	2	257.70	515.40	30.92	546.32	
7	11628R	Rotary Files	10	6.25	62.50	3.75	66.25	
8	10028W	Pencils - Box/12	8	2.65	21.20	1.27	22.47	
9	12018S	Heavy Duty Staplers	4	64.50	258.00	15.48	273.48	
10	12018A	Staples - Box/5000	3	7.95	23.85	1.43	25.28	
11	1512A		2050	0.10	205.00	12.30	217.30	
12				1.39	0.00	0.00	0.00	
13	First cell in last selected			16.00	0.00	0.00	0.00	
14	range is the active cell			0.50	0.00	0.00	0.00	
15								

Sheet1 / Sheet2 / Sheet3

To move the active cell within a selected range, press the Enter key to move down or the Tab key to move right, or hold the Shift key and press the Enter key or the Tab key to reverse direction.

You can deselect a cell or range of cells by selecting something else, by pressing an arrow key, or by clicking outside the selection. Be careful, however, that you do not click a part of the screen that will do something unexpected to your worksheet. It is best to click a blank cell.

IMPORTANT:

Excel's autocalculate feature automatically calculates the sum of a selected range of numbers and displays the sum on the status bar. You can right-click the calculation on the status bar and choose Average, Count, Count Nums, Max, Min, or None to display a calculation other than the sum.

Concept Builders

When you open a workbook, the cells that were active on the various worksheets when the workbook was last saved are the active cells.

S TEP-BY-STEP ▷ 1.1

1. To start Excel, click the **Start** button, click **Programs,** and click **Microsoft Excel.**

2. To activate cell D4 on Sheet1, be sure **Sheet1** is displayed in bold on its worksheet tab, and click the cell pointer on cell **D4.** The active cell has the bold border.

3. To activate cell **D3,** press the **up arrow** key.

4. To move to and activate cell A1, hold the **Ctrl** key and press the **Home** key.

5. To move the display down one row on the worksheet, click the down arrow on the vertical scroll bar. You see the next row, and row 1 is no longer displayed. You also do not see the active cell.

6. To move the display down one window on the worksheet, click the vertical scroll bar below the scroll box. You do not see the active cell.

7. To return to the active cell, hold the **Ctrl** key and press the **Backspace** key.

8. To move the display one window to the right, click the horizontal scroll bar to the right of the scroll box.

9. To move back one window to the left, click the horizontal scroll bar to the left of the scroll box.

10. To move the display one column to the right, click the right arrow on the horizontal scroll bar. You see the next column, and column A is no longer visible.

11. To make cell N5 the active cell, position the cell pointer on **N5** and click.

12. To display Sheet2, click the **Sheet2** tab. A1 is the active cell.

13. To return to Sheet1, click the **Sheet1** tab. Cell N5 is still the active cell on Sheet1.

14. To display and activate cell **Z36,** click the **Edit** menu and click **Go To.** Type **Z36** in the Reference text box and click **OK.**

15. To enter your initials in cell Z36, type *your initials* and press the **Enter** key.

16. To return the display to the beginning of the worksheet, drag the scroll box on the vertical scroll bar to the top of the scroll bar. Then drag the scroll box on the horizontal scroll bar to the left of the scroll bar. Again, you do not see the active cell, which is Z37.

 Did You Know?

If a dialog box hides data on the worksheet, you can move the box by clicking on its title bar and then dragging it to a different location.

17. To make A6 the active cell, click the cell pointer on **A6.**

18. To move to the cell with your initials, click the **Edit** menu and then click **Find.** Type *your initials* and click **Find Next.** Click **Close.**

19. To return the display and the active cell to the home position, A1, hold the **Ctrl** key and press the **Home** key.

20. To close the workbook, click its **Close Window** button. When asked if you want to save changes, click **No.**

Selecting Cells

Before you can enter data or use Excel commands, a cell or range must be selected.

A range is a group of cells. It can be a column, a row, or a group of cells forming a rectangle. A range is identified by the name of the cell in the upper left corner of the range and the cell in the lower right corner separated with a colon (:). For example, a range that includes all the cells between cells A1 and C5 is identified as A1:C5.

Excel lets you select nonadjacent cells or ranges (see Figure 1.4).

Excel identifies a selected range by using a different background color for the cells included in the range. However, the first cell you select in the most recently selected range is the active cell (see Figure 1.4) and does not change color. Table 1.2 contains instructions for selecting cells.

FIGURE 1.4
An Excel window displays nonadjacent selected ranges.

	A	B	C	D	E	F	G	H
1								
2			WILLIAMSON MANUFACTURING					
3			COMPANY					
4					TOTAL		GRAND	SHIPPING
5	STOCK	ITEM	QTY	COST	PRICE	TAX	TOTAL	CHARGE
6	2810A	Wall Cabinet	2	257.70	515.40	30.92	546.32	
7	11628R	Rotary Files	10	6.25	62.50	3.75	66.25	
8	10028W	Pencils - Box/12	8	2.65	21.20	1.27	22.47	
9	12018S	Heavy Duty Staplers	4	64.50	258.00	15.48	273.48	
10	12018A	Staples - Box/5000	3	7.95	23.85	1.43	25.28	
11	1512A		2050	0.10	205.00	12.30	217.30	
12				1.39	0.00	0.00	0.00	
13				16.00	0.00	0.00	0.00	
14				0.50	0.00	0.00	0.00	
15								

Select All button

Range

First cell in last selected range is the active cell

Step-by-Step 1-2 Basics

Sheet1 / Sheet2 / Sheet3

To move the active cell within a selected range, press the Enter key to move down or the Tab key to move right, or hold the Shift key and press the Enter key or the Tab key to reverse direction.

You can deselect a cell or range of cells by selecting something else, by pressing an arrow key, or by clicking outside the selection. Be careful, however, that you do not click a part of the screen that will do something unexpected to your worksheet. It is best to click a blank cell.

IMPORTANT:

Excel's autocalculate feature automatically calculates the sum of a selected range of numbers and displays the sum on the status bar. You can right-click the calculation on the status bar and choose Average, Count, Count Nums, Max, Min, or None to display a calculation other than the sum.

Concept Builders

When you open a workbook, the cells that were active on the various worksheets when the workbook was last saved are the active cells.

TABLE 1.2

Lesson ① Understanding Workbook Basics

PROCEDURES FOR SELECTING CELLS

TO SELECT	ACTION IS
A single cell	Click the cell pointer on it
A range of cells	Drag from the first cell (the cell in the upper left corner of the range) to the last cell (the cell in the lower right corner). Or, you can drag from the last cell to the first cell. You can click the first cell you want to select and then hold the Shift key and click the last cell in the range. You can also hold the Shift key and press the arrow keys to select a range of cells
Nonadjacent cells or ranges	Hold the Ctrl key as you click or drag through the additional cells or ranges.
An entire row	Click the row heading
An entire column	Click the column heading
All cells on the worksheet	Click the Select All button

STEP-BY-STEP ▷ 1.2

1. To open a workbook, click the **Open** button on the Standard toolbar, be sure the folder containing the course practice files appears in the Look in drop-down list, scroll down and double-click **Step-by-Step 1-2 Basics.**

2. To activate cell **B7,** click it.

3. To select cells **A7** and **A8,** drag across the two cells.

4. To select row **7,** click the **7** row heading.

5. To select column **B,** click the **B** column heading.

6. To move the active cell down one cell within the selection, press the **Enter** key.

7. To move the active cell up one cell, hold the **Shift** key and press the **Enter** key.

8. To select the range A7:C7 with the keyboard, click the cell pointer on **A7,** hold the **Shift** key and press the **right arrow** key twice.

9. To select row 7 and column B, click the row **7** heading, hold the **Ctrl** key and click the column **B** heading.

10. To select columns A, C, and E, click the **A** column heading, hold the **Ctrl** key and click the **C** and **E** headings.

11. To deselect, click on a blank cell on the worksheet.

12. To select the entire worksheet, click the **Select All** button.

13. To deselect, press the **up arrow** key.

Entering Data

You can enter data in Excel by typing the data in the active cell and pressing the Enter key. The cell below becomes the active cell. Or you can enter data and press the Tab key to make the cell to the right the active cell. You can also press an arrow key after typing data to move to the cell above, below, right, or left.

NOTE:

If you find you don't usually want to move to the cell below when you press the Enter key, you can change the direction or turn off the Move Selection After Enter option on the Edit tab in the Options dialog box.

As you enter data in a cell, it is displayed in the active cell and in the Formula Bar. As you begin entering data, the *Ready* message at the left side of the status bar changes to *Enter* and three small buttons appear in the formula bar (see Figure 1.5). You can click the Enter Formula (✔) button instead of pressing the Enter key to enter your data in the cell. You can click the Cancel Formula button (✗) or press the Esc key to cancel the entry you started to type. Click the Edit Formula button (=) to edit a formula. (You will learn more about formulas in Lesson 2.)

FIGURE 1.5
Notice the buttons on the Formula Bar for entering data or canceling data entry.

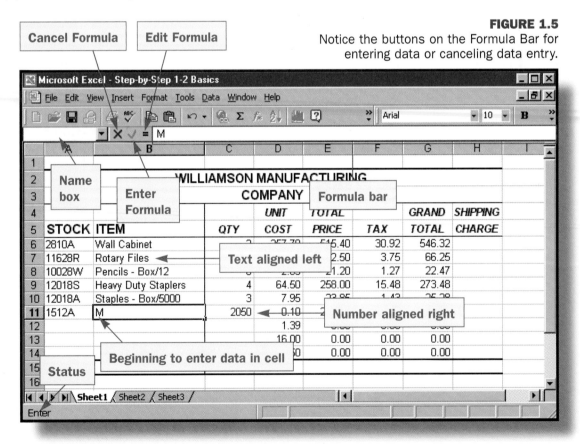

To enter data in a *selected* range, type the data in the active cell and:

- Press the Enter key to move down.

- Hold the Shift key and press the Enter key to move up.

- Press the Tab key to move right.

- Hold the Shift key and press the Tab key to move left.

You can repeat the same data in every cell in a newly selected range. Select the range, type the entry, and hold the Ctrl key and press the Enter key.

Understanding Types of Data

A cell can contain up to 32,000 characters. Data is normally categorized as text or numeric. Generally speaking, numeric data can be used in calculations whereas text normally is not. Excel automatically determines whether data is text or numeric as you enter it.

Text is aligned left in a cell and numbers are aligned right (see Figure 1.5). If you want to enter a number (such as a postal code) as text, you can type an apostrophe before the text to signal it is not a number to be used in calculations. Otherwise, a postal code such as 07458 would appear without the leading zero and be aligned right.

Hot Tips

The AutoCorrect feature automatically corrects common typing mistakes as you enter text in a cell. You will learn more about AutoCorrect in Lesson 3.

Entering Text

Text entries are often used as labels or headings that identify the numeric data you enter in a worksheet. When you enter text, it spills over into empty cells to the right unless those cells already contain data. If the cells to the right contain data, the text that you enter is truncated (cut off) in the display. The entire entry is still in the cell even though you don't see all of it. Text can also wrap within a cell.

Excel's AutoComplete feature automatically completes a text entry based on entries you've already made in the column. If, for instance, you have been entering department names including *Legal,* in a column, Excel enters the word *Legal* as soon as you key an *L* and as long as no other entry in the column begins with *L.* If you want to type another word, just keep typing over the entry.

NOTE:

Excel stores numbers with 15 digits of accuracy and uses the stored number in calculations. You can choose to display, for example, only whole numbers in a cell. If you want Excel to calculate the displayed values only, you can turn on the *Precision as displayed* option on the Calculation tab in the Options dialog box.

Entering Numbers

In addition to numbers, numeric data can include symbols such as +, –, (,), /, and %.

If a number is too long to fit in a cell, Excel displays the number in scientific notation (30984362282457 displays as 3.09844E+13).

If the format set for a cell makes a number too long to fit in the cell, Excel displays pound signs (###). Formatting data is covered in Lesson 4. As with text, even though you do not see the number

3 7

displayed, it is in the cell. You will learn to widen the column to accommodate the width of the number in Lesson 4.

You can include characters such as commas, dollar signs, or percent signs in numeric data as you enter it. However, it's usually more efficient to apply a numeric format to a range of cells after data has been entered.

Use a single period in a number to indicate a decimal point. Also, use a minus sign, not parentheses, to signal a negative number.

Entering Dates and Times

When you enter dates and times in a worksheet, Excel automatically converts them internally into a number value, or "serial number," that can be used in calculations. For example, you might want to calculate how many days passed between when an invoice was sent and when payment was received.

You can enter dates in many formats. Following are some of the commonly used formats:

- January 24, 2000

- 1/24/00

- 1/24/2000

- 4-Jan-2000

- 4-Jan-00

- 1/24

- Jan-24

Because Excel recognizes the slash mark (/) in dates, do not use it to enter fractions or Excel will treat the fraction as a date. Use mixed numbers (0 1/2) or decimals (.5) for fractions. The slash mark is also used to indicate the division operation in formulas. To ensure that Excel does not apply a date format, you must precede formulas with an equal (=) sign. You will learn more about entering formulas later in this lesson.

 IMPORTANT:

By default Windows 98's beginning date is January 1, 1930, and its ending date is December 31, 2029. Excel recognizes two-digit years from 00 to 29 as 2000 to 2029. Worksheets must be scrutinized to be sure they do not contain dates before January 1, 1930. You can use the Settings command on the Start menu to display the Regional Settings dialog box and change the default 100-year time span. Four digit years are not affected by these settings.

You can enter a time of day in a cell. Excel converts the time to a decimal fraction of a 24-hour day. Excel recognizes the following formats as times:

- 3:40 PM

- 3:40:40 PM

- 15:40

- 15:40:40

IMPORTANT:

If you want to use a menu command and you find many of the commands are dimmed, be sure you are not in the midst of entering data in a cell. Close the menu, press the Enter or Esc key if necessary, and the menu commands will be available.

Editing Cell Contents

To change the contents of a cell, activate the cell, type the new entry, and press the Enter key. The new entry replaces the original one.

You can also edit or delete the contents of a cell by:

■ activating the cell and pressing F2

■ activating the cell and clicking to position the insertion point in the formula bar

■ activating the cell, opening the Edit menu, choosing the Clear command, and then choosing Contents to delete

■ double-clicking on the cell

When you double-click on a cell, Excel positions the insertion point where you double-clicked. Then:

INTERNET An online service, such as Microsoft Network or America Online, provides its own services, content, and areas available to only their subscribers.

■ Use the left or right arrow keys to move the insertion point within the entry.

■ Type characters you want to insert to the left of the insertion point.

■ Drag the mouse pointer over characters to select them when you want to replace or delete them.

■ Use the Backspace key to delete a character to the left of the insertion point, or use the Delete key to delete a character to the right.

■ Double-click again to select the entire cell.

STEP-BY-STEP ▷ 1.3

C

1. To activate cell **B11,** click it.

2. To enter the word Markers, type **Markers.** The Cancel Formula, Enter Formula, and Edit Formula buttons appear next to the formula bar. As you type Markers, Excel displays your keystrokes in the cell and in the formula bar. Notice also Excel left-aligns the text within the cell. Press the **Enter** key.

3. To select cell **A12,** click it.

4. To enter the stock number, type **1005M.** Excel recognizes that the stock number is text and aligns it at the left of the cell.

5. To see how the menus react when you are in the midst of entering data in a cell, click the **File** menu, notice most commands are dimmed, click in a blank cell to close the menu, and enter the stock number.

(continued on next page)

6. To edit the contents of cell **B11,** click the cell, type **P.** Notice Excel entered Pencils – Box/12. Type **ens** and press the **Enter** key. You replaced the entire entry.

7. To select the range B12:B14, click **B12,** drag to **B14,** and release.

8. To enter data in the selected range, type **Rubber Bands,** press the **Enter** key, type **Magic Markers,** press **Enter,** type **Memo Books,** and press **Enter.**

9. To move back a cell in the selection, hold the **Shift** key and press the **Enter** key,

10. To activate cell **C12,** click it.

11. To enter the quantity, type **6** and press the **Enter** key. Notice Excel aligned the number to the right of the cell.

12. To select the range H6:H14, click on **H6,** drag to **H14,** and release. Notice row headings 6 through 14 are bold.

13. To enter the same shipping charge in each of the selected cells, type **4** and hold the **Ctrl** key and press the **Enter** key,

14. To save the changes, click the **Save** button on the Standard toolbar.

15. To close the workbook, click the document **Close Window** button on the menu bar.

Using Fill Features

You can use the fill handle on the lower-right corner of a selection (see Figure 1.6) or the Fill command on the Edit menu to copy the contents of a cell into adjacent cells. For example, in setting up an annual budget where the entry for your rent expense is the same for each of the months, you could enter the rent in the first month's cell and drag the cell's fill handle across the cells for the

FIGURE 1.6
Notice the cell fill handle.

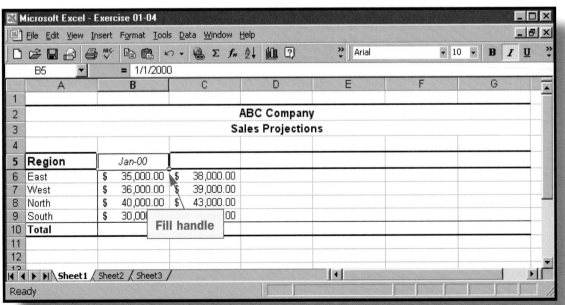

remaining months. Or, after you enter the first entry, select the range you want to fill and then select the Fill command on the Edit menu. From the Fill submenu, select the direction in which you want Excel to enter the fill.

 **IMPORTANT:**

The fill handle is available only if the Allow cell drag and drop option is turned on in the Edit tab of the Options dialog box.

You can also use the fill feature to create your own series of consecutive entries. For example, if you select a cell (or two cells) that contain a series of sequential values that Excel recognizes, such as months of the year, consecutive invoice numbers, or evenly incremented ordinal numbers, Excel will continue the series in the range you want filled.

FIGURE 1.7
Create a series in the Series dialog box.

To create a series, select the cell or range that contains the starting series of sequential values. Then drag the fill handle across the range you want to fill. If Excel recognizes the series, it will automatically complete the series across the range. Or, you can choose the Fill command on the Edit menu and then select Series. The Series dialog box appears (see Figure 1.7).

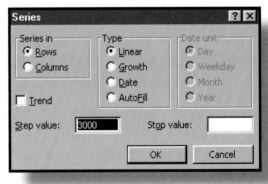

Using Undo and Redo

You can use the Undo command on the Edit menu to reverse your last command or action taken. The Undo command changes to show the most recent command or action. If the Undo command is not available, Can't Undo appears dimmed on the menu.

You can undo many Excel commands, but there are some that cannot be undone. When you choose a command that will change your data and cannot be undone, Excel will display a prompt before carrying out the command.

You can also use the Undo button to reverse the last 16 commands or actions taken. Click the Undo drop-down arrow to display a list of the last 16 actions. It is important to undo a mistake immediately because the drop-down list can be confusing. If you undo the third item on the list, the first two are undone as well. You may not remember what those actions were or see what happens when they are undone. Each of the actions is described briefly on the drop-down list.

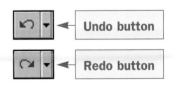

You can use the Repeat command on the Edit menu to repeat the last command you chose, including options you changed in a dialog box. When a command cannot be repeated, Can't Redo appears dimmed on the menu. You can also use the Redo button on the More Buttons drop-down list to reverse the action of the Undo command. When you use the Undo command, the Repeat command on the Edit menu changes to Redo.

1. To open one of the workbook practice files, click the **Open** button and double-click **Step-by-Step 1-4 Basics.**

2. To fill the months in the cells to the right of Jan-00, click cell **B5,** position the mouse pointer on the fill handle at the bottom-right corner of cell **B5** until the thin solid black crosshairs appears, and drag across to cell **G5.**

3. To remove the months you just entered, click the **Undo** button.

4. To undo the undo, click the **Edit** menu, click the **Expand** button if needed, and click **Redo AutoFill.**

5. To use the Fill command to enter the rest of the projections for the East, click **B6** and drag to **G6** to select a range B6:G6, click the **Edit** menu, click the **Fill** command, and click **Series.** Notice the dialog box shows Excel already knows from the selected cells to increment each cell by a Step value of 3000. There is no need to enter a Stop Value because the fill operation will end at the last cell in the range. Click **OK.**

6. To enter the projection figures for the remaining regions, select the range **B7:C9,** position the mouse pointer over the fill handle on the bottom-right corner of the selection until the crosshairs appears, and drag to **G9.**

7. To close Excel and save the changes to the file, click Excel's **Close** button and click **Yes** when asked to save changes.

Summary

You have now learned to select cells; enter text and numbers; use the Undo and Redo commands; and copy data using the fill handle and Fill command.

Try the exercises on the following pages to test how well you remember what you learned. Don't be afraid to go back and look up the answers, because that will help to reinforce what you learned.

LESSON 1 REVIEW QUESTIONS

TRUE / FALSE

Circle the T if the statement is true. Circle the F if it is false.

T F 1. Hold the Ctrl key as you click to select nonadjacent cells.

T F 2. You can press the Enter key or any of the four arrow keys to enter data in a cell.

T F 3. Excel recognizes text entries and aligns them to the right of the cell.

T F 4. Excel converts a date to a serial number.

T F 5. You should enter a fraction by typing 2/3.

T F 6. When many of the menu commands are dimmed, you may be in the midst of entering data in a cell.

T F 7. The easiest way to enter all the months of the year for column headings is to type each of them.

T F 8. You can undo many Excel commands by clicking the Undo button immediately after performing the task.

T F 9. You can use the AutoFill button to fill a range of cells with a series.

T F 10. When you cannot repeat a command, Can't Redo appears on the Edit menu.

COMPLETION

Complete the following sentences by writing the correct word or words in the blanks provided.

1. By default, a new workbook contains _____ sheets.

2. On a worksheet _____ are identified by letters of the alphabet, and _____ are identified by numbers.

3. The intersection of a row and column is called a(n) _____.

4. Use the Find command on the _____ menu to open the Find dialog box.

5. Text is aligned _____ when entered in a cell, and numbers are aligned _____.

6. The Save As command is on the _____ menu.

7. You can drag a cell's _____ handle to enter its data in adjacent cells.

8. The _____ feature lets you reverse your last 16 actions.

9. You can use the _____ feature to create a series of sequential values.

10. The _____ feature corrects common typing errors.

PROJECT 1A

To practice what you've learned in this lesson, complete the following project:

1. Start a new blank workbook.

2. Enter the data shown in Figure 1.8 in the cells indicated. For the months of the year, enter **Jul** in cell **C4** and then drag its fill handle to cell **H4** to enter the remaining months.

3. Save the workbook as **Data Entry Review** and close it.

FIGURE 1.8
Enter this data in a new workbook.

	A	B	C	D	E	F	G	H	I	J
1		Computer Sales								
2		July - December 2000								
3										
4		Employee	Jul							
5		Jim Smith	32843	29234	29472	21665	17222	39203		
6		Joe Lee	31232	29940	28794	19237	16694	40115		
7		Susan Valdez	38498	33618	31498	20411	20648	40961		
8		Totals								
9										

Sheet1 / Sheet2 / Sheet3 /

PROJECT 1B

To practice what you've learned in this lesson, complete the following project:

1. Open the **Data Entry Review** workbook.

2. Change the entry in cell **C6** to **31242**.

3. Change the entry in cell **H7** to **39440**.

4. Save and close the workbook. You will use it again in the next lesson.

Extra Challenges

Use Help to find information on editing cell contents. Review the information and print the Help topic.

SCANS

PROJECT 1C

Use the Microsoft on the Web command on the Help menu, and then click one of the listed options to see if you find anything that seems interesting to you. Discuss your findings with your classmates.

CRITICAL THINKING ACTIVITY

SCANS

Start a new workbook and create a worksheet for your personal budget for the next six months. A personal budget generally consists of income sources and expenses.

List all your sources of income for each month. Income may come from a job or from an allowance. Then, list your monthly expenses. Some of the expense items you'll want to track are rent, food, car payments, telephone and other utilities, and entertainment.

Save the workbook as **Critical Thinking Activity 1.** You will use it again at the end of the next lesson.

USING FORMULAS AND FUNCTIONS

Introduction

The real power of a spreadsheet program like Excel is its ability to perform simple and complex calculations on worksheet data. In this lesson, you will learn about how to enter formulas to perform calculations. You also will be introduced to Excel's functions—those predefined formulas that let you easily construct complex mathematical, statistical, financial, and other formulas.

Entering Formulas

A **formula** is a set of instructions to perform calculations in a cell. Formulas can set up relationships between two or more cells. You might, for instance, want Excel to total the numbers in a range of cells. You signal Excel that you are entering a formula by typing the equal sign (=).

A simple formula contains **operators** and the names of cells that contain the values you want calculated. Excel formulas follow a specific **syntax.** Syntax is the order which includes the equal sign followed by the values to be calculated which are separated by operators.

If you want to add the values in cells B9 through B12 and enter the result in cell B13, you can enter the formula =B9+B10+B11+B12 in cell B13 and press the Enter key. The formula is what is actually contained in the cell. You can see the formula in the Formula box when the cell is selected (see Figure 2.1).

 Concept Builders

To make it easy for Lotus 1-2-3 users to switch to Excel, Excel recognizes Lotus formulas and converts them to Excel formulas.

FIGURE 2.1
Formula result appears in cell and formula appears in Formula box.

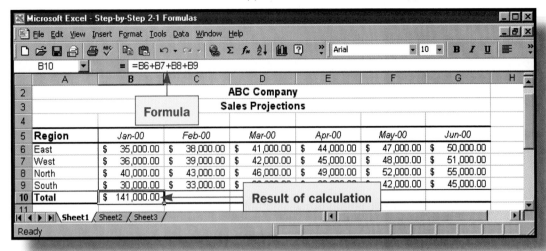

You can get the same result by activating cell B13, typing an =, clicking on cell B9, typing +, clicking on B10, typing +, clicking on B11, typing +, clicking on B12, and pressing the Enter key. That method of entering cell addresses in formulas is called *pointing*. Pointing eliminates the need to look up cell coordinates and avoids potential typographical errors.

 **NOTE:**

When you reference a cell in a formula by pointing to it, a marquee (moving dashes) appears around the cell so you can clearly see the cell address you are entering in the formula.

Worksheets usually have labels such as months, years, or departments for columns or rows. You can use these labels in formulas when you want to refer to the related data. The formula =SUM(March-00) makes it easier to enter the formula.

You can also use Excel's AutoSum button on the Standard toolbar to total a range of cells. There is usually no need to select a range because Excel will usually know from the active cell just which range you want to total.

Using Arithmetic Operators

You use arithmetic operators to signal that you want to add, subtract, multiply, or divide parts of a formula. The simplest operators are the arithmetic operators that perform basic mathematical operations to produce numeric results. Table 2.1 identifies the arithmetic operators.

When you use operators, Excel performs calculations in the normal algebraic precedence. That means the calculations are done from left to right in the following order:

a. Multiplication or division

b. Addition or subtraction

4 7

TABLE 2.1

ARITHMETIC OPERATORS			
OPERATOR	**OPERATION IT PERFORMS**	**OPERATOR**	**OPERATION IT PERFORMS**
+	Addition	/	Division
-	Subtraction	%	Percent
*	Multiplication	^	Exponentiation

If you want to change the order of evaluation, use parentheses to group expressions and to change the syntax in your formula. The example below shows how the order of evaluation can affect a formula.

3 + 7 * 2 = 17	(3 + 7) * 2 = 20
Multiplication calculation is done first, then addition: 7 x 2 = 14 + 3 = 17	Parentheses calculation is done first: 3 + 7 = 10 x 2 = 20

Using Reference Operators

There are two reference operators that you can use in worksheets:

- *Range* produces a single reference to all the cells between and including the two references separated by a colon; for example =SUM(B9:B12). The colon signals Excel to add all four cells from B9 through B12.

- *Union* produces a single reference that includes the two references separated by a comma; for example =SUM(B9:B11,C9:C11). The comma signals Excel to add the two ranges B9 through B11 and C9 through C11.

IMPORTANT:

You can group expressions in a formula and even have expressions within expressions. Be sure, however, that you have an equal number of parentheses. In some cases Excel will enter closing parentheses for you.

STEP-BY-STEP 2.1

1. Open the **Step-by-Step 2-1 Formulas** workbook.

2. To enter a formula in cell B10 to total the column, click cell **B10** to activate it, type **=B6+B7+B8+B9,** and press the **Enter** key.

3. To enter the formula in cell C10 by pointing to cells, click cell **C10,** type **=,** click **C6,** notice the marquee that appears so you can clearly see the cell address you are entering in the formula, type **+,** click **C7,** type **+,** click **C8,** type **+,** click **C9,** and press the **Enter** key.

4. To use the AutoSum button to total data in the rest of the cells, select cells **D10:G10** and click the **AutoSum** button.

5. To see the formula in cell C10, click **C10** and notice that the formula appears in the formula bar but the result appears in the cell.

6. To see the formula in D10, click cell **D10.** Notice the formula that appears in the Formula bar. It looks a little different from the formulas you entered in cells B10 and C10. This formula contains the SUM function. You will learn more about functions later in this lesson.

7. To save the workbook, click the **Save** button on the Standard toolbar.

8. To close the workbook, click its **Close** button.

Copying Formulas and Understanding Cell References

Excel uses relative, absolute, and mixed references cell references.

The default reference to a cell is called a **relative reference.** That means if cell B13 is active and you enter a formula telling Excel to add the cells from B9 through B12, you are telling Excel to add the four cells immediately above B13. When you copy or enter that same formula in another cell (for example, C13), Excel knows to add the values in the four cells immediately above that cell (namely, C9 through C12).

Absolute references are used to signal Excel you want a permanent reference to a cell and are indicated by a dollar sign ($B$9). Use absolute references when Excel must return to the same cell to find part of a formula. You can use the F4 key to rotate through the types of references you can use in your formula instead of typing the dollar signs yourself.

A **mixed reference** has either an absolute row or an absolute column reference. $B3 has an absolute column and a relative row; B$3 has a relative column and an absolute row.

A quick way to copy a formula down a column or across a row is to drag the fill handle of the cell containing the formula. You can also copy formulas with the Copy and Paste buttons on the Standard toolbar or the Copy and Paste commands on the Edit menu.

In the following exercise, you will do some more work with formulas for calculations necessary on the invoice shown in Figure 2.2.

Hot Tips

When Excel displays ######## because formatting prevents a number from fitting in a cell, you can easily widen the column with the Format menu's Column command. Just choose AutoFit Selection on the submenu.

FIGURE 2.2
Formulas will calculate the various totals on the invoice.

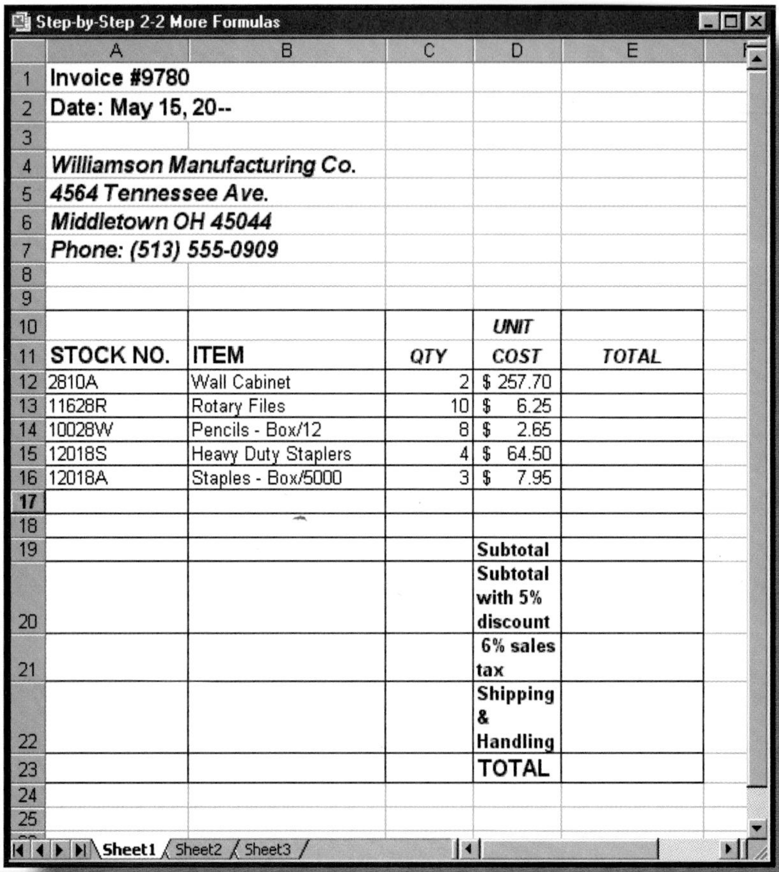

	A	B	C	D	E
	Step-by-Step 2-2 More Formulas				
1	Invoice #9780				
2	Date: May 15, 20--				
3					
4	Williamson Manufacturing Co.				
5	4564 Tennessee Ave.				
6	Middletown OH 45044				
7	Phone: (513) 555-0909				
8					
9					
10				UNIT	
11	STOCK NO.	ITEM	QTY	COST	TOTAL
12	2810A	Wall Cabinet	2	$ 257.70	
13	11628R	Rotary Files	10	$ 6.25	
14	10028W	Pencils - Box/12	8	$ 2.65	
15	12018S	Heavy Duty Staplers	4	$ 64.50	
16	12018A	Staples - Box/5000	3	$ 7.95	
17					
18					
19				Subtotal	
20				Subtotal with 5% discount	
21				6% sales tax	
22				Shipping & Handling	
23				TOTAL	
24					
25					

Sheet1 / Sheet2 / Sheet3 /

STEP-BY-STEP 2.2

1. Open the workbook **Step-by-Step 2-2 Formulas.**

2. To enter a formula to multiply the quantity by the cost per unit for the first item, click cell **E12.** Type **=,** click cell **C12,** type ***,** click cell **D12,** and then press the **Enter** key.

3. To copy the formula to cells E13:E16, be sure **E12** is still active and click and drag its fill handle down to cell **E16.** Click each of the cells and notice in the Formula bar how the references adapted to their location.

4. To calculate a subtotal in cell E19 that would include items in cells E17 and E18 if there were data there, click **E19,** click the **AutoSum** button on the toolbar, and press the **Enter** key.

5. To enter a discount of 5 percent on the subtotal so the new subtotal is 95% of the original one, click **E20,** type **=,** click **E19,** type ***95%,** and then press the **Enter** key.

6. To add a sales tax of 6 percent of the subtotal, click cell **E21** if it is not already active, type **=,** click **E20,** type ***6%,** and press the **Enter** key.

7. To enter a Shipping & Handling charge, click **E22** if it is not already active and type **45.**

8. To calculate the total for the invoice, click cell **E23,** click the **AutoSum** button, and press the **Enter** key.

9. To save and close the workbook, click the **Save** button on the Standard toolbar and then click the **Close** button.

Editing Formulas

If you want to change or edit a formula, you can activate the cell containing the formula, type your changes in the formula bar, and then press the Enter key. Or, you can double-click the cell containing the formula to activate Excel's Range Finder.

As you edit a formula, all cell and range references appear in different colors, and a cell border with a color matching its reference appears on the corresponding cells and ranges (see Figure 2.3). That way, you can easily see the data used in your formula. You can edit the formula right in the cell.

NOTE:

When Excel cannot calculate a formula properly, an error value appears. Error values always begin with a pound sign (#).

FIGURE 2.3
Notice the color-coded references and the absolute reference to cell A13.

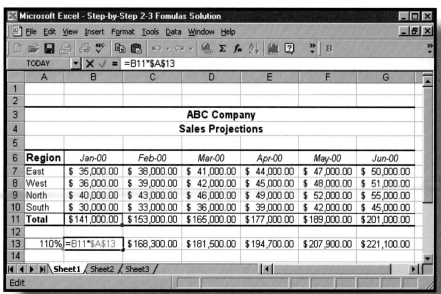

1. Open the workbook **Step-by-Step 2-3 Formulas.**

2. To enter a formula to calculate totals in row 11, click cell **B11,** click the **AutoSum** button, and press the **Enter** key. Notice the result of the calculation is too wide for the cell. You will fix that problem in a few seconds.

3. To copy the formula to cells C11:G11, click **B11** and drag its fill handle to **G11.**

4. To widen the columns so the formatted calculations fit in the cells, be sure B11:G11 is still selected, click the **Format** menu, click **Column,** and then click **AutoFit Selection.**

5. To enter a value to display a row with new totals as if sales were all 10% higher, click **A13,** type **110%,** and press the **Enter** key.

6. To use the F4 key to enter a formula with an absolute reference in row 13, select cells B13:G13, type **=,** click **B11,** type ***,** click **A13,** press the **F4** key to make the reference to A13 absolute, and press **F4** four more times while noticing the mixed, relative, and absolute references. Hold the **Ctrl** key and press the **Enter** key when you see the absolute reference ($A$13) in the formula box.

7. To activate the Range Finder, double-click cell **B13.** Notice the color-coded cell references and their corresponding cells on the worksheet.

8. To deactivate the Range Finder without making any changes in the cell, click in a blank cell.

9. Save and close the workbook.

Using Functions

Excel provides the user with built-in shortcuts called **functions** for entering formulas. You have already used the Sum function when you used the AutoSum button to enter a formula.

There are hundreds of functions available in the Excel program. Instead of typing all of the references and plus signs as you have in previous exercises, you can use a function in a formula to tell Excel to perform a calculation.

You can use the Function command on the Insert menu or click the Paste Function button on the the Standard toolbar to display the Paste Function dialog box (see Figure 2.4).

Excel groups functions by categories, as you can see in the Paste Function dialog box. There are Financial, Date & Time, Math & Trig, Statistical, Lookup & Reference, Database, Text, Logical, and Information functions.

Hot Tips

If you use Excel for worksheets containing Financial, Math & Trig, Statistical, or Logical calculations, be sure to look through the list of functions that can save you a great deal of time with your work.

Paste Function button

6. To add a sales tax of 6 percent of the subtotal, click cell **E21** if it is not already active, type **=,** click **E20,** type ***6%,** and press the **Enter** key.

7. To enter a Shipping & Handling charge, click **E22** if it is not already active and type **45.**

8. To calculate the total for the invoice, click cell **E23,** click the **AutoSum** button, and press the **Enter** key.

9. To save and close the workbook, click the **Save** button on the Standard toolbar and then click the **Close** button.

Editing Formulas

If you want to change or edit a formula, you can activate the cell containing the formula, type your changes in the formula bar, and then press the Enter key. Or, you can double-click the cell containing the formula to activate Excel's Range Finder.

As you edit a formula, all cell and range references appear in different colors, and a cell border with a color matching its reference appears on the corresponding cells and ranges (see Figure 2.3). That way, you can easily see the data used in your formula. You can edit the formula right in the cell.

NOTE:

When Excel cannot calculate a formula properly, an error value appears. Error values always begin with a pound sign (#).

FIGURE 2.3

Notice the color-coded references and the absolute reference to cell A13.

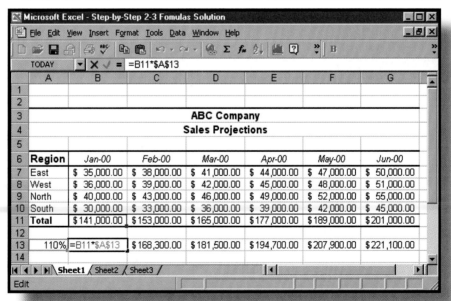

1. Open the workbook **Step-by-Step 2-3 Formulas.**

2. To enter a formula to calculate totals in row 11, click cell **B11,** click the **AutoSum** button, and press the **Enter** key. Notice the result of the calculation is too wide for the cell. You will fix that problem in a few seconds.

3. To copy the formula to cells C11:G11, click **B11** and drag its fill handle to **G11.**

4. To widen the columns so the formatted calculations fit in the cells, be sure B11:G11 is still selected, click the **Format** menu, click **Column,** and then click **AutoFit Selection.**

5. To enter a value to display a row with new totals as if sales were all 10% higher, click **A13,** type **110%,** and press the **Enter** key.

6. To use the F4 key to enter a formula with an absolute reference in row 13, select cells B13:G13, type **=,** click **B11,** type ***,** click **A13,** press the **F4** key to make the reference to A13 absolute, and press **F4** four more times while noticing the mixed, relative, and absolute references. Hold the **Ctrl** key and press the **Enter** key when you see the absolute reference ($A$13) in the formula box.

7. To activate the Range Finder, double-click cell **B13.** Notice the color-coded cell references and their corresponding cells on the worksheet.

8. To deactivate the Range Finder without making any changes in the cell, click in a blank cell.

9. Save and close the workbook.

Using Functions

Excel provides the user with built-in shortcuts called **functions** for entering formulas. You have already used the Sum function when you used the AutoSum button to enter a formula.

There are hundreds of functions available in the Excel program. Instead of typing all of the references and plus signs as you have in previous exercises, you can use a function in a formula to tell Excel to perform a calculation.

You can use the Function command on the Insert menu or click the Paste Function button on the the Standard toolbar to display the Paste Function dialog box (see Figure 2.4).

Excel groups functions by categories, as you can see in the Paste Function dialog box. There are Financial, Date & Time, Math & Trig, Statistical, Lookup & Reference, Database, Text, Logical, and Information functions.

Hot Tips

If you use Excel for worksheets containing Financial, Math & Trig, Statistical, or Logical calculations, be sure to look through the list of functions that can save you a great deal of time with your work.

Paste Function button

 **NOTE:**

When you click the Paste Function button or choose Function on the Insert menu, Excel automatically enters the equal (=) sign in the cell to signify that you are about to enter a formula.

Most functions require what is called an argument. An **argument,** which is usually enclosed in parentheses, lists the data on which the function is to be performed. Once you select a function in the Paste Function dialog box, click OK to open the Formula Palette (see Figure 2.5). The Formula Palette displays the name of the function, each of its arguments, the current result of a function, and the current result of the entire formula.

To enter cell references as an argument, you can click the collapse button (see Figure 2.5) to temporarily hide the dialog box. When you finish selecting cells for the argument, click the Expand button to redisplay the dialog box.

FIGURE 2.4
Excel's functions are listed in the Paste Function dialog box.

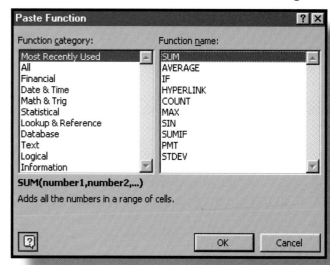

Concept Builders

Click the Edit Formula (=) button on the Formula bar to display the Formula Palette for a cell that has a function in its formula.

 ← **Expand button**

FIGURE 2.5
Use the Formula Palette to build a formula.

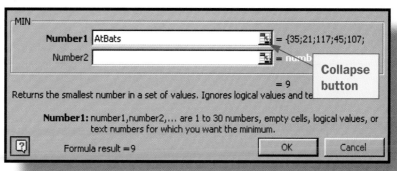

Collapse button

Naming Ranges

You can use the Name box at the left of the Formula bar to define a name for a range of cells that you will use in formulas. You can also use the Name command on the Insert menu to define a name for a range.

You can use the same Name command on the Insert menu to create a name using text in the worksheet. Names can make entering ranges in formulas much easier.

In the next exercise, you will name ranges and use some of Excel's functions to add some pertinent information to the baseball team stats (see Figure 2.6).

NOTE:

Dialog boxes that accept range references have a button that collapses the dialog box so its not in your way while you select a range. When you finish selecting, click the button that returns the dialog box to the screen.

INTERNET

Internet Service Providers (ISPs) provide access to the Internet usually via a local phone call. The software the ISP provides for you lets you actually work on the ISP computer but your screen shows what's happening on the computer you've dialed into.

FIGURE 2.6
Name ranges and use functions in this workbook.

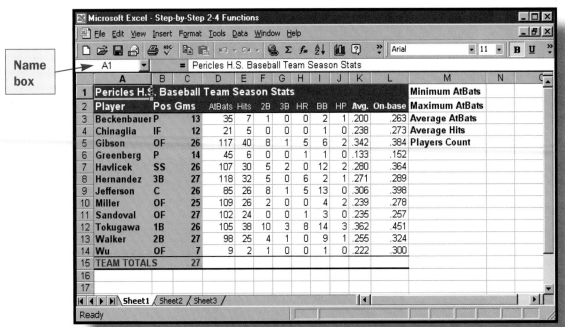

Name box

	A	B	C	D	E	F	G	H	I	J	K	L	M	N
		Pos	Gms	AtBats	Hits	2B	3B	HR	BB	HP	Avg.	On-base		
1	Pericles H.S. Baseball Team Season Stats												Minimum AtBats	
2	Player	Pos	Gms	AtBats	Hits	2B	3B	HR	BB	HP	Avg.	On-base	Maximum AtBats	
3	Beckenbauer	P	13	35	7	1	0	0	2	1	.200	.263	Average AtBats	
4	Chinaglia	IF	12	21	5	0	0	0	1	0	.238	.273	Average Hits	
5	Gibson	OF	26	117	40	8	1	5	6	2	.342	.384	Players Count	
6	Greenberg	P	14	45	6	0	0	1	1	0	.133	.152		
7	Havlicek	SS	26	107	30	5	2	0	12	2	.280	.364		
8	Hernandez	3B	27	118	32	5	0	6	2	1	.271	.289		
9	Jefferson	C	26	85	26	8	1	5	13	0	.306	.398		
10	Miller	OF	25	109	26	2	0	0	4	2	.239	.278		
11	Sandoval	OF	27	102	24	0	0	1	3	0	.235	.257		
12	Tokugawa	1B	26	105	38	10	3	8	14	3	.362	.451		
13	Walker	2B	27	98	25	4	1	0	9	1	.255	.324		
14	Wu	OF	7	9	2	1	0	0	1	0	.222	.300		
15	TEAM TOTALS		27											
16														
17														

STEP-BY-STEP 2.4

C

1. Open the workbook **Step-by-Step 2-4 Functions.**

2. To use the AutoSum button to enter formulas to total columns D through J,

select the range **D15:J15** and click the **AutoSum** button.

3. To name the range in the Name box, select **D3:D14,** click the **Name box,** type **AtBats,** and press the **Enter** key.

4. To name the range B3:B14 with a name different from its label (Pos), select **B3:B14,** click the **Insert** menu, click **Name,** click **Define,** and type **Position** in the **Names in workbook** text box. Click **Add.** Notice the range name is added to the list that already contains the range you named in step 3. Click **OK.**

5. To use the label in cell E2 as the name for the range E2:E14, select **E2:E14.** Click the **Insert** menu, click **Name,** and click **Create.** Click **Top row,** if necessary, and then click **OK.**

6. To see the list of named ranges, click the **Name box** drop-down button. Click elsewhere on the worksheet to close the list.

7. To enter a formula that uses the MIN function to find the fewest number of AtBats a player had, click cell **N1.** Click the **Insert** menu and click **Function.** Click **Statistical** in the Function category list box and scroll to and select **MIN** in the Function name list box. Review the function syntax and description at the bottom of the dialog box and click **OK.**

8. To complete the formula in the Formula Palette, type **AtBats** in the Number 1 text box. Notice the formula result (9) is displayed at the bottom of the dialog box. Click **OK.**

9. To enter a formula that uses the MAX function to find the greatest number of

AtBats a player had, click cell **N2.** Click the **Paste Function** button on the Standard toolbar. The Statistical Function category should still be selected. Scroll to and select the **MAX** function in the Function name list box. Review the syntax and description and click **OK.**

10. To complete the formula in the Formula Palette, type **AtBats** in the Number 1 text box and click **OK.**

11. To enter a formula that uses the AVERAGE function to find the average number of AtBats, select cell **N3.** Type **=AVERAGE(AtBats)** and press the **Enter** key.

12. To enter a formula that uses the AVERAGE function to find the average number of Hits, click cell **N4.** Click the **Paste Function** button, click the **AVERAGE** function, and click **OK.** In the Formula Palette, type **Hits** in the Number 1 text box and click **OK.**

13. To determine the number of players on the team by counting the number of entries in the Pos column, click cell **N5.** Type **=COUNTA(Position)** and press the **Enter** key.

14. To enter today's date using the TODAY function, click cell **M6.** Click the **Paste Function** button. Click **Date & Time** in the Function category list and then click **TODAY** in the Function name list box. Review the description and then click **OK.** When the Today message box appears, read it and click **OK.**

15. Save and close the workbook.

Using Comparison Operators in Formulas

Besides arithmetic and reference operators, Excel has two other types of operators that specify the type of calculation you want to perform on the elements of a formula.

Comparison operators let you compare two values to obtain a logical value, either True or False.

TABLE 2.2

COMPARISON OPERATORS

OPERATOR	MEANING	OPERATOR	MEANING
=	Equal to	>=	Greater than or equal to
>	Greater than	<=	Less than or equal to
<	Less than	<>	Not equal to

NOTE:

You may at times need to use (nest) a function as an argument in another function. A formula can have up to seven levels of nested functions, but the nested function must return the same type of value the argument uses. For instance if the first function returns a TRUE or FALSE value, the nested function must return a TRUE or FALSE.

Concept Builders

Another operator you should be aware of is the text concatenation operator, the ampersand (&). Use the ampersand to join (concatenate) one or more text strings to produce a single piece of text.

Displaying Formulas

You can use the Options command on the Tools menu to display formulas instead of values on your worksheet(see Figure 2.7). You might want to print a copy of your worksheet showing all the formulas so you can check to be sure the formulas are accurate. On the View tab click Formulas under Window options.

In Step-by-Step 2.5, you will use the Formula Palette (see Figure 2.8) to use the IF function and comparison operators to calculate grades.

FIGURE 2.7
Excel can display formulas on the worksheet.

Test5	Grade
98	=IF(AVERAGE(B6:F6)>=75,"Pass","Fail")
89	=IF(AVERAGE(B7:F7)>=75,"Pass","Fail")
84	=IF(AVERAGE(B8:F8)>=75,"Pass","Fail")
91	=IF(AVERAGE(B9:F9)>=75,"Pass","Fail")
93	=IF(AVERAGE(B10:F10)>=75,"Pass","Fail")

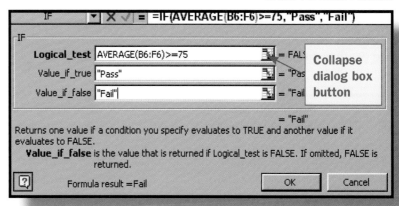

STEP-BY-STEP ▷ 2.5

1. Open the **Step-by-Step 2-5 Formulas** workbook.

2. To begin entering a formula to calculate a grade of Pass or Fail with passing grades being 75 or better, click cell **H6,** click the **Paste Function** button on the Standard toolbar, click **Logical** in the **Function category** box, click **IF** in the **Function name** box, and click **OK.**

3. To finish building the formula in the Formula Palette, type **AVERAGE(** in the **Logical_test** box, press the **Collapse** button in the Logical test box, select B6:F6, click the **Expand** button, type **)>=75,** press the **Tab** key, type **Pass** in the **Value_if_true** box, press **Tab,** type **Fail** in the **Value_if_false** box, and click **OK.**

4. To copy the formula, drag the **H6** fill handle to **H10.**

5. To display formulas on the worksheet, click the **Tools** menu, click **Options,** be sure the **View** tab is displayed, click **Formulas** in the Window options and click **OK.**

6. To return to the normal display, click the **Tools** menu, click **Options,** click **Formulas** in the Window options to deselect it, and click **OK.**

7. Save and close the workbook.

Summary

In this lesson, you learned more about entering and editing formulas, using operators, using relative, absolute, and mixed references, using functions, and naming ranges.

Try the exercises on the following pages to test how well you remember what you learned. Don't be afraid to go back and look up the answers, because that will help to reinforce what you learned.

TRUE / FALSE

Circle the T if the statement is true. Circle the F if it is false.

T   F   1. A formula is a set of instructions to perform calculations in a cell.

T   F   2. You can use the AutoSum button to quickly total a column of numbers.

T   F   3. Syntax of a formula refers to the structure or order of elements in the formula.

T   F   4. Excel completes addition and subtraction operations before it completes multiplication and division.

T   F   5. To change the order in which operations are carried out, you can use parentheses to group expressions in a formula.

T   F   6. The equation =3 + 5 * 2 - 4 would return a result of 12.

T   F   7. When the cell reference in a formula changes in relation to the location of the formula, it is a relative cell reference.

T   F   8. By default, cell references are absolute.

T   F   9. The only way to enter a function in a worksheet is to select it in the Paste Function dialog box.

T   F   10. Naming ranges makes it easier to enter formulas.

COMPLETION

Complete the following sentences by writing the correct word or words in the blanks provided.

1. You can press the _____ key to change a relative reference to an absolute reference.

2. You would use the _____ function to have Excel return the highest value in a range.

3. A function's _____ contain the data on which the function is to be performed.

4. One way to name a range is to select the range, click the _____ box, and then enter the name.

5. A(n) _____ between two cell references signals a range from the first cell to the last cell.

6. A(n) _____ between two cell or range references signals that each reference is to be combined.

FIGURE 2.8
Notice the IF function and comparison operators
in the Formula Palette.

7. You can drag a cell's _____ handle to copy a formula to adjacent cells.

8. The _____ helps you build formulas that contain functions.

9. One way to open the Paste Function dialog box is to select _____ on the _____ menu.

10. Double-clicking a cell that contains a formula activates the _____ feature, which assists you in editing a formula.

LESSON 2 PROJECTS

PROJECT 2A

To practice what you've learned in this lesson, complete the following project:

SCANS

1. Open a new, blank workbook in Excel. In cell **A1**, enter **Working with Order of Evaluation.**

2. Enter the equations as formulas as you see them in the list below and note carefully the result of each of the calculations. Enter formula *a* in cell **A3**, formula *b* in cell **A4**, formula *c* in cell **A5**, and formula *d* in cell **A6.**

    a. =4+6*2+3

    b. =(4+6)*2+3

    c. =(4+6)*(2+3)

    d. =4+6*(2+3)

3. Save the workbook as **Calculation Review** and close it.

PROJECT 2B

To practice what you've learned in this lesson, complete the following project:

1. Open the workbook **Project 2-B.**

2. Select the range **B5:B10** and rename it using the **Test1** label in the **Top row.** Do the same for the **Test2, Test3, Test4,** and **Test5** test scores.

3. In cell **B12,** enter a formula that uses the **AVERAGE** function and the **Test1** range to find the average score for test 1.

4. In cell **B13,** enter a formula that uses the **MAX** function and the **Test1** range to find the highest score for test 1.

5. In cell **B14,** enter a formula that uses the **MIN** function and the **Test1** range to find the lowest score for test 1.

6. Find the average, maximum, and minimum scores for the rest of the tests.

7. In cell **G6,** enter a formula that uses the **AVERAGE** function to find the average score for **L.E. Vator.** Copy the formula to the range **G7:G10** to find the average score for the other students.

8. In cell **D:1,** enter the DATE Date & Time function using the **Paste Function** button. Type the year, month, and day in the Date dialogue box, and click **OK.** Click the **Undo** button to undo DATE function.

9. In cell **E:1,** enter the NOW Date & Time function using the **Paste Function** button. Click **OK** in the NOW dialogue box. Click the **Undo** button.

Extra Challenges

Use Help to find information on using the Formula Palette to enter and edit formulas. Review and print the Help topic(s) you find.

10. Save and then close the workbook and exit from Excel.

PROJECT 2C

Open a new blank workbook and display the Web toolbar. Click the **Search the Web** button and search for information on **Current Interest Rates.** Go to one of the site matches and find the current interest rates for residential mortgages. Print a copy of what you find and then disconnect.

PROJECT 2D

Open a blank workbook, and using the **PMT** financial function, create a spreadsheet to calculate how much car payments will be for a $15,000 car with 48 monthly payments at 2.9% interest rate and also at 9% interest rate.

CRITICAL THINKING ACTIVITY

Open the **Critical Thinking Activity 1** workbook you created in Lesson 1. Add totals to your income and expenses to determine your financial standing. Save and close the workbook.

7. You can drag a cell's _____ handle to copy a formula to adjacent cells.

8. The _____ helps you build formulas that contain functions.

9. One way to open the Paste Function dialog box is to select _____ on the _____ menu.

10. Double-clicking a cell that contains a formula activates the _____ feature, which assists you in editing a formula.

LESSON 2 PROJECTS

PROJECT 2A

To practice what you've learned in this lesson, complete the following project:

SCANS

1. Open a new, blank workbook in Excel. In cell **A1,** enter **Working with Order of Evaluation.**

2. Enter the equations as formulas as you see them in the list below and note carefully the result of each of the calculations. Enter formula *a* in cell **A3,** formula *b* in cell **A4,** formula *c* in cell **A5,** and formula *d* in cell **A6.**

    a.   =4+6*2+3

    b.   =(4+6)*2+3

    c.   =(4+6)*(2+3)

    d.   =4+6*(2+3)

3. Save the workbook as **Calculation Review** and close it**.**

PROJECT 2B

To practice what you've learned in this lesson, complete the following project:

1. Open the workbook **Project 2-B.**

2. Select the range **B5:B10** and rename it using the **Test1** label in the **Top row.** Do the same for the **Test2, Test3, Test4,** and **Test5** test scores.

3. In cell **B12,** enter a formula that uses the **AVERAGE** function and the **Test1** range to find the average score for test 1.

4. In cell **B13,** enter a formula that uses the **MAX** function and the **Test1** range to find the highest score for test 1.

5. In cell **B14,** enter a formula that uses the **MIN** function and the **Test1** range to find the lowest score for test 1.

6. Find the average, maximum, and minimum scores for the rest of the tests.

7. In cell **G6,** enter a formula that uses the **AVERAGE** function to find the average score for **L.E. Vator.** Copy the formula to the range **G7:G10** to find the average score for the other students.

8. In cell **D:1,** enter the DATE Date & Time function using the **Paste Function** button. Type the year, month, and day in the Date dialogue box, and click **OK.** Click the **Undo** button to undo DATE function.

9. In cell **E:1,** enter the NOW Date & Time function using the **Paste Function** button. Click **OK** in the NOW dialogue box. Click the **Undo** button.

10. Save and then close the workbook and exit from Excel.

 Extra Challenges

Use Help to find information on using the Formula Palette to enter and edit formulas. Review and print the Help topic(s) you find.

SCANS

PROJECT 2C

Open a new blank workbook and display the Web toolbar. Click the **Search the Web** button and search for information on **Current Interest Rates.** Go to one of the site matches and find the current interest rates for residential mortgages. Print a copy of what you find and then disconnect.

PROJECT 2D

Open a blank workbook, and using the **PMT** financial function, create a spreadsheet to calculate how much car payments will be for a $15,000 car with 48 monthly payments at 2.9% interest rate and also at 9% interest rate.

CRITICAL THINKING ACTIVITY

SCANS

Open the **Critical Thinking Activity 1** workbook you created in Lesson 1. Add totals to your income and expenses to determine your financial standing. Save and close the workbook.

CREATING, PRINTING, AND DISTRIBUTING WORKSHEETS

LESSON 3

OBJECTIVES

When you complete this lesson, you will be able to:

■ Create a worksheet.

■ Use the AutoCorrect and spell checking features.

■ Use the AutoFormat command.

■ Rename sheets.

■ Use the Print Preview, Page Setup, and Print commands.

■ Identify buttons on the Web toolbar.

■ Publish worksheet data in HTML format.

■ Route and send documents.

🕐 **Estimated Time: 1½ hours**

Introduction

Now that you are familiar with Excel basics, you are ready to design your own worksheets. In this lesson you will learn how to produce professional-looking worksheets. You will use the AutoFormat command to apply one of Excel's preset formats to your worksheet. You will learn how to check spelling in a worksheet. You will discover how to preview a worksheet and print it. You also will become familiar with buttons on the Web toolbar and you will learn how to publish worksheet data on the Web.

Creating a New Worksheet

As you already know, you can use the New button to create a blank  New button
workbook.

Excel provides a set of templates for small businesses. A **template** is a master copy for a certain type of worksheet. You can access Excel's built-in templates for creating expense statements, invoices, and purchase orders from within the Excel program by opening the File menu, clicking the New command and looking on the Spreadsheet Solutions tab in the New dialog box (see Figure 3.1). You can also use the Village Software template to access information about a company that provides other Excel templates. You will work with an Excel template in Lesson 7.

6 1

FIGURE 3.1
The New dialog box contains templates for various types of workbooks.

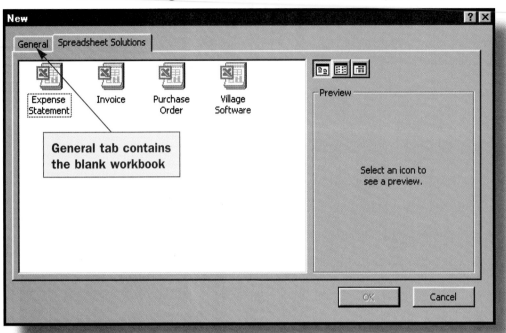

 **NOTE:**

If you are using Office, you can access the templates from the Windows desktop by clicking the New Office Document button on the Office Shortcut bar or by clicking the New Office Document command on the Windows Start menu.

Before you can plan or design a worksheet, you must determine what it is you want the worksheet to accomplish. You then need to give the worksheet a title, enter the labels for the data, enter the data itself, and enter the necessary formulas in the worksheet.

In Step-by-Step 3.1, you will create a new worksheet and enter the data shown in Figure 3.2.

 **Hot Tips**

When entering numbers, there is no need to type a comma. You will learn in Lesson 4 to use a formatting command to enter commas in numbers.

S TEP-BY-STEP ⟹ 3.1

1. To create a new workbook, click the **New** button on the Standard toolbar.

2. To enter a title for the worksheet in cell A1, type **Kayak Sales** and press the **Enter** key.

3. To enter a subtitle in A2 type **July–December 2000** and press the **Enter** key.

4. To activate cell B4, click it.

6 2

5. To enter the heading and employees' names, type **Employee,** press the **Enter** key, type **Jim Smith,** press **Enter,** type **Joe Lee,** press **Enter,** type **Sue Carlos,** and press **Enter.**

6. To enter the months, click cell C4, type **Jul,** press the **Enter** key, click **C4,** and drag **C4's** fill handle to **H4** and release.

7. To enter the sales figures for the three employees and the word **Totals,** copy from Figure 3.2.

8. To enter the formula to total each month's sales, select **C8:H8,** click the **AutoSum** button, and click in a blank area.

FIGURE 3.2

Your worksheet should look like the one pictured when you finish Step-by-Step 3.1.

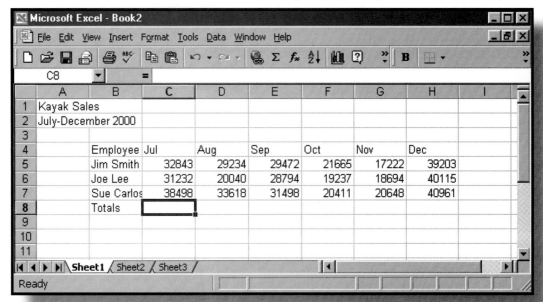

Using the AutoFormat Command

You can use the AutoFormat command on the Format menu to let Excel automatically format your worksheet. AutoFormat can quickly improve a worksheet's appearance without your knowing and using the many formatting commands available in the Excel application.

To use the AutoFormat command, simply select all the data and text you want to include in the Autoformat, open the Format menu and choose AutoFormat. You can scroll through the AutoFormat dialog box to display samples of preset formats (see Figure 3.3).

In Figure 3.4, Excel has applied the Classic 3 autoformat to the worksheet you created.

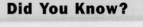
Did You Know?

You can choose None to remove an autoformat.

Naming a Sheet

You can give sheets in your workbooks descriptive names that better identify the data they contain. For instance, you might have several worksheets in one workbook that track sales for different products. You could name each sheet according to the product data on the sheet.

6 3

To rename a sheet, simply double-click the sheet name on the tab, type the new name and press the Enter key.

FIGURE 3.3
The AutoFormat dialog box lets you preview preset formats.

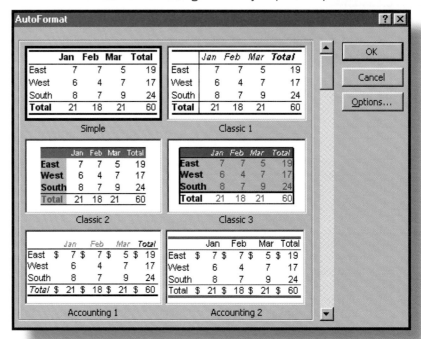

FIGURE 3.4
Your worksheet is displayed with the Classic 3 format.

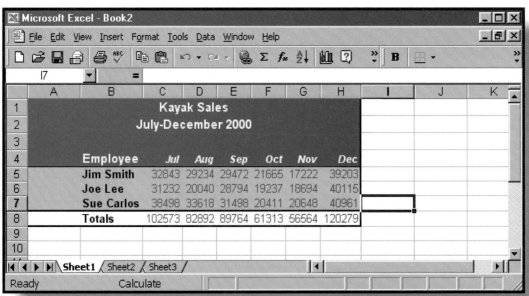

S TEP-BY-STEP ▷ 3.2

1. To select the cells containing the data you want Excel to format, drag across the range **A1:H8** and release.

2. To display the AutoFormat dialog box, click the **Format** menu and click **AutoFormat.**

3. To see the various formats from which you can choose, use the scroll bars to move down through the samples.

4. To use a format, click the Classic 3 format and click **OK.**

5. To deselect, click in a blank cell. Your worksheet should now look like the one shown in Figure 3.4.

6. To rename the sheet, double-click **Sheet1** on the sheet tab, type **Kayak,** and press the **Enter** key.

7. To save and close the workbook, click the **Save** button on the Standard toolbar, type **Step-by-Step 3.2 Solution,** be sure the correct folder for your files appears in the **Save in** box, click **Save,** and then click the **Close Window** button.

Using AutoCorrect

Excel's AutoCorrect feature may correct some of your typing errors. AutoCorrect contains a list of commonly misspelled words that Excel will correct if you enter them incorrectly. For example, it will correct two initial capitals (WHite). AutoCorrect also capitalizes the names of days of the week automatically.

You can use the AutoCorrect command on the expanded Tools menu to add words you often misspell. If entered incorrectly, Excel will correct them (see Figure 3.5). You can even use a short string of characters (for example, abc) to signal AutoCorrect to replace with a long entry you often use (American Business Corporation, Inc.). You can also remove a default AutoCorrect entry if you find it does not work well for you.

FIGURE 3.5
AutoCorrect contains commonly misspelled words and their corrections.

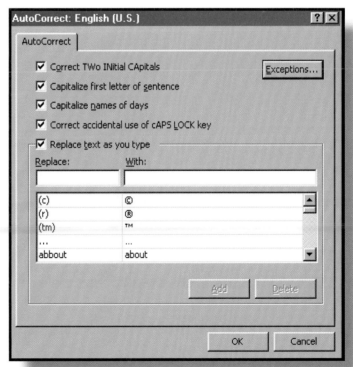

Checking Spelling

You can use the Spelling button or the Spelling command on the Tools menu to check your worksheet for spelling errors. The Spelling dialog box opens, as shown in Figure 3.6. Excel's main dictionary contains most commonly used words. If Excel finds a word in your worksheet that does not appear in its main dictionary, it gives you options for correcting the possible misspelling.

Spelling button

You probably will use some words that are not in Excel's main dictionary. When Excel selects such a word when you run check spelling, you can:

■ Add the word to a custom dictionary.

■ Ignore the word or ignore all occurrences of the word.

■ Change the word or change all occurrences of the word.

Concept Builders

If you are using Microsoft Office, Spelling uses the same dictionary for all the Office applications. The custom dictionary is also the same throughout the applications.

It is important to remember that the spelling check feature does not do away with the need to proofread a worksheet. If your typing error results in another English word (such as *form* instead of *from*), the spell checking feature will not notice it. You must always proofread carefully.

FIGURE 3.6
The Spelling dialog box shows the options available to you when you check spelling.

STEP-BY-STEP 3.3

1. Open the workbook **Step-by-Step 3-3 Tools.**

2. To set up the AutoCorrect feature to replace the letter Z followed by your initials with your full name, click the **Tools** menu, click

the **Expand** button if needed, and click **AutoCorrect**, type **Z***your initials* in the **Replace** text box, press Tab and type *your full name* in the **With** text box. Click **Add** and then click **OK.**

3. To add a subtitle to the worksheet, click cell **A2,** type **Z***your initials* and press the **Enter** key. Notice that Excel automatically entered your full name.

4. To remove the entry from AutoCorrect, click the **Tools** menu, click **AutoCorrect,** type a **Z** in the **Replace** text box, scroll to and click on **Z***your initials* in the **Replace** list box, press the **Delete** command button, and click **OK.**

5. To check the spelling in the worksheet, be sure **A3** is still the active cell, and click the **Spelling** button on the Standard toolbar.

6. To change **Employeee** with three e's to Employee, click the **Change** button.

7. To continue checking at the beginning of the sheet, click **Yes.**

8. To change the misspelled word Salez to Sales, accept Excel's suggestion that appears in the **Change to** text box by clicking the **Change** button.

9. To respond to the prompt that Excel is finished spell checking the sheet, click **OK.**

10. To save and close the workbook, click its **Close Window** button and click **Yes** when asked to save changes.

Making Printing Easy

You can use the Print Preview, Page Setup, Print Area and Print commands on the File menu and the Print button on the Standard toolbar to make printing your worksheets an easy task.

Previewing a Worksheet

Before you print a worksheet, it's a good idea to use the preview feature. Previewing your work lets you spot problems before you use time (and paper) printing documents that don't look exactly the way you want.

You can preview a worksheet by choosing Print Preview on the File menu. You can see a Print Preview in Figure 3.7.

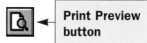

Print Preview button

NOTE:

Remember you can use the More Buttons button on the Standard toolbar to access the Print Preview button or add it to your toolbar if you use it often.

Notice the command buttons at the top of the screen. Each is explained below:

■ *Next:* Displays the next page if there is more than one page. You can also use the scroll bars and the arrow keys to move through pages. Notice that the status bar displays the number of pages in the worksheet.

■ *Previous:* Displays the previous page.

■ *Zoom:* Switches between a full-page view and a magnified view. When you click the magnifier pointer anywhere on the sheet, it is the equivalent of clicking the Zoom button. You can use the scroll bars or arrow keys to move around a page in a magnified view.

■ *Print:* Displays the Print dialog box.

FIGURE 3.7
The worksheet is displayed in Print Preview.

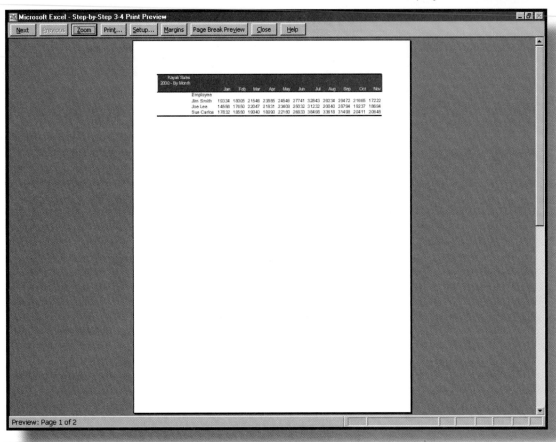

Microsoft Excel - Step-by-Step 3-4 Print Preview

Next | Previous | Zoom | Print... | Setup... | Margins | Page Break Preview | Close | Help

Preview: Page 1 of 2

- *Setup:* Displays the Page Setup dialog box. You will learn more about page setup options later.

- *Margins:* Displays page margin guides. The dotted lines (not shown in Figure 3.7) represent page margins and header and footer margins. Small black handles that also represent margins and columns appear as well. You can easily adjust margins or column widths by dragging the handles.

- *Page Break Preview:* Switches you to Page Break Preview where you can adjust page breaks on the worksheet, resize the print area, or edit the worksheet. The button name changes to Normal View if you were in Page Break Preview when you chose Print Preview.

- *Normal View:* Displays the active sheet in normal view.

- *Close:* Closes the preview window and returns you to the worksheet.

- *Help:* displays Help for the Print Preview buttons.

Concept Builders

When you return to Print Preview from Page Break Preview, the Page Break button changes to the Normal View button.

NOTE:

You cannot edit data in your worksheet while in Print Preview.

STEP-BY-STEP ▷ 3.4

1. Open the workbook **Step-by-Step 3-4 Print Preview.**

2. To apply an AutoFormat, select the range **A1:N7,** click the **Format** menu, click **AutoFormat,** click **Classic 2** on the Table format list, and click **OK.**

3. To see your sheet in Print Preview, click the File menu and then click **Print Preview.**

4. To zoom in on the worksheet data, click the magnifier pointer on the data.

5. To reduce the magnification and return to a full-page display, click on the data again or click the **Zoom** button.

6. To display the margins and header/footer boundaries and handles, click the **Margins** button.

7. To change the top margin from 1 to 1.5 inches, point to the second handle from the top of the page on the left or right edge.

Drag the handle until the status bar at the bottom left displays a measurement as close to **1.50** as you can get. Then release.

8. To see the worksheet in Page Break Preview, click **Page Break Preview.** Notice the dashed line where the page breaks and the dimmed Page 1 and Page 2 indicators. You may see a dialog box letting you know you can adjust where the page breaks are by dragging with the mouse. Click OK if you do.

Hot Tips

You can also use the Page Break command on the Insert menu to enter and remove page breaks.

9. To return to Print Preview, click the File menu and click **Print Preview.** Notice the Page Break Preview button is now the Normal View button. Click the **Normal View** button to return to that view.

Using the Page Setup Command

You can use the Page Setup command on the File menu (or click Setup in the Print Preview window) to open the Page Setup dialog box shown in Figure 3.8.

The Page Setup dialog box has four tabs: Page, Margins, Header/Footer, and Sheet. The options on each tab are explained below. We'll start with the Page tab shown in Figure 3.8:

- *Orientation* lets you print the sheet in Portrait (short edge of the paper is at the top) or Landscape (long edge of the paper is at the top).

- *Scaling* lets you enlarge or reduce the image that prints. You can reduce it to 10 percent of normal size or enlarge it up to 400 percent, depending on your printer. You can also reduce the sheet or selection so that it fits on a specific number of pages wide by tall.

- *Paper Size* lets you select letter, legal, 11x17, or other sizes depending on your printer.

- *Print quality* lets you select the resolution (number of dots per inch) for printing. The higher the number you select, the better the print quality. Some printers let you change that number.

- *First page number* lets you start page numbering at 1 or at a number of your choosing, if it is not the first page in the document you are assembling.

FIGURE 3.8

The Page Setup tabs control orientation, scaling, paper size,
print quality, and the starting page number.

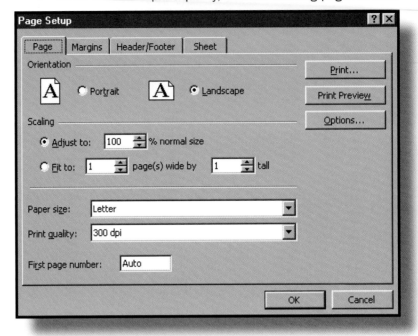

Figure 3.9 shows the Margins tab in the Page Setup dialog box. You can set the top, bottom, left, and right margins, set the header and footer positions, and center data horizontally, vertically, or both ways on the page.

The options on the Header/Footer tab are shown in Figure 3.10. A **header** is text that prints at the top of each page of a sheet; a **footer** is text that prints at the bottom. You can select an existing header or footer from the Header or Footer drop-down lists. Or, to create your own, click the Custom Header or Custom Footer buttons. A dialog box (either a Header or Footer dialog box) appears, as shown in Figure 3.11.

The Header or Footer dialog box allows you to place text in the left, center, or right parts of the page. You can enter text yourself or click one or more of the predefined buttons to insert text and other information. To format header and footer text, select it in the dialog box, and then click the Font button. You can select the font, font style, and size in the Font dialog box when it appears.

Hot Tips

When you have just one line or column that does not fit on a page, use the *Fit to* option on the Page tab to fit all the data on one page.

NOTE:

If you enter headers or footers and they do not print, try increasing the distance of the header or footer from the edge of the page on the Page Setup Margins tab.

The Sheet tab is shown in Figure 3.12. You can specify the area or range of the worksheet you want to print in the Print area text box. Remember you can click the Collapse Dialog button at the end of the Print area text box to select a range.

FIGURE 3.9

You can center worksheets horizontally and vertically on the page.

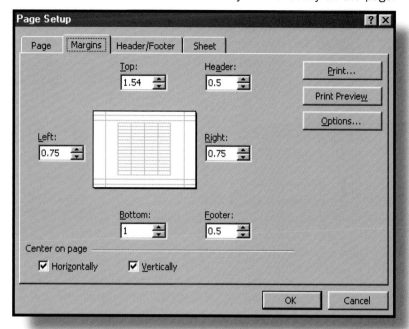

FIGURE 3.10

You can choose one of Excel's existing headers or footers or create your own using the Custom buttons.

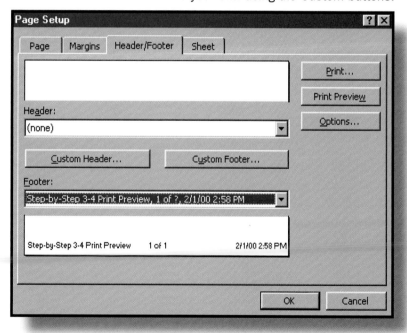

You can choose to print row and/or column titles at the top or left of each page when you are working with longer worksheets.

You can opt to print gridlines, which often make reading larger worksheets easier.

FIGURE 3.11

Create your own footer in the Footer dialog box.

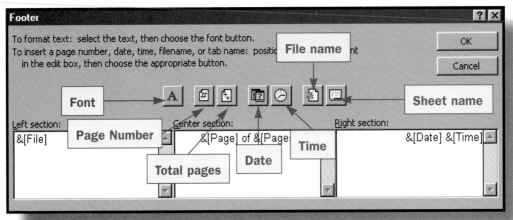

FIGURE 3.12

You can control what prints using options on the Sheet tab.

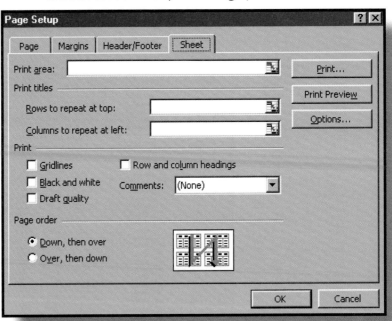

You can turn on the black and white option if you formatted your data in color, but you are not printing on a color printer.

Select Draft quality if you want to reduce printing time. Excel will not print gridlines or graphics.

You can opt to print comments and row and column headings. (You will learn more about comments in Lesson 7.)

Hot Tips

Options on the Sheet tab may be dimmed if the Page Setup dialog box is opened in the Print Preview window. Open Page Setup from the File menu to activate these options.

For worksheets that are more than one page wide, you can use the Page order options to control how pages print. You can choose to print from the first page to the pages below and then move to the right, or to print from the first page to the pages to the right and then move down.

 **NOTE:**

The Options button on each tab in the Page Setup dialog box contains additional choices that are geared to your selected printer.

STEP-BY-STEP ⊳ 3.5

1. To display the Page Setup dialog box, click the **File** menu, and click **Page Setup.**

2. To display the page options if they are not already displayed, click the **Page** tab.

3. To change the orientation of the page, click the **Landscape** option.

4. To display the margin options, click the **Margins** tab.

5. To center the data on the page, click the **Horizontally** and **Vertically** options at the bottom of the dialog box.

6. To display the header and footer options, click the **Header/Footer** tab.

7. To enter a custom footer, click **Custom Footer.**

8. To add the file name to the footer, click in the **Left section,** if necessary, and click the **File name** button (see Figure 3.11).

9. To enter the page number and total number of pages at the center of the page, click in the **Center section,** click the **Page Number** button, press the **Spacebar,** type **of,** press the **Spacebar,** and click the **Total Pages** button.

10. To enter a footer at the right side of the page, click in the **Right section** box (the blinking insertion point appears flush right).

11. To enter the printing date and time, click the **Date** button, press the **Spacebar,** click the **Time** button, and then click **OK.** Notice the Footer box now displays the information you added.

12. To display the sheet options, click the **Sheet** tab.

13. To preview the worksheet with the changes you've made, click the **Print Preview** command button on the dialog box. Notice Excel changed the orientation to Landscape, centered the data horizontally and vertically, and added the information you entered for the footer.

14. To close the Print Preview window, click the **Close** command button on the Print Preview button bar.

15. To save changes you've made to the workbook so far, click the **Save** button on the Standard toolbar.

Using the Print Command

You can use the Print command on the File menu to display the Print dialog box (see Figure 3.13). Choose All in the Print range box to print the entire document. Use the Pages option to print just the pages you specify.

Use the Selection option in the Print what box to print just the selected parts of the worksheet. Use the Entire workbook option to print the entire workbook. Excel will print only the sheets that contain data.

Use the Active sheet(s) option to print the selected sheets.

By default, Excel prints the active sheet or sheets.

You can click the Print button on the Standard toolbar when you want to print using the default settings in the Print dialog box. Excel sends your active worksheet(s) directly to the printer without opening the Print dialog box.

To select a second sheet for printing, hold the Shift key and click the second sheet's tab.

FIGURE 3.13
The Print dialog box lets you print a selection, selected sheets, or the entire workbook.

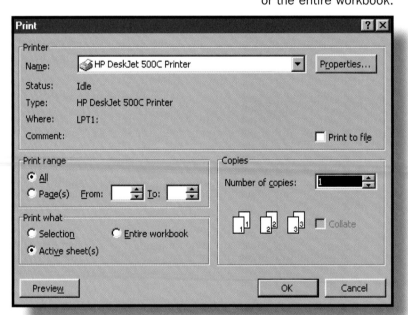

STEP-BY-STEP 3.6

1. To print the worksheet, click the **File** menu and click **Print.**

2. In the Print dialog box, make sure **All** is selected in the Print range options; **1** appears in the Number of copies text box; and **Active sheet(s)** is selected in the Print what options. Click **OK.**

3. Save the workbook.

Using Web Features

Excel 2000 has several features that make it really easy to work with HTML files either on the Web or on your intranet. Excel also has a wide variety of tools and features that can help you connect to the Internet, find information of all kinds, and even insert addresses directly in your documents so that the reader can jump to another file on your system, to a site on your intranet, or to the Internet.

Previewing and Saving as a Web Page

You can convert worksheet data into HTML (Hypertext Markup Language) format so that it can be published as part of an existing web page or as its own web page. HTML is the format used for Web pages. It enables Web users to open and access most files published on the Web, regardless of the browser they are using and the application used to create the Web page.

Excel saves any non-Web-supported formatting options so when you open your file in Excel, the standard formatting is still intact. Excel also saves all Web-supporting files in a folder with the same name as the file and can update and repair links.

INTERNET Contact your system administrator to publish a page on your intranet or your ISP to publish a page on the Internet.

To open your Web browser and preview a worksheet, use the Web Page Preview command on the File menu (see Figure 3.14).

FIGURE 3.14
You can see the worksheet data in HTML format.

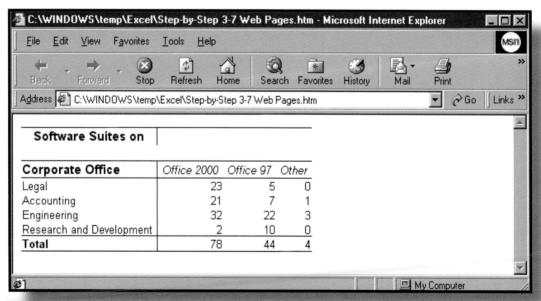

To convert worksheet data into HTML format in Excel, use the Save as Web Page command on the File menu (see Figure 3.15).

Use the Publish button in the Save as Web Page dialog box to display the Publish as Web Page dialog box (see Figure 3.16). You can add spreadsheet or pivot table interactivity so users can interact with the data.

7 5

FIGURE 3.15
This dialog box appears when you choose Save as Web Page.

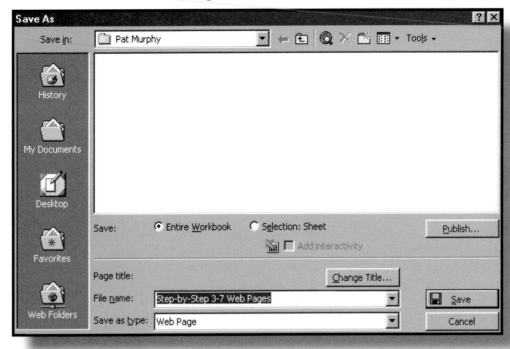

FIGURE 3.16
The Publish as Web dialog box is where
you can add interactivity.

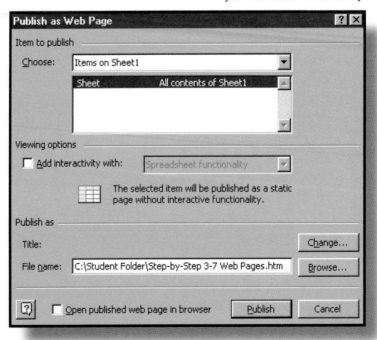

Use the Title button to set a page title that will be displayed in the title bar of the browser (see Figure 3.17).

FIGURE 3.17
Set a title for display in the browser title bar.

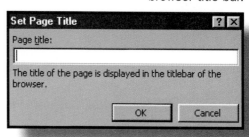

STEP-BY-STEP ▷ 3.7

1. Open the **Step-by-Step 3-7 Web Pages** workbook. To preview the worksheet data as a Web page in your browser, click the **File** menu and click **Web Page Preview.** Notice how the worksheet data looks in your browser.

2. To close your browser, click its **Close** button.

3. To save the the data as an HTML file, click the **File** menu, click **Save as Web Page.** Click the **Selection: Sheet** option.

4. To set a title to display in the browser title bar, click **Change Title,** type **Software by Department** in the **Title** text box, and click **OK.**

5. To save the file as a Web file, be sure the folder containing your files for the course is displayed in the **Save in** text box at the top of the dialog box and click Save.

6. To close the file, click its Close button.

Using the Web Toolbar

You can use the Toolbars command on the View menu to display or to turn off the Web toolbar (Figure 3.18).

The Web toolbar contains a number of buttons to help you easily negotiate the Web:

■ Use the Back and Forward buttons to move back to a previous site or forward to the following site.

Concept Builders

It is a good idea to save your open files before accessing the Internet.

FIGURE 3.18
The Web toolbar.

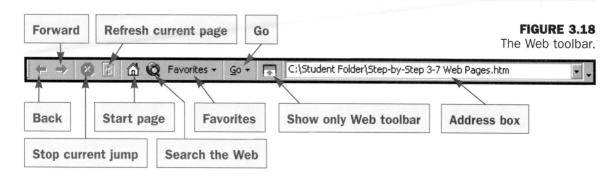

Forward · Refresh current page · Go · Back · Start page · Favorites · Show only Web toolbar · Address box · Stop current jump · Search the Web

C:\Student Folder\Step-by-Step 3-7 Web Pages.htm

- Use the Stop Current Jump button to cancel a jump. The button is especially useful if it seems to be taking a very long time to display a page.

- Use the Refresh Current Page button to update the current page by reloading it.

- Use the Start Page button to go to a starting page of your choosing. Use the Set Start Page command on the Web toolbar's Go menu to designate a start page.

INTERNET

Different search engines search Web sites differently so you should be aware how the engines available from your Internet access provider work.

- Use the Search the Web button to access the World Wide Web. From there you can use one of the search engines to find information about a subject of your choosing.

- Use the Favorites button to return to a site you have added to your favorites list or to enter a site as a favorite.

- Use the Go drop-down menu to access some of the Web toolbar commands as well as to set the start pages for the Web itself and for searching the Web.

- Use the Show Only Web Toolbar button to turn off the other Excel toolbars and display only the Web toolbar.

 Did You Know?

Most Internet Service Providers (ISPs) have software that will disconnect you after a specified period of inactivity.

- Use the Address box to enter a URL to go directly to a Web site or page of your choosing as well as to a page on your intranet or a document on your system.

 **IMPORTANT:**

You must have an Internet connection through a modem or a server to complete the following step-by-step exercises.

S TEP-BY-STEP 3.8

1. Open the **Step-by-Step 3-8 Hyperlinks** file.

2. To display the Web toolbar if it is not already on your screen, click the **View** menu, click **Toolbars,** and click **Web.**

3. To display the Microsoft Office home page, click the Address box on the Web toolbar and type **http://www.microsoft.com,** press the **Enter** key, and sign in and connect to

your Internet access provider if necessary. Read some of Microsoft's latest news about their company and their products.

4. To return to your Excel document, click the **Microsoft Excel** button for your document on the Windows taskbar. If you are asked to disconnect, click **No** because you will use the Internet access again.

5. To access the Web for a search, click the **Search the Web** button on the Web toolbar, type **Microsoft Office 2000** in the Search for box, click **AltaVista** if it is available as a search engine, and then click a hyperlink to see one of the category matches your search engine displays.

6. To return to the Excel document, click the **Microsoft Excel** button on the taskbar.

Creating Hyperlinks

You have already learned that hyperlinks are underlined or bordered words or graphics that have Web or other addresses embedded in them. You can also use hyperlinks to add additional or supporting information to Excel documents that will be read online. The hyperlink destination can be a file on your hard drive, on a company intranet, or on the Internet. You can even use hyperlinks to jump to multimedia files, such as videos and sounds.

When you click a hyperlink, Excel displays its destination object. You can use the Back button on your browser's toolbar or the workbook's button on the Window's taskbar to return to the original location in the Excel document.

IMPORTANT:

The reader must have access to the hyperlink addresses you insert in documents or the hyperlinks will be useless. You should not, for instance, put a hyperlink to a document on your drive to which the reader does not have access.

You can insert a hyperlink by simply typing a URL address in your document. Excel recognizes it as a hyperlink and formats it automatically.

To delete a hyperlink, right-click the hyperlink, click Hyperlink on the shortcut menu, click Edit Hyperlink, and click Remove Link in the Edit Hyperlink dialog box (see Figure 3.19).

You can use the Hyperlink command on the Insert menu to add a hyperlink to your Excel document:

■ Select the text or graphic you want to use to indicate the hyperlink.

■ Choose Hyperlink on the Insert menu.

■ Decide if you want to link to an existing file or Web page, a different place in your Excel document, a new document, or an e-mail address.

■ Enter or select the location information needed for the hyperlink.

■ Enter a ScreenTip if you want your own ScreenTip instead of the path to the linked-to file or page.

In the exercise below, you will insert hyperlinks that will let the user jump to Microsoft Office information on the Web.

FIGURE 3.19
Type or select an address for a hyperlink in this dialog box.

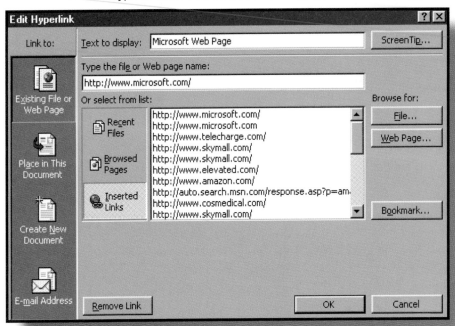

STEP-BY-STEP 3.9

C

1. To insert a hyperlink in a cell, click **A10,** type **http://www.microsoft.com,** and press the **Enter** key. Notice Excel recognized the address as a URL and added hyperlink formatting.

2. To see the ScreenTip for the hyperlink, slide the hand pointer on it until the ScreenTip appears.

3. To test the hyperlink, click it with the hand pointer.

4. To return to the Excel workbook, click its button on the taskbar.

5. To insert a hyperlink that displays text other than the URL, click **A11,** type, **Microsoft Web Page,** press the **Enter** key, click cell **A11** again, click the **Insert** menu, and click **Hyperlink.** Be sure **Existing File or Web Page** button is selected in the **Link to** box. Click **http://www.microsoft.com** if it appears on the list. Otherwise type it in the **Type the file or Web page name** text box, and click **OK.**

6. To test the hyperlink, click it.

7. To return to the Excel file, click its button on the taskbar.

Sending Documents Electronically

You can use the options on the File menu's Send To command to send an e-mail message in the "universal" HTML format. A message can include animated graphics, multimedia objects, and anything else you can put on a Web page.

IMPORTANT

To e-mail a message in HTML format, you need Excel 2000 and either Outlook 2000 or Outlook Express 5.0 or later. To e-mail or route a document as an attachment in Excel format, you need Excel 2000 *and* a 32-bit e-mail program compatible with the Messaging Application Programming Interface (MAPI) *or* a 16-bit e-mail program compatible with Vendor Independent Messaging (VIM).

To view an e-mail message or document in HTML format, the recipient needs a Web browser or e-mail program that can read documents in HTML format.

To view a document sent as an attachment in Excel format, recipients need Excel 97 or later.

You can use the commands on the File menu's Send To submenu to deliver documents electronically. When you use the Mail Recipient or Routing Recipient commands, your document is included as an attachment to an e-mail message and displays as an icon, as shown in Figure 3.20. The recipient simply double-clicks the document icon to open it.

■ Use the Mail Recipient command to send a document to an individual or group of individuals. All recipients get the document at the same time. You enter the recipients' e-mail addresses, the subject, additional documents, and a message. Microsoft recommends you use this option when you want to distribute a document quickly to a specific list of reviewers.

FIGURE 3.20
Your document appears as an attachment in the message.

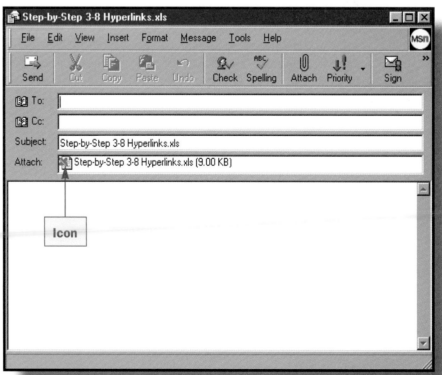

- Use the Routing Recipient command to send a document to a group of recipients who will receive the document in the order you specify. When a reviewer finishes reviewing and adding comments to the document and clicks the Send To command, Next Routing Recipient appears on the submenu so the next recipient can get the document. When the last reviewer finishes with the document, Excel returns it to you. You will learn more about reviewers' comments in Lesson 7.

Concept Builders

E-mail really speeds up the process of delivering Excel data when compared to the time it takes to print out files and address envelopes for regular mail delivery.

- Use the Exchange Folder command to post a document to a Microsoft Exchange public folder so others can access the document over the network. You might use this command when you have a document, such as a company manual, that needs to be available to many network users.

STEP-BY-STEP 3.10

1. To attach the open workbook to an e-mail message, click the **File** menu, click **Send To**, and click **Mail Recipient (as Attachment)** on the submenu.

2. To send the workbook to yourself via e-mail, type your e-mail address in the To box, position the I-beam in the message area, press the **Enter** key, and type **This is the workbook I mentioned when we spoke earlier today.** Press the **Send** button. You may have to reconnect to your Internet provider if the connection has been broken.

3. To close the Excel document, click the **Microsoft Excel** button on the taskbar, and click the document's **Close** button.

4. To check on how an e-mail message with an attachment works, wait until the mail has been sent and received in your in box. Then open the message by double-clicking the document icon.

5. Close your mail application and return to Excel.

Summary

You have now learned how to create and enhance a worksheet by using the AutoFormat command, the spell checking feature, and Excel's AutoFormats. You also learned how to use the various printing and page setup options. And, you learned how to work with Web features and send workbooks electronically.

Try the exercises on the following pages to test how well you remember what you learned. Don't be afraid to go back and look up the answers, because that will help to reinforce what you learned.

LESSON 3 REVIEW QUESTIONS

TRUE / FALSE

Circle the T if the statement is true. Circle the F if it is false.

T F 1. The AutoFormat dialog box contains preset worksheet formats you can apply to your data.

T F 2. You can use the Save As command to rename a sheet in your workbook.

T F 3. You do not have to proofread data if you use Excel's Spelling command.

T F 4. You can edit data in your worksheet in Print Preview.

T F 5. AutoCorrect will capitalize the days of the week automatically.

T F 6. You can change margin settings in Print Preview.

T F 7. You can begin page numbering at a number other than one.

T F 8. You can opt to print a sheet or selection so it fits on a specified number of pages.

T F 9. To view a workbook sent as an e-mail attachment in Excel format, recipients need Excel 97 or later.

T F 10. You can save an entire workbook or just selected data in HTML format.

COMPLETION

Complete the following sentences by writing the correct word or words in the blanks provided.

1. To rename a worksheet, double-click the _____ and type the new name.

2. Use the _____ command on the _____ menu to apply a preset Excel format to your worksheet data.

3. Use the _____ command on the _____ menu to see how your worksheet data will look on a page before you print it.

4. You can display the _____ tab in the Page Setup dialog box to change the orientation of the page.

5. You can display the _____ tab in the Page Setup dialog box to center data horizontally and vertically on a page.

6. You can display the _____ tab in the Page Setup dialog box to turn off gridlines when printing.

7. You can display the _____ tab in the Page Setup dialog box to add or edit headers or footers.

8. You can click the _____ button in Print Preview to display margin and header/footer boundaries and handles.

9. You can click the _____ command on the Send To command's submenu to send a copy of a workbook to a public folder.

10. The _____ feature corrects some typographical errors as you enter them.

LESSON 3 PROJECTS

PROJECT 3A

To practice what you've learned in this lesson, complete the following project:

1. Open the workbook **Project 3-A.**

2. Rename Sheet1 as **Test Grades.**

3. Check the spelling on the sheet. Do not change any proper names.

4. Select the range **A1:G10** and use the **AutoFormat** command to apply the **List 2** format to the range.

5. Select the range **A1:G10** again if needed, click the **Edit** menu, move to **Clear,** and click **Formats** to remove the AutoFormat.

6. Open the AutoFormat dialog box again. Select the **List 1** format and click **OK.**

7. Select the range **A1:G10.** Click the **File** menu and click **Print.** From the Print what options, click **Selection.** Click **OK.**

8. Choose **Save As** on the File menu and save the workbook as **AutoFormat Review.** Then, close the workbook.

PROJECT 3B

To practice what you've learned in this lesson, complete the following project:

1. Open the workbook **Project 3-B.**

2. Select range **A1:D7.**

3. Click **File,** choose **Print Area,** and click **Set Print Area.**

4. Click the **Print Preview** button. Click **Close.**

5. Click **File,** choose **Print Area,** and click **Clear Print Area.**

6. Click the **Print Preview** button.

7. To break the pages between the June and July figures, click **Page Break Preview.** If you see a message box, click **OK.** Click on and drag the **vertical heavy blue page marker** on the right edge so you see part of **Page 2.** Click and drag the dashed blue page break marker so it's between the Jun and Jul columns.

8. To exit from Page Break Preview, choose **Normal** on the **View** menu. Then, click the **Print Preview** button on the Standard toolbar.

9. To change the orientation, click **Setup.** Click the **Page** tab and click Landscape orientation. Click the **Margins** tab and click the **Horizontally** option.

10. To add a header, click the **Header/Footer** tab. Click **Custom Header.** Click in the **Left section** and then click the **Date** button. Click in the **Right section** and then click the **Page Number** button. Click **OK** to close the Header dialog box and click OK again to close the Page Setup dialog box. Then, click **Close** to close the preview window.

Extra Challenges

Use help to find information creating a hyperlink to an existing file. Read and print the information you find.

11. To set rows and columns to repeat on each page, on the File menu, click **Page Setup.** Click the **Sheet** tab. Click the **Collapse Dialog** button at the end of the **Rows to repeat at top** text box. On the worksheet, select rows **1** and **2.** A moving dotted line appears around rows 1 and 2. Click the Expand Dialog button in the collapsed Page Setup dialog box to reopen it. Click the **Collapse Dialog** button at the end of the **Columns to repeat at left** text box. On the worksheet, select column **A.** Reopen the Page Setup dialog box and then click **OK.**

12. To preview and print, click **Print Preview** again. Click **Next** and then click **Previous.** Click **Print.** In the Print dialog box, click **OK.**

13. Save the workbook as **Printing Review.** Then, close the workbook.

PROJECT 3C

SCANS

Start a new blank workbook and display the Web toolbar. Click the **Search the Web** button and search for information on spreadsheets. You might want to use a couple of different search engines. You will get different results when using different search engines. Print any topics you feel are relevant and share them with classmates.

CRITICAL THINKING ACTIVITY

You manage the Island Water Sports Pier where you rent kayaks, windsurfers, and wave runners. Start a new workbook and create a worksheet using the data shown in Figure 3.21. Add totals for each of the months and for each of the rental types. Rename the sheet **98 Sales.** Apply the **3D Effects 1** AutoFormat to the data.

FIGURE 3.21
Enter this data in a new workbook.

	A	B	C	D	E	F	G	H	I
1	In-Season 2000 Sales								
2									
3		Apr	May	Jun	Jul	Aug	Sep	Total	
4	Kayaks	9432	10678	11890	15345	14876	11341		
5	Windsurfers	7123	8567	8678	10238	10678	9098		
6	WaveRunners	14987	15321	15765	18869	17240	16350		
7	Total								
8									

Sheet1 / Sheet2 / Sheet3 /

Center the data horizontally and vertically and in landscape orientation. Preview the worksheet. Print the worksheet.

Add a hyperlink to Step-by-Step 3-4 Print Preview. Send the workbook to a classmate if you have the e-mail software.

Save the workbook using the file name **Critical Thinking Activity 2,** and then close the workbook.

FORMATTING AND EDITING THE WORKSHEET

OBJECTIVES

When you complete this lesson, you will be able to:

■ Adjust column width and row height.

■ Format cells.

■ Copy formats.

■ Apply conditional formatting.

■ Use styles.

■ Insert cells, rows, and columns.

■ Copy and move data.

■ Use the Find and Replace commands.

🕐 **Estimated Time: 1½ hours**

Introduction

Now that you know how to create and print a worksheet, you will learn more about how to use Excel's editing and formatting tools to enhance the appearance of a worksheet. In this lesson, you will learn to adjust column widths; use fonts; align data in cells; use borders, colors, and patterns; insert and delete cells, rows, and columns; copy and move data; and find and replace data.

Adjusting Column Width and Row Height

When you create a new workbook, columns are set to a default width. You can change that setting for all columns or for just selected columns.

Excel provides several ways to adjust column width. You can drag a column heading border—the line separating column letters—to the width you want. Double-click the right side column heading border so Excel sets the column width to make the longest entry fit. Choose the Column command on the Format menu and then choose Width, Auto Fit Selection, or Standard Width on the submenu.

If you choose Width on the submenu, the Column Width dialog box appears (see Figure 4.1), and you can set a specific width. The width is measured by the number of characters in the standard font that can be entered in the cell.

If you choose AutoFit Selection on the submenu, the column adjusts to automatically fit the longest entry. Note that you must select the entire column, the range of cells in the column that you want adjusted, or the cell containing the longest entry for this option to work.

If you choose Standard Width, the Standard Width dialog box opens where you can enter a width of your choosing as the default width. The Hide and Unhide commands on the Column submenu are discussed in Lesson 5.

Row height can be adjusted with similar procedures. When you enter data in a worksheet, rows automatically adjust to accommodate wrapped text or the largest font size applied to data in the row. (You will learn more about font size later in this lesson.)

You can change the height of a row with one of the following procedures. Drag the border of the row heading until the row is the height you want. Choose the Row command on the Format menu and then choose Height or AutoFit on the submenu.

When you choose Row Height on the submenu, the Row Height dialog box appears (see Figure 4.2). You can set a specific height for a specified row(s) or all rows (height is measured in points, which will be covered later in this lesson). When you choose the AutoFit command on the submenu, the row height adjusts to fit the largest font size or the wrapped data of a specified row(s) or all rows.

FIGURE 4.1
Set the column width in the Column Width dialog box.

Concept Builders

You will usually not need to use the Row Height commands since Excel changes the height to accommodate the data and font size.

FIGURE 4.2
The 12.75 row height accommodates a 10 point font.

STEP-BY-STEP 4.1

1. Open the workbook **Step-by-Step 4-1 Column Width.**

2. To widen the column to fit the names because some of them are not fully displayed, click the **B** column heading, click the **Format** menu, click **Column,** and click **AutoFit Selection.** Notice column B is now wider than the others.

3. To return to the original width, click the **Undo** button.

4. To change the column width to fit the longest entry in column B, click on a blank cell to deselect the column, position the mouse pointer on the right border of the column **B** heading until you see a double-headed arrow pointer. Then double-click. Notice column B is now wide enough for the longest entry.

5. To return to the previous width, click the **Undo** button.

6. To change the width of column B to one of your choosing, drag the right border of the column B heading until you think it is wide enough for the longest entry, and then release.

7. To increase the height of row 1, be sure a cell in row **1** is active, click the **Format** menu, click **Row,** click **Height,** type **20** in the Row Height dialog box, and click **OK.** Notice the increased height of row 1.

8. To return to the original height, click **Undo.**

9. To increase the height of row 1 with the mouse, point to the bottom border of the row **1** heading until you see a vertical double-headed arrow, and drag until the row is about twice its size. Notice the ScreenTip that appears showing the height of the row as you drag.

10. To return to the previous row height, click the **Undo** button.

Formatting a Worksheet

In the previous lesson, you learned about Excel's AutoFormat feature and how it's a useful tool for quickly applying attractive formats to your worksheets. Excel has a whole range of additional formatting tools that let you change and enhance the appearance of a worksheet.

To format data and cells, you must first select them. Then, you can use buttons on the Formatting toolbar (see Figure 4.3). The most often used formatting features are on the Formatting toolbar. You can use many formats without opening the dialog box.

The More Buttons button contains many other formatting buttons that you can add to your Formatting toolbar if you use them often.

 **Hot Tips**

Remember you can drag the vertical bar at the left of the toolbar to place it on a line of its own to display more buttons.

FIGURE 4.3

The Formatting toolbar contains buttons for the most often used formatting features.

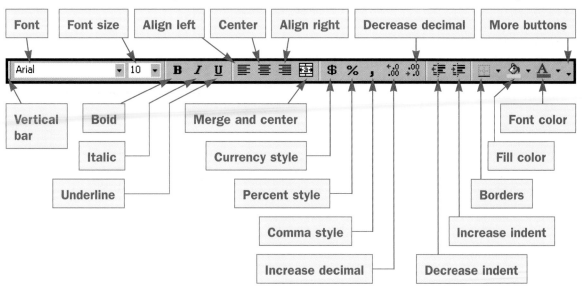

The Cells command on the Format menu is where you can access many formatting features available to you. The Format Cells dialog box contains six tabs containing the various options.

The Number Tab

When you enter a number in a cell, Excel automatically applies the General format. The General format displays numbers as integers, decimal fractions, or scientific notation if the number is longer than the width of the cell. To change to a different number format, you can select one of the built-in formats in the Category list on the Number tab (see Figure 4.4).

Concept Builders

Notice in Figure 4.4 that the Euro currency symbol is available for you to use in your worksheets.

FIGURE 4.4
Format Cells dialog box is the "command center" for formatting operations.

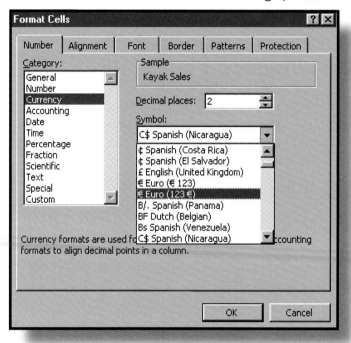

When you select a format in the list, additional options specific to that format appear in the right part of the dialog box, along with a description and sample of the format. Formatting does not change internal storage or calculations.

NOTE:

When you enter a number with a dollar sign or a percent sign, Excel changes the cell format from General to a currency or percentage format.

In addition to the formats Excel provides, you can create a custom number format. For example, you might want to format dates or times differently from the formats Excel provides. Choose the Custom category, choose an existing format code, and alter it using Excel's number format codes.

STEP-BY-STEP ▷ 4.2

1. To put the Formatting toolbar on a row by itself at the top of the worksheet if it is not already so positioned, drag its vertical handle to a position just below its current row.

2. To display commas as 1000 separators for the numbers in cells C5 through H7, select **C5:H7.** If you see the Comma Style button on the Formatting toolbar, click it.

3. To delete the two decimal places that the comma style automatically added, be sure

C5:H7 is still selected and then click the **Decrease Decimal** button twice.

4. To display dollar signs and commas with the numbers in the Totals row, select **C8:H8,** click the **Format** menu, and click **Cells.** In the Format Cells dialog box, make sure the **Number** tab is selected. Click **Currency** in the Category list box, click the **down** button in the **Decimal places** spin box until it displays **0,** and click **OK.**

The Alignment Tab

As you have learned, Excel aligns numbers at the right of the cell and text at the left. The Alignment tab in the Format Cells dialog box (shown in Figure 4.5) lets you determine horizontal and vertical alignment of data, the orientation, and whether to wrap text in cells. Changing the alignment of data does not change the data or the data type.

From the Horizontal drop-down list, you can choose:

■ *General* to align text to the left, numbers to the right, and logical and error values in the center (the default horizontal alignment).

■ *Left (Indent)* to align cell contents to the left. (If you enter a number in the Indent spin box, Excel indents the data the specified number of character spaces.)

■ *Center* to align cell contents in the center of the cell.

■ *Right* to align cell contents to the right.

■ *Fill* to repeat the contents of the left-most selected cell across a selected range of blank cells.

FIGURE 4.5
You can see the various alignment options on the Alignment tab.

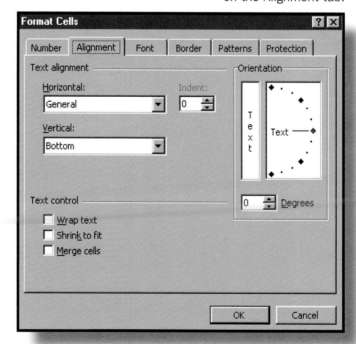

- *Justify* to align and wrap data within a cell at both the right and left of the cell. You won't see this unless you have more than one line of text.

- *Center Across Selection* to center the contents of the leftmost cell in a selection across the selected range. When you center data across a selected range, the data is still only in the original cell even though it appears to be in the other cells. You have to click the original cell to display the cell contents in the formula bar.

From the Vertical drop-down list, you can choose:

- *Top* to align cell contents along the top of the cell.

- *Center* to center cell contents in the middle of the cell.

- *Bottom* to align cell contents along the bottom of the cell (the default vertical alignment).

- *Justify* to align and wrap data evenly from the top to the bottom of the cell.

From the Text control options, you can choose:

- *Wrap text* to display cell contents on multiple lines within a cell. You can left-align, right-align, center, or justify wrapped text in a cell.

- *Shrink* to fit to reduce the displayed size of the data so it fits within the width of the cell.

- *Merge cells* to combine two or more cells into a single cell. The reference of the merged cell is the upper left cell in the original range.

The *Orientation* option lets you rotate cell contents to a specified degree. To set the degree of rotation, use a positive number in the Degrees spin box to rotate counter clockwise. Use a negative number to rotate clockwise.

You can also use the alignment buttons on the Formatting toolbar, shown in Figure 4.3. The Merge and Center button merges selected cells and centers contents of the upper left-most cell across a selected range.

The Font Tab

The Font tab in the Format Cells dialog box (see Figure 4.6) lets you change the characteristics or attributes of the data entered in cells. A **font** (also called a typeface) is the design of the characters you enter. Some examples are:

Times New Roman

Arial

BernhardMod BT

Courier

The fonts available on your computer are displayed in the Font list box. Fonts are listed alphabetically. The ⊤ icons that appear in front of some fonts indicate whether they are TrueType resident fonts. TrueType fonts can be displayed

FIGURE 4.6

Change font styles and sizes on the Font tab.

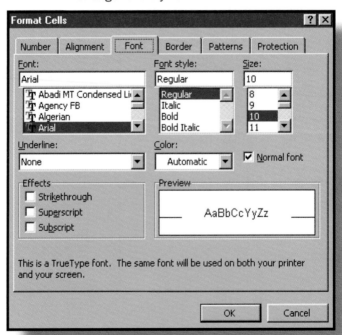

9 2

and printed in any size and are the fonts displayed on your screen.

You can apply the following styles to a font in the Font style list box: Regular, *Italic,* **Bold,** and ***Bold Italic.***

You can change the size of a font by selecting the size in the Size list box or by entering the size in the Size text box. The size of a font is measured in points. **Point size** measures the height of characters. A point is approximately equal to 1/72 of an inch. A 10 point font size, for example, is approximately 10/72 of an inch high when printed. The size of the text you are reading right now is 11 points.

In the Underline drop-down list, you can select from the following underlining formats: None, Single, Double, Single Accounting, and Double Accounting.

Use the Color drop-list to change the font color.

You can also apply the following special effects:

~~Strikethrough~~

Super^{script}

Sub$_{script}$

You can see a preview of any font options in the Preview box.

Hot Tips

The Arial font is the default font applied to worksheet data. The default size is 10 pt.

STEP-BY-STEP ▷ 4.3

C

1. To center the months in their cells, select **C4:H4** and click the **Center** alignment button.

2. To rotate the months in their cells, be sure **C4:H4** is still selected, click the **Format** menu, click **Cells,** click the **Alignment** tab, and click the **up** button in the **Orientation** spin box until it reaches **45.** Click **OK.**

3. To add the bold style to the data in row 4, select **B4:H4** and then click the **Bold** button.

4. To add the bold style to the word *Totals,* click cell **B8** and click the **Bold** button.

5. To center the title across the columns containing data, select **A1:I1** and click the **Merge and Center** button.

6. To center the subtitle across the columns containing data, select **A2:I2** and click the **Merge and Center** button.

7. To format the title text, click **A1,** click the **Format** menu, click **Cells,** and click the **Font** tab. In the Font list box, scroll to and click **Arial Narrow.** In the Font style list box, click **Bold Italic.** In the Size box, scroll to and click **16.** Click the Color drop-down button, and click a dark blue color. Click **OK.** Notice the row height increased for all of row 1.

8. To format the subtitle text, select cell **A2,** click the **Font** drop-down button on the Formatting toolbar and click **Arial Black,** click the **Font Size drop-down** button, click **12,** and then click the **Italic** button.

The Border Tab

The Border tab in the Format Cells dialog box (see Figure 4.7) lets you add borders to any side of a cell or range of cells. You can choose a line style for the border from the Style list box. Then, you can choose from one of the preset borders or create your own by clicking individual border buttons. The sample window illustrates where the border will be placed. To remove a border, simply click it in the sample window. You can also choose a color to apply to the border.

You can also click the Borders button on the Formatting toolbar to display a drop-down menu with various border options.

FIGURE 4.7
Excel displays various borders options on the Border tab.

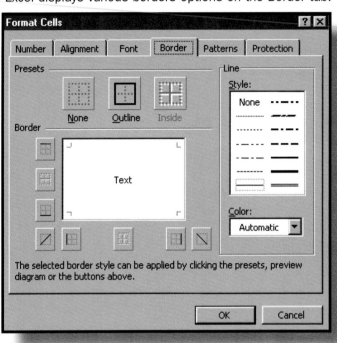

The Patterns Tab

The Patterns tab (see Figure 4.8) contains options for adding a background color and/or a pattern to a cell or range of cells. Color can add an extra dimension to your worksheet. For instance, you can use different colors for different products, sales reps, and so on. Excessive use of color, however, can be distracting.

FIGURE 4.8
Select colors and patterns for cells on the Patterns tab.

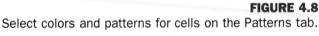

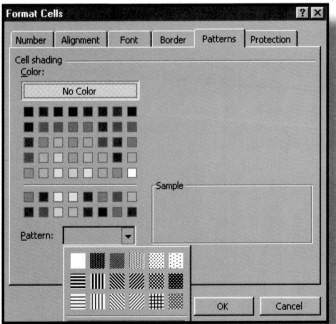

The Protection Tab

The Protection tab in the Format Cells dialog box lets you apply Excel's security features to data in certain cells. You will learn more about protecting data in Lesson 7.

INTERNET ISDN (Integrated Services Digital Network) lets us connect at high speeds to the Internet via existing telephone lines. The faster the Internet connection, the better it is for the user. In some parts of the country it is expensive, and in other areas it can be more reasonably prices.

S TEP-BY-STEP ▷ 4.4

C

1. To add a border around the data, select **B4:H8,** click the **Format** menu, click **Cells,** and click the **Border** tab. Click the fifth line style (medium solid) in the right-hand column in the Line Style box, click the **Outline** option under **Presets,** and click **OK.** Click outside the selection to see the border.

2. To add a gridline effect to the data, select **B4:H8,** click the **Borders** drop-down button on the Formatting toolbar, and click the second option (All Borders) on the left on the bottom row of the palette.

3. To add a heavier border, be sure **B4:H8** is still selected, click the **Borders** drop-down button and click the **Thick Box Border** on the bottom right corner of the palette.

4. To add a light shading to the cells containing the months, select **C4:H4,** click the **Format** menu, click **Cells,** click **Patterns,** click the lavender color, and click **OK.**

5. To add color to the data in column B, select **B4:B8,** click the **Fill Color** drop-down button on the Formatting toolbar, and select a light yellow shade.

6. To save your formatting changes, click the **Save** button.

Using Conditional Formatting

You can highlight formula results or other cell data that you want to be aware of without reading every cell on the worksheet. This feature is useful if, for instance, you want sales above or below a given figure to stand out.

To display the Conditional Formatting dialog box (see Figure 4.9), choose Conditional Formatting on the Format menu.

From the Cell Value Is drop-down list, you specify whether you want to use values in selected cells or the results of a formula as the formatting criteria. You then select the type of comparison to make (for example, equal to or between), then enter a value(s) to which Excel can compare the data.

To determine the formats if the conditions are met, click the Format button to display the Format Cells dialog box.

You can use the Add >> button in the Conditional Formatting dialog box to specify up to three conditions for one conditional format.

FIGURE 4.9

Specify conditions that data must meet to apply conditional formatting.

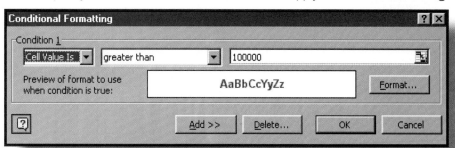

Use the Delete button in the dialog box to remove conditional formatting. You can also use the Clear command on the Edit menu and choose Formats on the submenu to clear all formats.

STEP-BY-STEP ⟹ 4.5

1. To begin applying conditional formatting to the Totals data, select **C8:H8,** click the **Format** menu, and click **Conditional Formatting.**

2. To add the conditions, be sure **Cell Value Is** is selected, click **greater than** in the center drop-down list, and type **100,000** in the right text box.

3. To choose the conditional formatting, click the **Format** button, be sure the **Font** tab is

displayed, click **Bold** in the Font style list box, click the Color drop-down button, and click a bright red. Click **OK** to close the Format Cells dialog box and then click **OK** to close the Conditional Formatting dialog box. Notice conditional formatting is applied to the totals for July and December.

4. To save your formatting changes, click the **Save** button.

Copying Formats

You can use Excel's Format Painter button to copy formats from one cell to another. To paint a format:

Format Painter button

■ Select the cell or range containing the formats you want to copy.

■ Click the Format Painter button on the Standard toolbar.

■ Click the cell or drag across the range to which you want to copy the formats.

You can double-click the Format Painter button so the Format Painter stays active while you format more than one cell or range. You must click the Format Painter button again or press the Esc key to turn it off.

Using Styles

A named combination of formats is called a **style.** Excel initially formats all cells in a workbook with the Normal style. You can see in Figure 4.10 the formats that make up the Normal style.

FIGURE 4.10
The Style dialog box displays the features a style includes.

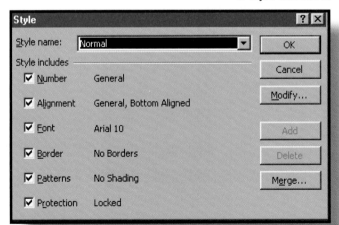

In addition to the Normal style, Excel provides several other pre-defined styles (see Figure 4.11).

To create a style:

■ Select a cell that has the formats you want to use.

■ Choose the Style command on the Format menu.

■ Enter a name for the style in the Style name text box.

■ Clear any of the cell formats (such as Border or Patterns) from the Style Includes (By Example) list you want to remove from the new style.

FIGURE 4.11
You can see a list of Excel's built-in styles.

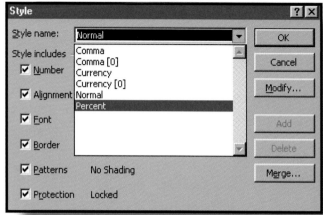

■ Click Modify if you want to change any of the style's formatting.

■ Click Add to save the style to the list of styles.

To apply a style:

■ Select the cells to which you want to apply the style.

■ Choose the Style command on the Format menu.

■ Select the style you want from the Style name drop-down list.

■ Click OK.

S TEP-BY-STEP ▷ 4.6

1. To paint the currency format of the numbers in row 8 to the numbers in row 5, click **D8,** click the **Format Painter** button, and drag the paintbrush pointer over cells **C5:H5.**

2. To begin to create a style based on the conditionally formatted Totals in row 8, click **C8,** click the **Format** menu, click **Style,** type **Highs** in the Style name box, click the **Number** box to remove its check but keep the remaining formats, and click **Modify.** Because the conditional formats do not appear in the Style list, you must add them to the style.

3. To add the formats, click the **Font** tab, click **Bold** in the Font style list box, click the Color drop-down button, click the same bright red, and click **OK.** In the Style dialog box, click **Add,** and then click **OK.**

4. To apply the style to the highest sales for each employee, click **H5:H7** (each employee's highest sales were in the month of December), click the **Format** menu, and click **Style.** Click the Style name drop-down button, click **Highs,** and click **OK.**

(continued on next page)

5. To preview and print the workbook, click the **Print Preview** button on the Standard toolbar, click the **Setup** button, click the **Margins** tab, click **Horizontally,** click **Vertically,** click the **Page** tab, click the Fit to option button, click **OK,** and click the **Print** button on the toolbar. Click **OK** on the Print dialog box.

6. To save and close the workbook, click the **Save** button and then click the workbook **Close** button.

Inserting and Deleting Cells, Rows, and Columns

You can change the structure of a worksheet by inserting or deleting cells, rows, or columns. You can insert blank cells, rows, or columns anywhere on your worksheet. When you insert cells, rows, or columns, other cells, rows, or columns shift to make a place for the insertion.

Inserting Rows or Columns

You can use the Rows or Columns command on the Insert menu to insert rows or columns. Blank rows are inserted above the currently selected cell. Blank columns are inserted to the left of the currently selected cell. When you want to insert more than one row or column at a time, select the same number of rows or columns as you want to insert before choosing the command.

When you insert a row or column, the existing rows or columns shift down or right to make room for the new cells.

Inserting Cells

You can use the Cells command on the Insert menu to insert cells. To insert cells:

■ Select a range of cells with the same number of cells as the number of cells you want to insert.

■ Choose the Cells command on the Insert menu. The Insert dialog box opens (see Figure 4.12).

■ Choose the direction you want to shift the existing cells (Right or Down) and click OK. You can also opt to insert a row or column in the Insert dialog box.

Deleting Cells, Rows, or Columns

When you delete rows or columns, the rows beneath the deleted row and the columns to the right of the deleted column automatically shift up or left to fill in the space. To delete a row or column, select the row or column and click Delete on the Edit menu. To delete a cell or range, select it and click Delete on the Edit menu to display the Delete dialog box (see Figure 4.13). You decide

FIGURE 4.12
Make insertion decisions in the Insert dialog box.

FIGURE 4.13
Determine how deletions affect the worksheet in the Delete dialog box.

whether surrounding cells shift up or left to fill the space. You can also choose to delete an entire row(s) or column(s) in the Delete dialog box.

IMPORTANT:

When you want to delete just the data in a cell, be sure to use the Clear command, the Backspace key, or the Delete key, not the Delete command. The Delete command deletes the data and the cell itself.

Using the Clear Command

You can use the Clear command on the Edit menu (see Figure 4.14) to clear the contents, formats, comments, or all three from a cell or range. (You will learn more about cell comments later in this course.) When you use the Clear command, you do not delete the cell itself, only its contents, comments, and/or formats.

FIGURE 4.14
Use the Clear command to delete contents, formats, and/or comments.

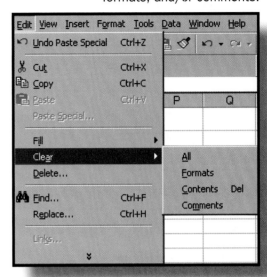

S TEP-BY-STEP 4.7

1. Open the workbook **Step-by-Step 4-7 Inserts.**

2. To insert a row between rows 6 and 7, click **C7,** click the **Insert** menu, and click **Rows.**

3. To enter a sales figure in C7, type **18648** and press the **Enter** key. The total in cell C9 increases and the formatting in cell C7 matches the existing formats.

4. To insert a row before the Totals row, click **C9,** click the **Insert** menu, and click **Rows.**

5. To delete the newly inserted row, click anywhere in row **9,** click the **Edit** menu, click **Delete,** click **Entire row,** and click **OK.**

6. To insert a column for June sales, click **C6,** click the **Insert** menu, and click **Columns.** Excel inserts the new column with the formatting of the column to its left.

7. To enter a sales figure in C7, click **C7,** type **34222,** and press the **Enter** key. Notice the comma formatting is not there.

8. To delete column C, be sure **C7** is still selected, click the **Edit** menu, click **Delete,** and double-click **Entire column.**

9. To delete row 7, be sure **C7** is still selected, click the **Edit** menu, click **Delete,** and double-click **Entire row.**

(continued on next page)

10. To insert another column, click **D4,** click the **Insert** menu, and click **Columns.**

11. To move July figures to the right, select **C4:C8,** point to a border of the selected cells until you see the left-pointing arrow, drag to the right one column, and release.

12. To paint the column D formats to column C, be sure **D4:D8** is still selected, click the **Format Painter** button, and drag across **C4:C8.**

13. To clear all contents from a cell, click **E7,** click the **Edit** menu, click **Clear,** and click **All.**

14. To see the formatting is no longer there, type **43561** and press the **Enter** key. To return the original data and formatting, click the **Undo** button **twice.**

15. To insert a cell, select **A11,** click the **Insert** menu, click **Cells,** and double-click **Shift cells right.**

16. To clear the contents of D7, select **D7,** click **Edit,** click **Clear,** and click **Contents.** Notice the empty cell is still there.

17. To undo the clear, click the **Undo** button.

18. To delete cell D7, be sure **D7** is still selected, click the **Edit** menu, click **Delete,** double-click **Shift cells up.** Notice the entire cell is gone and the cells below have shifted up.

19. To undo the delete, click the **Undo** button.

20. To delete the data in row 6, click the row heading, click the **Edit** menu, and click **Delete.** To undo the delete, click the **Undo** button.

21. To delete column C, click the column heading, click the **Edit** menu and click **Delete.** To undo the delete, click the **Undo** button.

22. To save your changes and close the workbook, click the **Save** button and then click the workbook's **Close** button.

Finding and Replacing Data

You already learned to use the Find command to quickly locate data on your worksheet. You can use the Replace command to find and replace data in your worksheets (see Figure 4.15).

When using the Replace command on the Edit menu, be very careful that you do not replace items you do not want to replace. The next exercise has a good example of why you should be very careful when you use the Replace All button in the Replace dialog box.

Enter the data you want to find in the Find what text box and the text you want to replace it

FIGURE 4.15
Use the Replace dialog box to replace existing data.

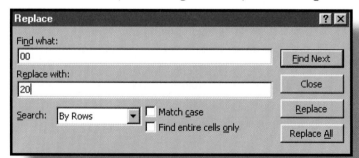

with in the Replace with text box. Click Find Next to start the search. When Excel finds an occurrence of the text, you are prompted to replace it. You can click Find Next if you don't want to replace it, Replace to replace just the selected occurrence, or Replace All to replace all occurrences of the text.

In this step-by-step exercise, you will use the Replace command for a commonly needed procedure to see how careful you must be when using the command.

Concept Builders

To move a dialog box that hides an area of the worksheet you want to see, position the mouse pointer on the title bar and drag the dialog box to a new location.

 IMPORTANT:

Check your worksheets very carefully when changing from twentieth to twenty-first century dates with the Replace command.

STEP-BY-STEP ▷ 4.8

1. Open the **Step-by-Step 4-8 Replace** workbook.

2. To see the contents of C3 in the formula bar, click **C3** and notice the complete date in the formula bar.

3. To open the Replace dialog box and start with the first cell, click **A1,** click the **Edit** menu and click **Replace.**

4. To replace the year **98** with **00,** type **98** in the **Find what** text box, press the **Tab** key, type **00** in the **Replace with** box, and click **Find Next.** On the first six occurrences of *98,* click **Replace.**

5. To leave the number *98* in C6 as is, click **Find Next.**

6. To leave the number *98* in E6 as is, click **Find Next.**

7. To close the Replace dialog box when it is alternating between the cells you do not want to change, click its **Close** button.

8. To check the contents of C3 in the formula bar again, click **C3** and notice the date in the formula bar.

9. To change the year to 2000, type **Jul 2000,** press the **Enter** key, click **C3** and drag its fill handle across the other months.

10. To print a copy of the sheet, click the **Print** button.

11. To save and close the file, click the **Save** button and then click the workbook's **Close** button.

Copying and Moving Data

Excel offers two different clipboards you can use to move or copy data—the Windows Clipboard and the Office Clipboard. A clipboard is an area of memory that stores cut or copied selections.

Using the Windows Clipboard

When you *move* a cell, you remove (cut) the contents (data and formatting) from a cell and paste them in another cell. When you copy a cell you put an identical copy of the cell contents in a new location. When you cut or copy, Excel stores a copy of the cut or copied item in the Windows Clipboard.

You must be very careful to check that your formulas are what you expect them to be when moving or copying worksheet data.

IMPORTANT:

Excel does not keep the last cut or copied data in the Windows Clipboard as is done with other Windows applications. As long as the marquee appears around cells you cut or copy, you can continue pasting. You can paste an item as often as you like, as long as you do not go on to other tasks.

You can use the Cut, Copy, and Paste commands on the Edit menu, the Cut, Copy, and Paste buttons on the Standard toolbar (see Figure 4.16), or the drag-and-drop feature explained next to move cells.

When you want to copy or move data to a distant part of the worksheet, to a different worksheet in the workbook, or to another window or application not visible on your screen, use the Cut, Copy, and Paste commands on the Edit menu or shortcut menu, or the Cut, Copy, and Paste buttons on the toolbar instead of using drag-and-drop. Select the cell or range you want to move or copy and use one of the Cut or Copy options. You need only select the top left cell of the paste area because Excel will set the paste area the same size and range as the cells you are pasting.

When you paste, any data that existed in the cell(s) into which you paste is overwritten. Be sure to use the Undo button immediately if you accidentally write over data.

Concept Builders

Remember, the AutoFill feature is much faster when you want to copy data or formulas to adjacent cells.

FIGURE 4.16
Cut, Copy, and Paste buttons are on the Standard toolbar.

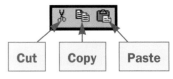

Copying and Moving with Drag-and-Drop

To move or copy a cell or range using drag-and-drop, select the cell or range you want to copy, position the mouse pointer over the border of the selection until you see the move arrow (see Figure 4.17). While you drag, the selection is surrounded by a hatched line box and Excel displays the range for the drop (see Figure 4.18).

FIGURE 4.17
Point to border of selected range to drag and drop.

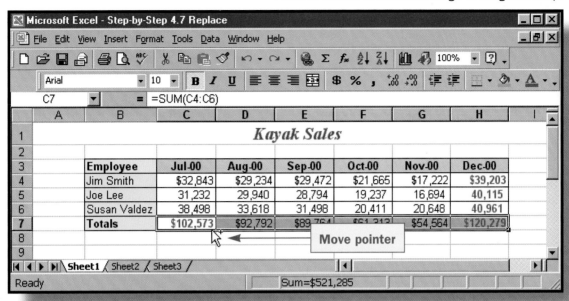

FIGURE 4.17
Point to border of selected range to drag and drop.

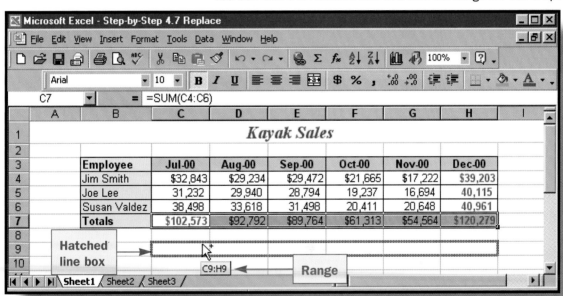

FIGURE 4.18
You can see the hatched line box and the range for the drop.

- To move a selection, drag the selection to a new location.

- To copy a selection, hold the Ctrl key as you drag to the new location. When you use the drag-and-drop method to copy, Excel displays a message asking if you want to overwrite existing data.

 **Hot Tips**

Use the Cut, Copy, and Paste commands and buttons rather than drag-and-drop to move or copy to another workbook or a long distance in a sheet.

- To insert a selection between existing cells, hold the Shift key (for move) or hold the Shift key and press the Ctrl key (for copy) as you drag.

- To drag to a different sheet hold the Alt key and drag over a sheet tab to display the sheet.

 Did You Know?

When you move or copy a selection using the drag-and-drop method, the selection is not stored in either Clipboard.

Using the Paste Special Command

You can use the Paste Special command on the Edit menu to display the Paste Special dialog box (see Figure 4.19). You can then specify which attributes of a cell are to be pasted. The Paste Special command is not available when you use the Cut command.

You can use the Paste Special command to:

- Paste only a cell's formula, value, format, comment, validation checks, or everything except its borders. (You will learn more about comments and validations checks later in this course.)

- Combine the contents of the copy and paste areas by choosing Add, Subtract, Multiply, or Divide in the Operation box.

- Transpose the copied selection so that a column of data is displayed as a row, and vice versa.

- Prevent overwriting destination cells when the copy cell is a blank cell.

- Create a link between the source of the copied cell (or range) and the destination.

FIGURE 4.19
The Paste Special dialog box offers many paste options.

Using the Office Clipboard

You must use the Toolbars command to turn on the Office Clipboard toolbar to use the Office Clipboard (see Figure 4.20). The Office Clipboard can hold up to 12 items instead of the single item the Windows Clipboard holds. You can copy items from any program that has copy-and-cut functionality. However, the Office Clipboard cannot paste items in applications other than Microsoft Office applications.

Each time you cut or copy an item, it is added to the Office Clipboard. To see up to the first 50 characters of each item, slide the mouse pointer over the item on the Clipboard until its ScreenTip appears.

FIGURE 4.20
The Office Clipboard can hold up to 12 items.

To paste an individual item from the Clipboard, click the cell where you want to paste the item and then click the item on the Office Clipboard toolbar. Excel pastes only the value in the cell not a formula even if the original cell contained a formula.

When you want to paste all items in the Office Clipboard, use its Paste All button. In Excel, you cannot use the Paste All button if any of the collected items is a drawing or a picture.

Use the Clear Clipboard button on the Clipboard toolbar to clear the entire Office Clipboard contents.

IMPORTANT:

The Office Clipboard toolbar must be displayed for its procedures to work.

 **Hot Tips**

If the Clipboard is docked (attached) to another toolbar, click the Item's drop-down button to see a ScreenTip.

STEP-BY-STEP ▷ 4.9

1. Open the **Step-by-Step 4-9 Move & Copy** workbook.

2. To display the Office Clipboard, click the **View** menu, click **Toolbars**, click **Clipboard.**

3. To copy the data in the Totals row to another position, select **C7:H7,** click the **Edit** menu, and click **Copy.** Notice the marquee surrounding the copied cells. Click **C9,** click the **Paste** button on the Standard toolbar. Notice Excel copied the formulas, with their relative references to three cells above, and the formatting in the original cells.

4. To undo the paste, click the **Undo** button on the Standard toolbar.

5. To paste the values in the copied cells instead of the formulas, be sure **C9:H9** is still selected and the marquee still surrounds cells **C7:H7,** click the **Edit** menu, click **Paste Special,** click **Values,** and click **OK.** Notice Excel did not paste the formats.

6. To paste the formats, be sure **C9:H9** is still selected and the marquee still surrounds cells **C7:H7,** click the **Edit** menu, click **Paste Special,** click **Formats,** and click **OK.** Notice Excel did paste the formats, but it takes two separate operations to do it.

7. To move Joe Lee's data to the row above **B5:H5** so the names are in alphabetical order, select **B5:H5,** hold the **Shift** key, point to the border of the selection near the Joe Lee cell until you see the move pointer, drag until you see the ScreenTip **B4:H4,** and release. If you see a message asking if you want to overwrite the cells, Excel thinks you are copying rather than moving. If your move succeeds, notice your formulas are now incorrect.

8. To undo the move, click the **Undo** button.

9. To copy all the information on the worksheet to **Sheet2,** select **A1:I7,** click the **Copy** button on the Standard toolbar, click the **Sheet2** tab, be sure **A1** is the active cell, and click **Paste.** Notice the Office Clipboard now has two entries.

10. To paste all the entries in the Office Clipboard, select **A:9** and click the Clipboard's **Paste All** button.

11. To undo the Paste All, click **Undo** twice.

12. To close the worksheet without saving changes, click its **Close** button and respond **No** when asked to save changes.

Summary

You have now learned to adjust column width and row height, to format cells, to copy formats, to use styles, to insert cells, rows, and columns, to copy and move data, and to use the Replace command.

Try the exercises on the following pages to test how well you remember what you learned. Don't be afraid to go back and look up the answers, because that will help to reinforce what you learned.

LESSON 4 REVIEW QUESTIONS

TRUE / FALSE

Circle the T if the statement is true. Circle the F if it is false.

T F 1. You can double-click on the right border of a column heading to adjust the width of a column to fit the longest entry.

T F 2. When you increase font size, you have to adjust the row height.

T F 3. Most formats can be applied using buttons on the Standard toolbar.

T F 4. When you enter a number with a dollar sign, Excel automatically formats the cell for currency.

T F 5. You cannot create custom number formats.

T F 6. When you use the Center Across Selection alignment option, the cell(s) in which the data appears to be displayed actually contains the data.

T F 7. When you double-click the Format Painter button, it stays active until you turn it off by clicking the button again or by pressing the Esc key.

T F 8. Excel formats all data you enter with the Normal style unless you choose another.

T F 9. You can apply conditional formatting to cells that contain only formulas.

T F 10. The Paste Special command lets you paste only a cell's format.

COMPLETION

Complete the following sentences by writing the correct word or words in the blanks provided.

1. You can use the _____ command on the _____ menu to adjust column width.

2. You can use the _____ tab in the Format Cells dialog box to add color to cells.

106

3. You can use the _____ button to copy formats.

4. You can use the _____ command on the _____ menu to insert rows.

5. You can use the _____ tab in the Format Cells dialog box to format cells for currency.

6. You can use the _____ button to add commas to your numbers.

7. You can use the _____ button to reduce the number of decimal places displayed.

8. You can use the _____ command on the _____ menu to find occurrences of a group of characters and change them.

9. You can use the _____ button to add color to fonts.

10. You can use the _____ button to add color to cells.

LESSON 4 PROJECTS

PROJECT 4A

To practice what you've learned in this lesson, complete the following project:

1. Open the workbook **Project 4-A.**

2. Center the three title rows across the columns containing data.

3. Change the font in cell **A1** to **Arial Black,** size **16,** and **Bold** style.

4. Increase the font size of the data in cell **A2** to **14** and the data in cell **A3** to **12.**

5. Use the italic style for the names of the students in column A.

6. Center the data in the range **A5:G5** and then apply the **Bold** style to it.

7. Select the range **B6:G10** and apply the **Percent Style.**

8. Select the range **A5:G10.** Apply an **Inside** border format to the range and then add the Thick Box border.

9. Select the range **G5:G10** and add a light yellow color to the cells' background.

10. Center the data horizontally on the page and then print a copy of the worksheet.

11. Save the workbook as **Formatting Review.** Then, close the file.

PROJECT 4B

To practice what you've learned in this lesson, complete the following project:

1. Open the workbook **Project 4-B.**

2. Apply the **Percent Style** to the range **B6:B11.**

3. Use the Format Painter to copy the format from **B6:B11** to the range **C6:G11.**

Extra Challenges

Use Help to find information about custom number formats. Review the information and print the Help topic(s).

4. Select cell **A5** and change the font to **Arial Narrow,** the font size to **12,** and the style to **Bold.** Create a style based on the formats in cell A5 named **Column Labels** and apply the style to the range **B5:G5** and then to cell **A11.**

5. Wrap the contents of cell **G5.**

6. Center the data in the range **A5:G5.**

7. Adjust the column width for column A.

8. Add a thick line border to the bottom of the range **A5:G5** and to the bottom of the range **A10:G10.**

Did You Know?

The Arial font is a sans serif font which is the font type traditionally used in worksheets. Use the different Arial fonts in your worksheets.

9. Apply conditional formatting to the range **G6:G10** that highlights the student scores that are greater than or equal to 90. (When entering the value in the Conditional Formatting dialog box, be sure to enter **90%** rather than 90.) Choose a font color.

10. Format the titles in the range **A1:A3** using formats of your choice.

11. Select row **3** and insert a blank row above it.

12. Center the data horizontally on the page and then print a copy of the worksheet.

13. Save the workbook and then close the file.

PROJECT 4C

SCANS

Start a new blank workbook and display the Web toolbar. Use the **Search the Web** button on the Web toolbar to search for *Edmund's* used car price list. Review **Edmund's Used Car Pricing Examples.** Search for information on a **1995 Honda Civic.** Print the **Edmund's Pricing, Equipment Adjustment,** and **Mileage Adjustment** sections (the first three to four pages). Don't forget to disconnect when you are finished.

CRITICAL THINKING ACTIVITY

SCANS

Open the **Critical Thinking Activity 3** workbook you created in the last lesson. Use the formatting and editing features you learned in this lesson to enhance the appearance of the **2000 Sales** worksheet. You will probably want to clear the existing AutoFormat.

When you are finished formatting, print the worksheet, save the workbook as **Critical Thinking Activity 4** and close it.

LESSON

5

USING EXCEL'S WORKBOOK FEATURES

OBJECTIVES

When you complete this lesson, you will be able to:

- Group worksheets.

- Insert and delete sheets.

- Move and copy sheets.

- Use the Consolidate command and 3-D references.

- Use various features that control worksheet displays.

- Use additional saving and printing features.

⏱ Estimated Time: 1½ hours

Introduction

You now know how to enter, edit, and format data on a worksheet. In this lesson, you will learn how to organize worksheets in a workbook. You will learn how to add and delete sheets from a workbook, how to copy sheets, and how to group sheets. You also will discover how to use various display and printing options related to workbooks.

Understanding Workbooks

Workbooks are ideal for organizing related data. For example, if you own a chain of sporting goods stores, you might want a workbook that contains budget sheets for each location. Excel offers great flexibility for adding, deleting, and organizing worksheets in a workbook.

As you have learned, each new workbook you create in Excel contains three worksheets. By default, each sheet is named consecutively (Sheet1, Sheet2, Sheet3, and so on), and the name appears on the sheet tab. You can rename a sheet by double-clicking the sheet tab and typing the new name.

To move to a sheet, simply click its sheet tab. If you have many sheets in a workbook and cannot see all the sheet tabs, use the tab scrolling buttons to the left of the sheet tabs (see Figure 5.1). To scroll several tabs at once, hold the Shift key while clicking one of the middle tab scrolling buttons.

To display a sheet shortcut menu, right-click a sheet (see Figure 5.2).

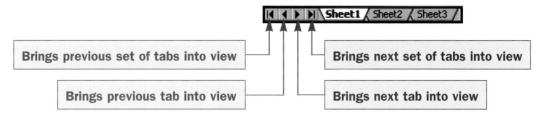

Brings previous set of tabs into view	Brings next set of tabs into view
Brings previous tab into view	Brings next tab into view

FIGURE 5.2
You can see the sheet shortcut menu.

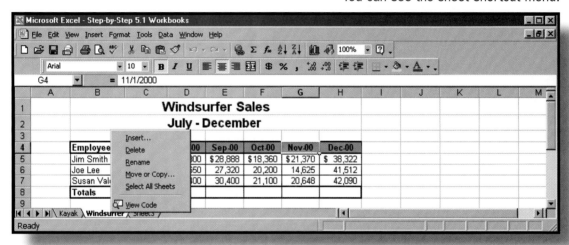

STEP-BY-STEP ▷ 5.1

1. Open the workbook **Step-by-Step 5-1 Workbooks.**

2. To display Sheet2, click the **Sheet2** tab. To redisplay Sheet1, click the **Sheet1** tab.

3. To rename Sheet1, double-click the **Sheet1** tab, type **Kayak,** and press the **Enter** key.

4. To display and rename Sheet2, double-click the **Sheet2** tab, type **Windsurfer,** and press the **Enter** key.

Grouping Worksheets

Y ou can select more than one sheet and perform tasks on all selected sheets at the same time. You can, for example, enter the same data on several worksheets at once, apply formats to grouped sheets, check spelling, and enter formulas.

To group sheets:

- For any number of adjacent sheets, click the first sheet tab, hold the Shift key, and click the last sheet tab.

- For nonadjacent sheets, click the first sheet tab, hold the Ctrl key, and click the other sheet tabs you want to select.

- To select *all* sheets, right-click any sheet tab to display the sheet shortcut menu. Choose the Select All Sheets command.

- To cancel a group selection, right-click any sheet tab in the group to display the sheet shortcut menu and choose Ungroup Sheets or click a sheet tab that is not part of the group.

    When you group sheets, the title bar displays [Group] after the file name. All sheet tabs in the group appear with a white background instead of gray.

NOTE:

You can use the General tab in the Options dialog box to change the number of sheets created in new workbooks. The maximum number of sheets you can have in a workbook is limited by the amount of memory in your system.

Inserting and Deleting Sheets

Excel makes it simple to add and remove sheets from a workbook.

- To add a sheet to an existing workbook, click the tab for the sheet you want to *follow* the inserted sheet and choose Worksheet on the Insert menu.

- To delete a sheet from an existing workbook, click its sheet tab and then click Delete Sheet on the Edit menu. A message box appears asking you to confirm the deletion.

- You can also use the Insert and Delete commands on the sheet shortcut menu to insert or delete sheets.

Hot Tips

Remember, if you don't see a command on a menu you may have to expand the menu.

Moving and Copying Sheets

Just as you can move or copy cells within a workbook or worksheet, you can move or copy sheets either within the workbook or to another workbook.

    You can move a sheet or group of sheets within a workbook by selecting its tab or one of the sheet tabs in the group and dragging along the row of tabs to where you want to insert the sheet(s). Excel displays a filled black triangle where it will insert the sheet(s) (see Figure 5.3).

FIGURE 5.3
Notice the filled black triangle that shows where Excel will drop the sheet.

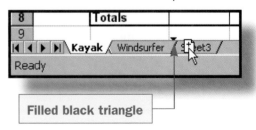

Filled black triangle

You can copy a sheet or sheets within a workbook by selecting one or more sheets, holding the Ctrl key, and dragging the selection to where you want to insert the copy. If selected sheets are nonadjacent, Excel inserts the copied sheets together. Excel renames the copy of the sheet—*Sheet1* becomes *Sheet1 (2)*. There is no undo function when you move or copy sheet(s).

You can use the Move or Copy Sheet command on the Edit menu to move or copy one or more selected sheets to another open workbook or to a new workbook. The Move or Copy dialog box opens, as shown in Figure 5.4.

From the To book drop-down list, select the workbook (if it's not the current one) to which you want to move or copy the sheet(s). In the Before sheet list box, select the sheet that you want to *follow* the new sheet.

Select the Create a copy check box to copy rather than move the selection.

You can also copy sheets between workbooks by displaying both workbooks and dragging the selected sheet tabs across workbook windows. You will learn more about displaying multiple windows later in this lesson.

NOTE:

If a sheet you move to another workbook has the same name as a sheet already there, Excel renames the moved sheet. For example, *Kayak* becomes *Kayak (2)*.

FIGURE 5.4
Choose the location to which you want to move or copy a sheet.

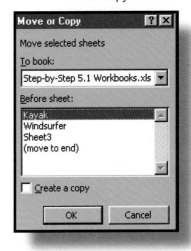

STEP-BY-STEP ▷ 5.2

C

1. To group the Kayak and Windsurfer sheets, be sure the Windsurfer sheet is still displayed, hold the **Shift** key and click **Kayak. [Group]** appears on the title bar.

2. To insert a row before row 1 on both sheets, click **A1,** click the **Insert** menu, and click **Rows.**

3. To enter text in cell B1 in both sheets, click **B1,** type **Water Sports, Inc.,** and press the **Enter** key.

4. To see that Excel entered the text in both sheets, click the **Kayak** tab.

5. To center *Water Sports, Inc.* over columns B through H, select **B1:H1** and click the **Merge and Center** button on the Formatting toolbar.

6. To format the text you just entered, be sure it is still selected, click the **Font Size** drop-down button, click **18,** and click the **Bold** button.

(continued on next page)

7. To add formulas to C9 through H9 in both sheets, select **C9:H9** and click the **AutoSum** button.

8. To see that the formatting and formulas are in both sheets, click the **Windsurfer** tab.

9. To insert two sheets before the Windsurfer sheet, click the **Insert** menu and click **Worksheet.** Excel inserts two sheets because two sheets were grouped when you chose the Insert command. Notice also that one of the newly inserted sheets is displayed and your sheets are now ungrouped.

10. To delete Sheet2, click its tab, click the **Edit** menu, click the **Expand** button if necessary, click **Delete Sheet,** and click **OK** in the message box.

11. To return to the Kayak sheet, click the **Kayak** tab.

12. To copy the Kayak sheet to a position before Sheet3, click the **Edit** menu, click the **Expand** button if necessary, click **Move or Copy Sheet,** click **Sheet3** in the **Before sheet** list box, click the **Create a copy** check box, and click **OK.** Notice you now have a Kayak(2) sheet before Sheet3.

13. To delete Sheet1, right-click the **Sheet1** tab, and click **Delete** on the shortcut menu. Click **OK** to confirm the message.

14. To rename Kayak(2), double-click the **Kayak(2)** tab, type **JetSki,** and press the **Enter** key. On the Jetski sheet, click cell **B2,** double-click the word Kayak on the formula bar, type **JetSki,** and press the **Enter** key.

15. To copy the Kayak and JetSki sheets to a new workbook, be sure the Kayak sheet is still selected, hold the **Ctrl** key, and click the **JetSki** tab. The title bar displays *[Group]* after the file name to let you know you have selected more than one sheet. Click the **Edit** menu, click **Move or Copy Sheet,** click the **To book** drop-down button, click **(new book),** click the **Create a copy** check box, and click **OK.**

16. To close the new workbook without saving it, click the **File** menu and click **Close.** Respond **No** when asked to save changes.

17. To ungroup the sheets, click the **Windsurfer** tab.

18. Save the workbook.

Consolidating Data

One of the biggest advantages of having data organized and stored in workbooks is the ability to consolidate the data. Using our example, you might, for instance, want to consolidate the budgets for the chain of sporting goods stores we mentioned earlier.

Using 3-D References to Consolidate Data in the Same Workbook

Use a **3-D reference** when you want to analyze data that is in the same position on multiple worksheets in the same workbook. A 3-D reference includes a range of worksheet names and a reference to a single cell or range of cells. Simply select the cell where you want to enter the function, type the equal (=) sign to signal Excel you are entering a formula, type the name of the function, type the opening parenthesis, group the sheets to be referenced, select the cell or range to be referenced, and complete the formula (see Figure 5.5).

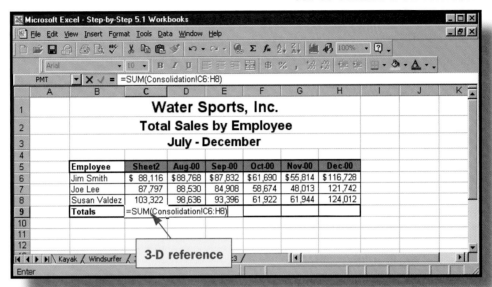

Using the Consolidate Dialog Box to Consolidate from Different Source Files

Use the Consolidate command on the Data menu to summarize large amounts of data (from up to 255 sources). With the Consolidate command you can consolidate data that exists in the same worksheet, in the same workbook, in separate workbooks, or even in Lotus 1-2-3 files.

Choose Consolidate on the Data menu to open the Consolidate dialog box (see Figure 5.6).

References to cells in other workbooks are called external references. References to data in other programs are called remote references.

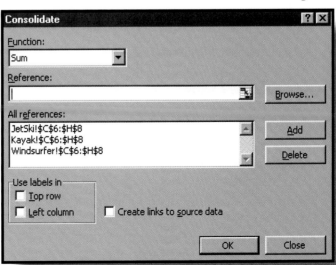

NOTE:

You can also use the Consolidate dialog box to reference source areas that are on worksheets with different layouts.

In this step-by-step exercise, you will use both consolidation methods to combine data in the same workbook. Notice, the formula that consolidates the totals from the other worksheets references the cells containing the data rather than the cells that contain formulas.

STEP-BY-STEP 5.3

1. To set up a summary sheet in the workbook that uses the same formats and structure as the Kayak, Windsurfer, and JetSki sheets, make sure the Windsurfer tab is still selected and click the **Edit** menu, click **Move or Copy Sheet,** click **Sheet3** in the **Before sheet** list box, click the **Create a copy** check box, and click **OK.**

2. To rename the Windsurfer(2) sheet, double-click its sheet tab, type **Consolidation,** and press the **Enter** key.

3. To replace the title, click cell **B2,** type **Total Sales by Employee,** and press the **Enter** key.

4. To clear the sales data and make room for the consolidation data, select **C6:H9,** click the **Edit** menu, click **Clear,** and click **Contents.**

5. To use the Consolidate command to total the sales data for each employee for each of the three product types, click the **Data** menu, click the **Expand** button if needed, and click **Consolidate.** Be sure **Sum** is displayed in the Function box.

6. To add the first Reference, click the **Collapse Dialog** button at the end of the **Reference** text box, click the **Kayak** sheet tab, select **C6:H8,** click the **Expand Dialog** button in the collapsed dialog box, and click **Add** in the Consolidate dialog box.

7. To add the second reference, click the **Collapse Dialog** button at the end of the **Reference** text box again, click the **Windsurfer** sheet tab, select **C6:H8** if necessary, click the **Expand Dialog** button to return to the dialog box, and click **Add.**

8. To add the last reference, click the **Collapse Dialog** button again, click the **JetSki** sheet tab, select **C6:H8** if necessary, click the **Expand Dialog** button, and click **Add.** Click **OK.** The data from the three sheets is combined on the Consolidation sheet.

9. To adjust the column widths, select **C9:G9,** click the **Format** menu, click **Column,** and click **AutoFit Selection.**

10. To use 3-D formulas to combine each employee's monthly sales for each of the product types, click cell **C9** on the Consolidation sheet, type **=SUM(.** Click the **Kayak** sheet tab, hold **Shift** and click the **JetSki** sheet tab, select the range **C6:C8,** click the **Consolidation** sheet tab, enter the closing parenthesis in the 3-D formula, and press the **Enter** key.

11. To copy the 3-D formula, click cell **C9** and drag its fill handle to cell **H9.** Adjust the column widths if necessary.

12. Save and close the workbook.

Using Windows Features to Change the Display

Excel offers several ways for you to change how sheets and workbooks display on screen. It can make it easier to work with large worksheets or with multiple sheets in a single workbook or even with multiple workbooks.

In the Getting Started lesson you learned to use the Arrange command to arrange all open *workbooks* on your screen.

Hot Tips

When you open a workbook, Excel displays the view in effect when you last saved the file.

Splitting Sheet Windows

You can split a window into two or four panes in order to simultaneously view different parts of the same *worksheet.* Figure 5.7 shows a window split horizontally in two panes. You can access the entire worksheet in each of the panes.

To split a window horizontally, position the pointer on the split box at the top of the vertical scroll bar (see Figure 5.8). When you see the double-crossed arrow pointer, drag the split box down to a position of your choosing on the worksheet.

To split a window vertically, drag the split box at the right end of the horizontal scroll bar (see Figure 5.8) to a position of your choosing on the worksheet.

To remove a split, use the Remove Split command on the Window menu, or double-click the split bar, or drag the split bar to the edge of the window.

You can work in any pane simply by clicking in it. Use the scroll bars to bring data in a pane into view. If you print a worksheet with a split window, Excel prints the worksheet normally.

FIGURE 5.7
You can horizontally split a worksheet window.

FIGURE 5.8
Notice the Split boxes.

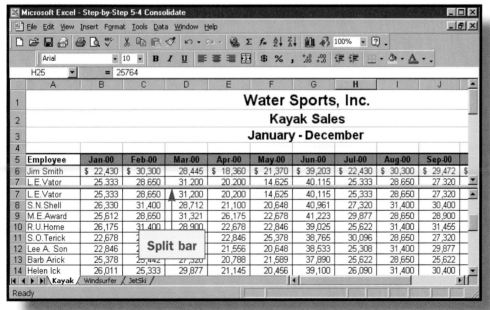

1. Open **Step-by-Step 5-4 Display.**

2. To split the window horizontally at row 9, point to the split box at the top of the vertical scroll bar until you see a double-crossed arrow pointer, and then drag it down to the bottom of row 9.

3. To see that each window contains the entire worksheet, click the **up** scroll button in the bottom pane until you see the top of the worksheet.

4. To remove the split, position the pointer on the split until it turns into a double-headed arrow pointer and double-click it.

5. To split the window vertically between columns **G** and **H,** point to the split box at the right end of the horizontal scroll bar until you see a double-crossed arrow pointer and drag it to the left to the border between columns **G** and **H.**

6. To split the window in four panes, point to the split box at the top of the vertical scroll bar and drag to place a horizontal split between rows **5** and **6.**

7. To remove the splits, click the **Window** menu and then click **Remove Split.**

Freezing Panes

You can use the Freeze Panes command on the Window menu when you want to keep certain data visible as you scroll through the worksheet (see Figure 5.9). The Freeze Panes command is useful for large spreadsheets when you want to keep your row and/or column titles visible (or "frozen") while scrolling through or viewing other parts of the worksheet.

■ To freeze a row or rows of data, select a cell in the row *below* the row(s) you want to freeze. Then, choose Freeze Panes on the Window menu.

■ To freeze a column or columns of data, select a cell in the column to the *right* of the column(s) you want to freeze, then choose Freeze Panes on the Window menu.

■ To freeze both, click the cell below and to the right of the row(s) and column(s) you want to freeze, and choose Freeze Panes on the Window menu.

■ To unfreeze rows or columns, choose the Unfreeze Panes command on the Window menu.

You can edit or enter data in any cells of the worksheet, whether they are frozen or not.

1. To freeze the column containing employee names and the row containing the months, click cell **B6,** click the **Window** menu, and click **Freeze Panes.** You should see a dark vertical line and a horizontal line that indicate the freeze lines.

2. To display the December figures for each employee, click the right scroll arrow until you see the *Dec-00* heading. Notice the data in column A remains visible when column B scrolls off the screen.

3. To see the row headings remain in place, click the down scroll arrow until you see the data in the top rows scroll off the screen.

4. To unfreeze panes, click the **Window** menu and click **Unfreeze Panes.**

FIGURE 5.9
Notice the frozen panes.

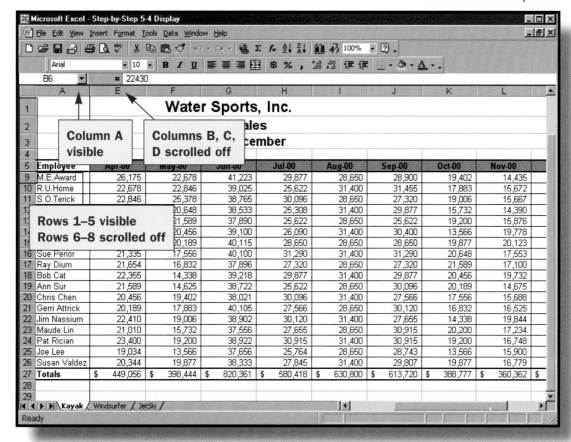

Viewing Multiple Sheets

To view multiple worksheets, use the New Window command on the Window menu to open a new window for each sheet you want to display (see Figure 5.10).

When you open a new window for a workbook, the title bars display the name of the workbook followed by a number indicating the number of the window.

After creating the new windows for the workbook, you must use the Arrange command and click the Windows of active workbook check box to display them.

You can organize the windows in one of four ways:

■ *Tiled,* which proportionately displays each window on the screen.

■ *Horizontal,* which displays the windows horizontally across the screen.

■ *Vertical,* which displays the windows vertically across the screen.

■ *Cascade,* which layers each window so that title bars are visible.

To move from one window to another, simply click a window to make it active. To remove a window, click its Close button. To restore a window to its full size, click its Maximize button.

1 1 9

FIGURE 5.10
Create new windows and arrange them to display more than one sheet.

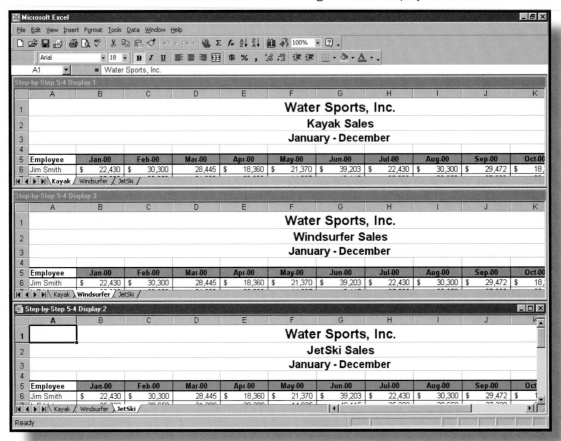

 **NOTE:**

You can choose Custom Views on the View menu to save a display you set up as a view. You can add a view or select a view to display in the Custom Views dialog box.

STEP-BY-STEP 5.6

1. To open two new windows so you can view the Kayak, Windsurfer, and Jetski sheets at the same time, click the **Window** menu, click the **Expand** button if needed, and then click **New Window.** Click **Window** again and click **New Window.**

2. To arrange the windows, click the **Window** menu, click **Arrange**, click **Horizontal,** click

Windows of active workbook, and click **OK.**

3. To display the Windsurfer sheet, click in window **2** to make it active and click the **Windsurfer** tab.

4. To display the JetSki tab, click in window **3** to make it active and click the **JetSki** tab.

5. To see that you are viewing all three sheets, click and scroll through each window.

6. To close windows 1 (Kayak sheet active) and 2 (Windsurfer sheet active), click their **Close** buttons. Notice as you close

windows, the window numbers change on the remaining windows.

7. To maximize the remaining window (JetSki sheet active), click its **Maximize** button.

Hiding and Unhiding Data

Excel lets you hide rows and columns to temporarily remove them from view (see Figure 5.11). Even when you print, the data remains hidden. By hiding rows or columns, you can:

■ Prevent others from seeing certain columns or rows.

■ Save and display different versions of the same worksheet.

■ Print different versions of the same worksheet.

To hide a row or column, select the row(s) or column(s) you want to hide, open the Format menu, choose either Row or Column,

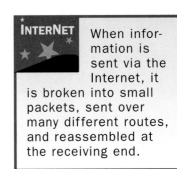

INTERNET

When information is sent via the Internet, it is broken into small packets, sent over many different routes, and reassembled at the receiving end.

FIGURE 5.11
You can see the results of hiding rows and columns.

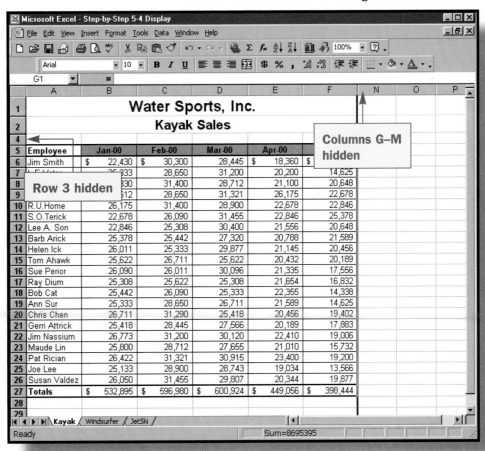

and choose Hide. The row or column and its row number or column letter is removed from view. The border where the column or row has been hidden is slightly darker.

NOTE:

Anyone who knows how to use Excel will be able to unhide columns or rows.

To unhide a row or column, select the rows or columns on both sides of the hidden row or column. Open the Format menu, choose Row or Column, and choose Unhide.

IMPORTANT:

If you've hidden row 1 or column A, you must select the whole sheet by clicking the Select All button above the row numbers and to the left of the column letters before you choose Unhide.

STEP-BY-STEP 5.7

1. To hide columns H through M on the Kayak worksheet, click the **Kayak** worksheet tab, select columns **H** through **M,** click the **Format** menu, click **Column,** and click **Hide.**

2. To hide row 3, select row **3,** click the **Format** menu, click **Row,** and click **Hide.**

3. To print the sheet as it is displayed, click the **Print** button.

4. To unhide row 3, select rows **2** and **4,** click the **Format** menu, click **Row,** and click **Unhide.**

5. To unhide columns H through M, select columns **G** and **N,** click the **Format** menu, click **Column,** and click **Unhide.**

Saving a Workspace

You can use the Save Workspace command to save all open workbooks. Excel saves their sizes and positions on the screen so the screen will look the same the next time you open the workspace file.

To save a workspace, open the workbooks that you want to save as a group. Size and position the windows, open the File menu and choose Save Workspace. Enter a name for the workspace and select the location to which you want to save it.

You open a workspace the same as you open an individual workbook. However, you must continue to save changes to individual workbooks.

Concept Builders

Remember, you can view both windows by clicking Window and then Arrange.

S TEP-BY-STEP ▷ 5.8

1. The *Step-by-Step 5-4 Display* file should still be open. Open the workbook **Step-by-Step 5-8 Workspace.**

2. To save the two workbooks as a group, click the **File** menu, click **Save Workspace,** type **My Workspace,** be sure the Save in text box contains the name of the folder for your class files, and click **Save.**

3. To close each of the workbooks, click its **Close** button.

4. To open the workspace, click the **Open** button on the toolbar and be sure you are in

the same folder you used to save My Workspace. Notice that the *My Workspace* file is identified in the file list by a special workspace icon and/or a different file extension (depending on the selected view). Also notice that both the *Step-by-Step 5-4 Display* and *Step-by-Step 5-9 Workspace* workbooks still exist as individual files. Double-click **My Workspace** to open it.

5. To close the workspace, click each workbook's **Close** button.

Summary

You have now learned to group worksheets, to insert and delete sheets, to move and copy sheets, to consolidate data in a workbook, to use various features to display worksheets, and to save a workspace.

Try the exercises on the following pages to test how well you remember what you learned. Don't be afraid to go back and look up the answers, because that will help to reinforce what you learned.

LESSON 5 REVIEW QUESTIONS

TRUE / FALSE

Circle the T if the statement is true. Circle the F if it is false.

T F 1. You can select several worksheets and perform tasks on all of them at the same time.

T F 2. You cannot select nonadjacent sheets for copying.

T F 3. You can enter formulas that reference more than one worksheet.

T F 4. You can easily tell when more than one sheet is selected because the sheet tabs all appear in gray.

1 2 3

T F 5. You can drag a sheet tab to move the sheet to another location within a workbook.

T F 6. To freeze a row or rows of data, select the row *above* the row(s) you want to freeze. Then, select Freeze Panes on the Window menu.

T F 7. You can create only one duplicate of a window for looking at different parts of a worksheet.

T F 8. Saving a number of workbooks as a workspace means you have to open only one file to open all the workbooks.

T F 9. You can hide columns and rows of data so they don't appear on screen, but the hidden data will still print.

T F 10. You can use the Freeze Panes command when you want column and row titles to remain on the screen as you scroll to other areas of the worksheet.

COMPLETION

Complete the following sentences by writing the correct word or words in the blanks provided.

1. You can use the _____ command on the sheet shortcut menu to cancel a group selection of sheets.

2. You can use the _____ command on the _____ menu to move or copy sheets.

3. You can click the _____ command on the _____ menu to delete a sheet from a workbook.

4. You can use the _____ command on the _____ menu to add a sheet to a workbook.

5. A(n) _____ reference is to a cell or range on at least one other workbook.

6. To split a window vertically, drag the split box at the right end of the _____ scroll bar.

7. You can use the _____ command on the _____ menu when you want to open a second window on the workbook.

8. You can use the _____ command on the _____ menu when you want to arrange open windows on the screen.

9. You can use the _____ command on the _____ menu to save a group of workbooks as a unit.

10. The Hide command on the _____ submenu on the _____ menu temporarily removes a column of data from view.

1 2 4

S TEP-BY-STEP ⯈ 5.8

1. The *Step-by-Step 5-4 Display* file should still be open. Open the workbook **Step-by-Step 5-8 Workspace.**

2. To save the two workbooks as a group, click the **File** menu, click **Save Workspace,** type **My Workspace,** be sure the Save in text box contains the name of the folder for your class files, and click **Save.**

3. To close each of the workbooks, click its **Close** button.

4. To open the workspace, click the **Open** button on the toolbar and be sure you are in the same folder you used to save My Workspace. Notice that the *My Workspace* file is identified in the file list by a special workspace icon and/or a different file extension (depending on the selected view). Also notice that both the *Step-by-Step 5-4 Display* and *Step-by-Step 5-9 Workspace* workbooks still exist as individual files. Double-click **My Workspace** to open it.

5. To close the workspace, click each workbook's **Close** button.

Summary

You have now learned to group worksheets, to insert and delete sheets, to move and copy sheets, to consolidate data in a workbook, to use various features to display worksheets, and to save a workspace.

Try the exercises on the following pages to test how well you remember what you learned. Don't be afraid to go back and look up the answers, because that will help to reinforce what you learned.

LESSON 5 REVIEW QUESTIONS

TRUE / FALSE

Circle the T if the statement is true. Circle the F if it is false.

T F 1. You can select several worksheets and perform tasks on all of them at the same time.

T F 2. You cannot select nonadjacent sheets for copying.

T F 3. You can enter formulas that reference more than one worksheet.

T F 4. You can easily tell when more than one sheet is selected because the sheet tabs all appear in gray.

T F 5. You can drag a sheet tab to move the sheet to another location within a workbook.

T F 6. To freeze a row or rows of data, select the row *above* the row(s) you want to freeze. Then, select Freeze Panes on the Window menu.

T F 7. You can create only one duplicate of a window for looking at different parts of a worksheet.

T F 8. Saving a number of workbooks as a workspace means you have to open only one file to open all the workbooks.

T F 9. You can hide columns and rows of data so they don't appear on screen, but the hidden data will still print.

T F 10. You can use the Freeze Panes command when you want column and row titles to remain on the screen as you scroll to other areas of the worksheet.

COMPLETION

Complete the following sentences by writing the correct word or words in the blanks provided.

1. You can use the _____ command on the sheet shortcut menu to cancel a group selection of sheets.

2. You can use the _____ command on the _____ menu to move or copy sheets.

3. You can click the _____ command on the _____ menu to delete a sheet from a workbook.

4. You can use the _____ command on the _____ menu to add a sheet to a workbook.

5. A(n) _____ reference is to a cell or range on at least one other workbook.

6. To split a window vertically, drag the split box at the right end of the _____ scroll bar.

7. You can use the _____ command on the _____ menu when you want to open a second window on the workbook.

8. You can use the _____ command on the _____ menu when you want to arrange open windows on the screen.

9. You can use the _____ command on the _____ menu to save a group of workbooks as a unit.

10. The Hide command on the _____ submenu on the _____ menu temporarily removes a column of data from view.

LESSON 5 PROJECTS

PROJECT 5A

To practice what you've learned in this lesson, complete the following project:

1. Open the workbook **Project 5-A.**

2. The three sheets in the workbook contain each student's grades for a Word Processing, Spreadsheet, and Database course. Rename Sheet1 to **Word Processing,** Sheet2 to **Spreadsheets,** and Sheet3 to **Database.**

3. To enter the average grade for each test on each worksheet, group the three worksheets. In cell **A11** on any of the sheets, enter **Average.**

4. In cell **B11** on any of the sheets, enter the function **AVERAGE(B6:B10).** Use the handles to copy the formula from cell B11 to the range **C11:F11.** Select each of the worksheets to see that the changes were made on all of them.

5. Move the **Word Processing** sheet so it follows the Database sheet.

6. Insert a sheet between the Database sheet and the Word Processing sheet. Name the sheet **Presentations.**

7. Delete the **Presentations** sheet you just inserted.

8. Print the entire workbook.

9. Save and then close the workbook.

PROJECT 5B

To practice what you've learned in this lesson, complete the following project:

1. Open the workbook **Project 5-B.**

2. Rename Sheet1 to **Rentals** and rename Sheet2 to **Shop.**

3. Split the window vertically between columns G and H. Then, remove the split.

4. Freeze column **A** and scroll through all the months. Then, unfreeze the column. (*Hint:* Do not select the column you want to freeze.)

5. Use the **Move or Copy Sheet** command on the **Edit** menu to copy the **Shop** sheet and place the copy before **Sheet3.** Rename the sheet **Summary.**

6. On the Summary sheet, change the title text in cell **A1** to **Receipts and Rentals.** Clear the contents of the range **B5:M8.**

7. On the Summary sheet, open the Consolidate dialog box to add the values in the range **B5:M7** on the **Rentals** sheet and on the **Shop** sheet.

8. In cell **B8** on the Summary sheet, enter a 3-D reference that sums the range **B5:B7** on the **Rentals** sheet and on the **Shop** sheet. Copy the formula to the range **C8:M8.** Adjust column widths, if necessary.

9. Group the three sheets.

Extra Challenges

Use Help to find information on sharing workbooks. Review and print the Help topic(s) you find. If your system is set up so you can share workbooks with others, open one of your existing workbooks and practice sharing it with others on your network.

10. Select **Page Setup** on the File menu. On the Page tab, select **Landscape** orientation and click the option to **Fit to 1 page(s) wide by 1 page tall.** Click **Print Preview.**

11. Look through the preview pages for the workbook. Then, click the **Print** button.

12. Save and close the workbook.

SCANS

PROJECT 5C

Connect to the Internet and enter the URL http://www.cnn.com or any other major news provider to read up on current news. Don't forget to disconnect.

CRITICAL THINKING ACTIVITY

Let's pretend you're the owner of a chain of sporting goods stores. Since you haven't been in business long, let's say you have only two locations right now. Create a new workbook that documents quarterly expenses for each location. Create a separate worksheet for each location. Set up the structure for each worksheet so they are identical and can easily be consolidated on a third summary sheet. Some of the items you'll want to include on each worksheet are:

Rent	Equipment/Supplies
Utilities	Marketing
Labor	Miscellaneous

Remember, you want to track expenses on a quarterly basis. Come up with a name for the chain and a location for each. Then format the three sheets using the formatting options you've learned. Consolidate the expenses for each location on the summary sheet. When you are finished, print the three sheets, save the workbook as **Critical Thinking Activity 5,** and then close the workbook.

WORKING WITH CHARTS

OBJECTIVES

When you complete this lesson, you will be able to:

- Create a chart.
- Select charts for sizing, moving, and deleting.
- Activate charts for editing.
- Insert objects and pictures in a chart.
- Print and save a chart.

⏱ **Estimated Time: 1½ hours**

Introduction

You can use Excel charts to quickly create graphic representations of your worksheet data. Charts can often make data clearer, more interesting, and easier to read and understand. Charts are visually appealing and can make it easy for users to see at a glance whether sales are rising or falling.

Identifying Parts of a Chart

Before you proceed with this lesson, take a good look at Figure 6.1 and Table 6.1 so you are familiar with the parts of a chart with which you will work.

 **Hot Tips**

Excel will display a ScreenTip if you point to parts of the chart.

Creating Charts

You can use Excel's Chart Wizard to create a chart. A **Wizard** is a series of dialog boxes that guide you through the steps to accomplish certain tasks. To start the Chart Wizard, use the Chart Wizard button on the Standard toolbar or open the Insert menu and then choose Chart.

The Chart Wizard—Step 1 of 4—Chart Type dialog box is shown in Figure 6.2.

 ← **Chart Wizard button**

127

FIGURE 6.1
Parts of a chart.

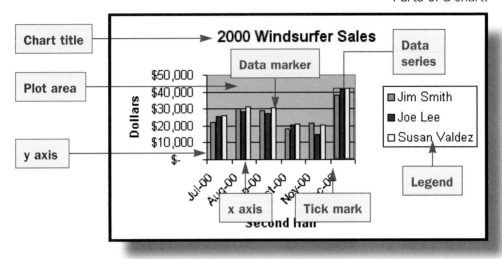

TABLE 6.1
Some parts of a chart.

CHART ELEMENTS

ELEMENT	DESCRIPTION
Chart and Chart Frame	The area inside of a chart. This includes the plot area, titles, axes, legend, and any other objects.
Plot Area and Plot Frame	Used to plot values from the worksheet. This area includes the axes and data series.
Axes (X and Y)	The horizontal axis (X) is used for showing categories, and the vertical axis (Y) is used for plotting values.
Data Marker	This can be a dot, a bar, or a symbol used to represent one number from the worksheet.
Data Series	A series of related values from the worksheet. The data series is comprised of related data markers.
Legend	A written description for understanding the various data series that appear in the plotted area.

Excel provides many types of charts from which you can choose. The Standard Types tab lists the common types of charts available. Select a chart in the Chart type list box and the variations available for that chart appear in the Chart sub-type window. A description of how data is charted for

128

the selected sub-type appears below the variations. When you press and hold the Press and Hold to View Sample button, the Chart Wizard displays how your selected data appears in the chart type you selected.

The Custom Types tab lists more specialized types of charts available in Excel.

The Step 2 of 4—Chart Source Data dialog box is shown in Figure 6.3. On the Data Range tab, you specify the cells that contain the data for the chart. If you want the column and row labels used in the chart, include them in your range selection. If you selected the range before starting the Chart Wizard, the range appears in the Data range text box. If you did not select the range, you can click the Collapse Dialog button at the end of the text box to return to the worksheet and make your selection.

The Series tab lets you further manipulate how the data you select is charted.

NOTE:

If you have questions about any of the options or choices in a Chart Wizard dialog box, click the Help button to display the Office Assistant. You can then request information on the dialog box options.

FIGURE 6.2
Chart Wizard—Step 1 of 4—Chart Type dialog box.

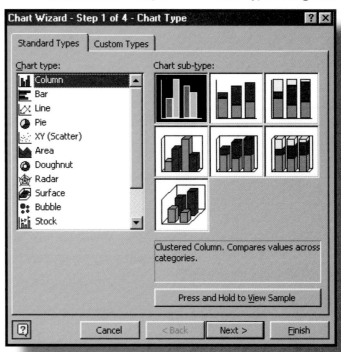

FIGURE 6.3
Chart Wizard—Step 2 of 4—Chart Source Data dialog box.

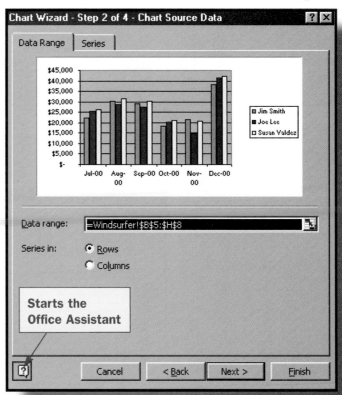

The Chart Wizard—Step 3 of 4—Chart Options dialog box is shown in Figure 6.4. You can change the settings and options for parts of the chart (see Figure 6.1) by clicking the various tabs. As you make changes, you can see them in the preview window.

The Chart Wizard—Step 4 of 4—Chart Location dialog box is shown in Figure 6.5. Here you specify whether you want to place the chart on the same sheet with the data—called an embedded chart—or on a new sheet—called a chart sheet.

An embedded chart is a graphic object that is saved as part of its worksheet. Use an embedded chart when you want to display and print one or more charts with the worksheet. The chart is placed on your worksheet where you can move, resize, edit, and format it (see Figure 6.6).

Concept Builders

You can create a chart on its own worksheet in one step: Select the data to be charted and press the F11 key. The data is plotted in the default column chart type and is placed on its own worksheet named Chart1.

FIGURE 6.4
Chart Wizard—Step 3 of 4—Chart Options dialog box.

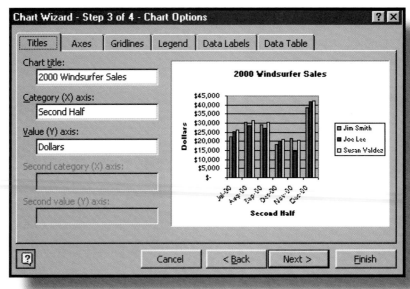

FIGURE 6.5
Chart Wizard—Step 4 of 4—Chart Location dialog box.

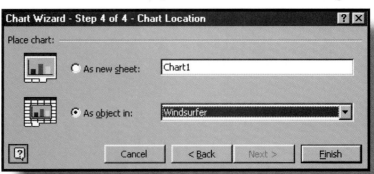

FIGURE 6.6
Handles indicate a chart is selected.

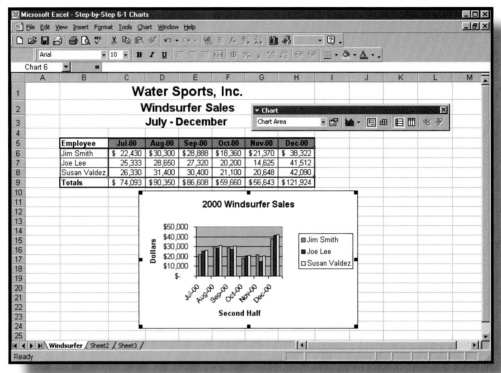

A chart sheet is a separate sheet in your workbook, and it has its own name. Use a chart sheet when you want to print or work with your chart separately.

When you create a chart, Excel links the chart to its related data on the worksheet. When the data in the worksheet changes, Excel automatically updates the chart.

 **Hot Tips**

You can return to a previous dialog box in the Chart Wizard and change your selections by clicking the Back button.

STEP-BY-STEP ▷ 6.1

1. Open the workbook **Step-by-Step 6-1 Charts.**

2. To begin creating a chart for Windsurfer sales that shows each of the employee's sales for each of the months, select **B5:H8** and click the **Chart Wizard** button.

3. To select a chart type, click the **Column** Chart type and click the first Chart sub-type. Preview the chart with your data by pressing the **Press and Hold to View Sample** button. Then click **Next.**

4. To accept the range =*Windsurfer!$B$5:$H$8,* that the series is in rows, and move to the next step, click **Next.**

5. Click in the **Chart title** text box and key **2000 Windsurfer Sales**, press the **Tab** key, type **Second Half,** press **Tab,** and type **Dollars.**

(continued on next page)

6. To move back a step, click **Back.**

7. To move forward without making any changes, click **Next.** Then click **Next** again.

8. To finish and display the chart, check that the **As object in** option is selected and click **Finish.** Notice the chart appears on the Windsurfer sheet and it is selected (eight handles around it). Don't worry about text being cut off or missing. You will learn how to fix this later in the lesson. The Chart toolbar usually displays automatically as well.

9. To change the chart to a 3-D chart, click the **Chart** menu (it has been added to the menu bar), click **Chart Type,** click the 3-D column chart (the bottom one in the Chart sub-type box, and click **OK.** The chart changes to 3-D.

10. To return to the original chart, click **Chart** on the menu, click **Chart Type,** click the first Chart sub-type, and click **OK.**

11. To deselect the chart, click a blank cell.

Sizing, Moving, and Deleting Charts

Before you can size, move, or delete a chart, you must select it.

To select a chart, position the mouse pointer on a blank area of the chart and click it. Excel indicates a chart is selected by placing eight black handles on the boundaries of the chart.

To resize a selected chart proportionally, hold the Shift key and drag one of the chart's corner handles.

To make a chart taller or wider, drag a middle handle.

To move a selected chart, position the mouse pointer on the background area of the selected chart (but not on a handle) and drag to the new location.

To delete a selected chart, press the Delete key.

1. To select the chart, click a blank area on the chart.

2. To move the chart to a new location on the sheet, drag it so its top left corner is in cell **B12.**

3. To resize the chart proportionally, be sure it is still selected, hold the **Shift** key, and drag the handle in the bottom right corner to cell **H28.**

4. To save what you've done so far, click the **Save** button.

Formatting the Chart

You can change any of the options you selected in the Chart Wizard with the Chart Type, Source Data, Chart Options, and Location commands on the Chart menu. Excel displays a dialog box corresponding to a Chart Wizard dialog box when you choose one of the commands.

Using the Chart Toolbar

You can also change chart options with tools on the Chart toolbar (see Figure 6.7).

To format a specific part of a chart, you must first select it. You can position the pointer on a part of a chart until a ScreenTip appears identifying the part. Then click the part to select it. You can also display the Chart Objects drop-down list on the Chart toolbar and select a chart part on the list.

 **Hot Tips**

If the Chart toolbar does not automatically appear when you place a chart on a worksheet, open the View menu, choose Toolbars, and choose Chart.

FIGURE 6.7
Buttons on the Chart toolbar.

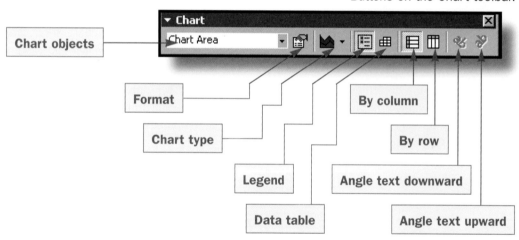

To open a selected object's Format dialog box, click the Format button on the Chart toolbar. Excel displays a dialog box corresponding to the object selected that contains formatting options specific to that object.

The rest of the buttons on the Chart toolbar let you manage specific parts of a chart.

STEP-BY-STEP ▷ 6.3

1. To display the Chart toolbar if it is not already displayed, click the **View** menu, click **Toolbars,** and click **Chart.**

2. To display the Format Axis dialog box for the X-axis or category axis labels (the month

names), click the **Chart Objects** drop-down button on the Chart toolbar and click **Category Axis.** Click the **Format Axis** button on the Chart toolbar.

(continued on next page)

133

3. To change the font size, click the **Font** tab, click **8** in the Size box, and click **OK**.

4. To angle the text downward, be sure the X-axis (Category Axis) is selected, click the **Angle Text Downward** button on the Chart toolbar.

5. To format the Y-axis or Value axis labels (the dollar amounts), click the **Value-axis** labels on the chart and then click the **Format Axis** button. Click the **Font** tab if needed, click **10** in the Size box, click the **Number** tab, click **General** in the **Category** list box, click the **Scale** tab, click the **Display units** drop-down button, click Thousands, and click **OK**.

6. To format the chart title, click it. Click the **Font** drop-down button on the regular Formatting toolbar and click **Arial Black**. Click the **Font Size** drop-down button and click **14**.

7. To format the legend, click it and then click the **Format Legend** button on the Chart toolbar. In the Format Legend dialog box, click the **Font** tab, click the **Bold Italic** font style, click **11** in the Size box, and then click **OK**.

8. To format the plot area, display the **Chart Objects** drop-down list on the Chart toolbar and click **Plot Area**. Then, click the **Format Plot Area** button. On the **Patterns** tab, select a color of your choice (a light color is the best choice) for the plot area background, and click **OK**.

9. To format the chart area, click the **Chart Objects** drop-down list and click **Chart Area**. Click the **Format Chart Area** button. Click the **Patterns** tab, click a different color (from the one you choose above) for the chart area background, and click **OK**.

10. To save your work, click the **Save** button.

Changing Chart Values and Text

The easiest way to change values or text in a chart that is linked to worksheet data is to change the data in the worksheet. Excel updates the chart immediately.

When you select a chart or its plot area, the corresponding data on the worksheet is color-coded (see Figure 6.8).

- Data used for the X-axis categories and data points is outlined in purple.

- Data used for the data series is outlined in green.

- Data used for the categories and data series is outlined in blue.

With Excel's "drag-and-plot" capabilities, you can add data to a chart and it automatically adjusts to accommodate the new data. Just select the data you want to add, and drag it to the chart's plot area.

INTERNET Browsers, such as Internet Explorer, display information on your computer by interpreting or translating the Hypertext Markup Language (HTML).

FIGURE 6.8
The chart selection is color coded on the worksheet.

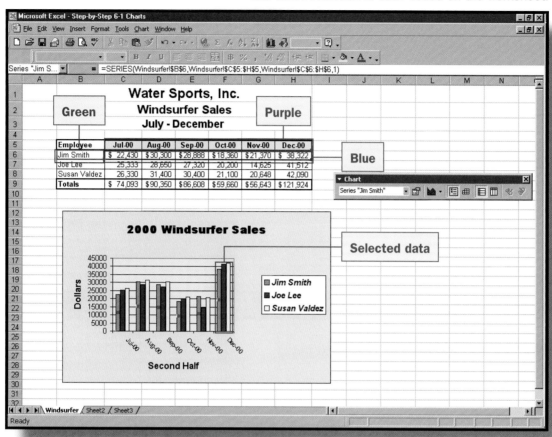

STEP-BY-STEP ▷ 6.4

1. To see the worksheet data, scroll to the top of the worksheet.

2. To remove the hyphen and year from each of the months, click **C5**, type **Jul** and press the **Enter** key. Click **C5** and drag its fill handle to cell **H5**. Notice the labels are automatically updated to reflect the change.

3. To insert a row in the worksheet, click **B8**, click the **Insert** menu, and click **Rows**.

4. To enter data in the inserted row, click **B8**, type **Kat Murphy**, press the **Tab** key, type **19745**, press **Tab**, type **18200**, press **Tab**, type **20087**, press **Tab**, type **19233**, press

Tab, type **12235**, press **Tab**, type **26788**, and press the **Enter** key.

5. To drag the data to the chart, select **B8:H8**, point to a border of the range until you see the drag-and-drop arrow, drag the range to the plot area on the chart, and release. Notice the new data series appears in the chart and Kat Murphy's name is added to the legend.

6. To widen columns **D** and **E**, select **D10:E10**, click **Format**, click **Column**, and click **AutoFit Selection.**

7. Click the **Save** button to save your work.

135

Enhancing a Chart with Graphics

You can add graphic objects to worksheets and charts. The graphics can be other files, drawing objects, clip art, pictures, or WordArt.

Using the Drawing Toolbar

C

To display the drawing toolbar, click the Drawing button on the Standard toolbar or choose Toolbars on the View menu and choose Drawing on the submenu. To create a drawing object, click one of the drawing tools on the Drawing toolbar (see Figure 6.9). You will learn to use some of the drawing tools in the next step-by-step exercise.

← Drawing button

FIGURE 6.9
Notice the various buttons on the Drawing toolbar.

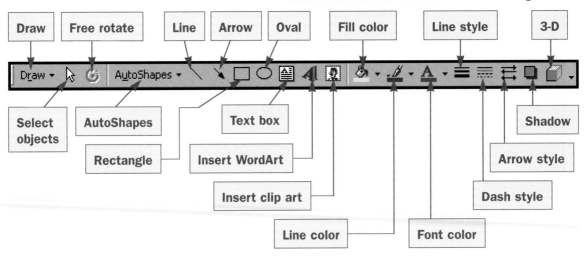

A text box is an object you can place on the chart when you want to enter text that will display and wrap.

To add a text box, click the Text Box button. Click on the chart approximately where you want the text box, and begin typing the text. The box's size adjusts to fit the text as you are typing (see Figure 6.10). You can also click in the chart and drag to create a box approximately the size you want and begin typing the text.

To resize a text box, select it and drag its handles. To move or reposition the text box, drag it by one of its borders. To format text in the text box, select the text and then use the text formatting commands you have learned. To delete a text box, select it and press the Delete key.

 Did You Know?

Hold the Shift key while drawing lines, arrows, ovals, or rectangles to draw straight lines, circles, or squares.

Selecting, Grouping, and Overlapping Objects

You can select an object by clicking it. It is sometimes better, however, to use the Select Objects button on the Drawing toolbar so only objects, such as a chart, picture, or text box, and not cells are

FIGURE 6.10
Notice the text box and the arrow to the December series.

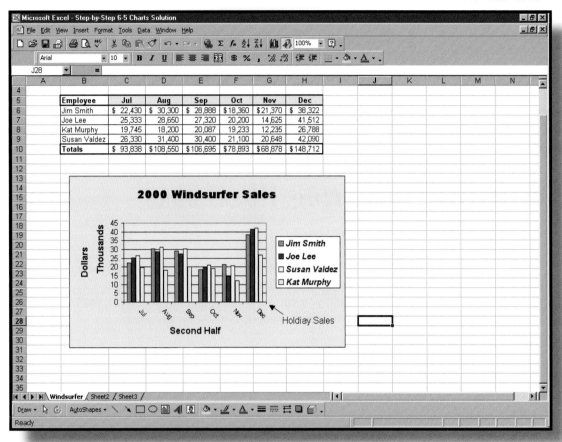

selected, and so a group of objects can be selected. Because the Select Objects button selects only objects, you need not worry about anything else being selected.

To select an object with the Select Objects button, click the Select Objects button so it is active and click the object. To select more than one object at a time, drag to surround the objects you want to select.

You can group objects for formatting, moving, sizing, copying, or deleting by selecting two or more objects and clicking the Group command on the Draw button's pop-up menu.

Drawing objects are placed one over the other in the order you create them. You can use Order commands on the Draw button's pop-up menu to change the order of drawing objects. You can bring objects to the front, send them to the back, or move them forward or backward with the options on the Order submenu.

Inserting Pictures in a Chart

In addition to text boxes, you can use the Picture command options on the Insert menu to place other graphic objects in a chart. The different types of pictures you can insert include:

■ Predesigned graphics from the Microsoft Clip Art Gallery.

■ Graphics files created in a graphics program. Excel displays a Picture toolbar when you insert such a graphics file that contains tools for editing and manipulating the image.

- Basic shapes like lines, arrows, callouts, etc., from the AutoShapes collection. Excel displays an AutoShapes palette containing basic shapes and variations on each.

- Special text treatments from the WordArt Gallery. Excel displays a WordArt toolbar that lets you edit and format your WordArt selection.

Taking Pictures of Charts or Worksheets

You can create picture objects of embedded charts or cells and then put the picture object on a different sheet or in a document created in another application.

To create a picture object, select the chart or cells you want to capture, hold the Shift key and open the Edit menu. Then choose the Copy Picture option.

Saving and Printing Workbooks with Charts

When you save your workbook, any embedded charts or chart sheets are automatically saved. When you print a worksheet, any embedded charts print with the worksheet data. If you create charts on separate sheets in the workbook, you can select the chart sheet and the worksheet and use any of Excel's print commands to print the active sheets.

STEP-BY-STEP 6.5

1. To display the Drawing toolbar if it is not already displayed, click the **Drawing** button on the Standard toolbar.

2. To add a text box to the chart to explain the December figures, click the **Text Box** button, and then click at the bottom of the chart to the right of Dec (see Figure 6.10), type **Holiday Sales,** and click outside the chart.

3. To draw an arrow to the December series, click the **Arrow** button, hold the **Shift** key and drag the crosshairs from the top of the text box to the bottom right of the December numbers (see Figure 6.10).

4. To take a picture of the chart, be sure it is selected, hold the **Shift** key and click the **Edit** menu, click **Copy Picture**, and click **OK** to accept the default settings.

5. To paste the picture on Sheet2, click the **Sheet2** tab, hold the **Shift** key and click the **Edit** menu, and click **Paste Picture.**

6. To preview the Windsurfer sheet, including the data and the chart, click the Windsurfer sheet tab, click outside the chart to be sure it is not selected. (If the chart is selected, the Preview window will display only the chart). Click the **Print Preview** button.

7. Click the **Close** button on the Print Preview menu bar.

8. Click the **Save** button and then close the workbook.

Summary

You have now learned to create a chart; select a chart for sizing, moving, and deleting; modify parts of a chart; and insert objects and pictures on a chart.

Try the exercises on the following pages to test how well you remember what you learned. Don't be afraid to go back and look up the answers, because that will help to reinforce what you learned.

LESSON 6 REVIEW QUESTIONS

TRUE / FALSE

Circle the T if the statement is true. Circle the F if it is false.

T F 1. You can click the Previous button in a Chart Wizard dialog box to return to the previous dialog box.

T F 2. You must select the range of data you want to chart before starting the Chart Wizard.

T F 3. An embedded chart always appears on the same worksheet as its corresponding data.

T F 4. One way to change data on a chart when it is linked to a worksheet is to change the data in the worksheet.

T F 5. Your chart must be selected before you can modify or format it.

T F 6. You can create a chart on its own worksheet in one step by selecting the data for the chart and pressing **F1.**

T F 7. You can resize a selected chart proportionally by holding down the **Ctrl** key and dragging one of the chart's corner handles.

T F 8. To change the chart type, you must reselect the data and start the Chart Wizard again.

T F 9. You can insert a text box on a chart.

T F 10. You cannot use drawing tools on worksheet cells.

COMPLETION

Complete the following sentences by writing the correct word or words in the blanks provided.

1. Excel's _____ will walk you through the steps needed to create a chart.

2. Before you can size, move, or delete a chart, you must _____ it.

1 3 9

3. A(n) _____ chart is placed on the same sheet as its related data.

4. You click _____ in a Wizard dialog box to proceed to the next step.

5. You click _____ in a Wizard dialog box to return to a previous step.

6. To resize a selected chart proportionally, hold down the _____ key and drag one of the chart's corner handles.

7. To select a specific chart part, you can display the _____ drop-down list on the Chart toolbar.

8. Using _____ you can select and move data directly from the worksheet to the chart's plot area and Excel automatically adjusts the chart.

9. You can use the _____ command options on the Insert menu to place graphic objects in a worksheet.

10. Use the _____ button on the Drawing tool to enter text that will wrap on a worksheet.

LESSON 6 PROJECTS

PROJECT 6A

To practice what you've learned in this lesson, complete the following project:

1. Open the workbook **Project 6-A.**

2. Select cells **A4:G7** on the New Home Sales sheet.

3. Start the Chart Wizard to create an area chart.

4. Create an **Area** chart using the selected default Chart sub-type. Advance through the Chart Wizard—Step 2 of 4 dialog box. In the Step 3 of 4 dialog box, enter **New Home Sales (July-December)** as the Chart title. Place the chart on the **New Home Sales** worksheet.

5. Center the chart below the sheet data. Resize it so it fits within the range **B11:F23.**

6. Change the font size for the chart title to **14** points. Break it after *Sales* into two lines and change the font size of the second line to **10** points.

7. Change the color of **Jane Grey's** data series to bright red.

8. Add a text box positioned near Jane Grey's August sales to let readers know she was on vacation. Enter the text **Vacation causes slight dip.** Format the text appropriately.

9. Change the font size of the **X-axis (category axis)** and **Y-axis (value axis)** labels to **8** and the style to **Bold.**

Extra Challenges

Use Help to find out how to add data labels to a chart. Review and print the Help topic(s) you find.

10. Add a background color to the **Chart Area.**

11. Change the font size of each of the names in the legend to **10.**

12. Print a copy of the worksheet, save and then close the workbook.

PROJECT 6B

To practice what you've learned in this lesson, complete the following project:

1. Open the workbook **Project 6-B.**

2. Format the worksheet to enhance its appearance.

3. Create a chart of your choosing for B5:C11. To enhance the chart's appearance, use any of the tools available.

4. Print, save, and close the workbook.

PROJECT 6C

SCANS   Access the http://www.nasdaq.com or another stock exchange site on the Web and check the price of Microsoft's stock today. Find the history of the stock's performance over the past year.

CRITICAL THINKING ACTIVITY

SCANS   1. Start a new workbook and create a worksheet using the data below. Compute the totals for each type of rental.

Rental Receipts			
	Jun	Jul	Aug
JetSkis	42,640	43,900	42,610
Windsurfers	38,115	37,655	34,235
Kayaks	31,405	32,720	29,630

2. Use AutoFormat to format the data.

3. Select the cells containing the three rental types and the cells containing the totals for each type.

4. Prepare a 3-D pie chart showing the percentage of the total for each of the rental types.

5. Print a copy of the worksheet data and chart. Save the workbook as **Critical Thinking Activity 6** and close the file.

AUTOMATING, PROTECTING, AND ENHANCING WORK

OBJECTIVES

When you complete this lesson, you will be able to:

■ Record and run a macro.

■ Find special data.

■ Set validation checks on data.

■ Use the various Excel features for protecting data.

■ Share workbooks.

■ Insert comments.

■ Insert hyperlinks to another workbook.

■ Use an Excel template.

■ Use the online collaboration feature.

🕐 **Estimated Time: 1½ hours**

Introduction

Now that you are familiar with many of Excel's features, you can create some pretty intricate worksheets for your data. In this lesson, you will learn how to use macros to automate tasks that you find yourself doing repeatedly. You will learn how to protect your workbooks, worksheets, and data from access by others and from changes by others. You will discover how to insert text boxes, cell comments, hyperlinks and other objects in your worksheets. You also will take a look at Excel's templates.

Recording and Running a Macro

A **macro** is a recording of a series of commands and actions. For example, if you want to enter a footer that consists of the file name at the left side of the page and the page number at the right side of the page on every worksheet, you could create a macro to do the job for you. After you create a macro, you can assign a menu command, toolbar button, or shortcut key to it to make running the macro easy.

To create a macro, open the expanded Tools menu, choose Macro, and then Record New Macro. You can see the Record Macro dialog box in Figure 7.1.

You then enter a name and a description for your macro and assign the shortcut keys. Be sure the shortcut key you assign to a macro is not already used for a menu command.

You can also choose whether you want to store your macro:

- In a personal macro workbook, which is always available.

- In the current workbook, so the macro is available only in this workbook.

- In a new workbook.

When you click OK, Excel displays the Stop Recording box (see Figure 7.2). The word "Recording" appears in the bottom left of the status bar. Use the Stop Recording button to signal you are finished recording.

When recording a macro, try to think of anything that might interfere with your macro. Do not make any assumptions that certain dialog boxes or buttons will be on the screen. For example, in the macro you enter in the next exercise, you will have to click the Header/ Footer tab in the Page Setup dialog box even if it is already displayed. It may not always be the displayed tab when you run a macro.

To run a macro, either enter the shortcut key command or choose Macro on the Tools menu and then choose Macros. The Macro dialog box opens as shown in Figure 7.3. Select a macro and click Run.

If your macro does not work properly, you can click Step Into in the Macro dialog box. Excel then runs the macro one step at a time to help you isolate any problems.

IMPORTANT:

Excel might display a warning message whenever you open a workbook that contains macros that lets you disable the macros. This prevents any computer viruses that may be stored in a macro from "infecting" your computer or network. If a macro is disabled, the virus cannot spread.

FIGURE 7.1
Enter a name, shortcut keys, and description for the macro.

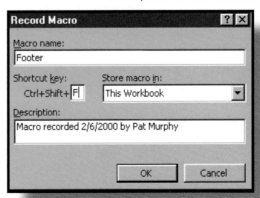

FIGURE 7.2
When you begin recording, Excel displays the Stop Recording button.

FIGURE 7.3
Select a macro to run in the Macro dialog box.

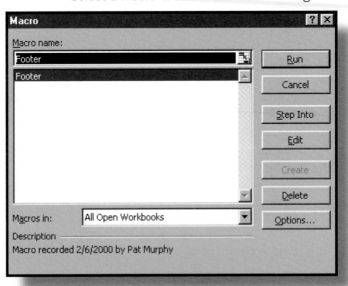

You can click Edit in the Macro dialog box to open the macro in Microsoft Visual Basic, which is the language used to write the macro. There, you can edit your macro if you already know Microsoft Visual Basic. To delete a macro, select it in the Macro dialog box and click Delete.

STEP-BY-STEP ▷ 7.1

1. Open the workbook **Step-by-Step 7-1 Macro.**

2. To display the Record Macro dialog box, click the **Tools** menu, click **Macro,** and click **Record New Macro.**

3. To name the macro, type **Footer.**

4. To assign a shortcut key, press the **Tab** key, hold the **Shift** key and type **F.** (Note that Excel will record the shortcut key for this macro as **Ctrl + Shift + F.**)

5. To store the macro in the current workbook, be sure **This Workbook** is displayed in the **Store macro in** list box.

6. To begin recording, click **OK.** Excel displays the Stop Recording box on your worksheet.

7. To enter the footer, click the **File** menu, click **Page Setup,** click the **Header/Footer** tab (even if it is already displayed), click the **Footer** drop-down list button, scroll to and

click the **Step-by-Step 7-1 Macro, Page 1** macro, and click **OK.**

8. To stop recording, click the **Stop Recording** button on the Stop Recording toolbar.

9. To preview and print the Kayak sheet with the new footer, click the **Print Preview** button. Click the **Print** button and click **OK.**

10. To use the macro to add the footer to the Windsurfer sheet, click the **Windsurfer** tab, hold the **Ctrl** and **Shift** keys and press **F** (Ctrl-Shift-F).

11. To print the Windsurfer sheet, click the **Print** button.

12. To add the footer and print the JetSki sheet, click the **JetSki** tab, hold the **Ctrl** and **Shift** and **F** keys, and then click the **Print** button.

13. Click the **Save** button and then close the workbook.

Finding Cells with Special Types of Contents

You already know how to use Excel's Find and Replace commands to find data in a worksheet. You can also conduct a search to find cells that contain certain types of data using the Go To command on the Edit menu. The Go To dialog box opens. Click the Special button to open the Go To Special dialog box shown in Figure 7.4.

You can find and select all cells containing constant values, formulas, comments, objects, or blanks. The Go To command searches the entire worksheet if you do not select a specific area for it to search.

In addition to the specific contents just mentioned, you can select:

- *Current region,* which selects a range of cells around the active cell bounded by any combination of blank rows and blank columns.

INTERNET Spam is unsolicited e-mail or junk mail. Some e-mail applications let you block junk mail.

- *Current array,* which selects the entire array, if any, to which the active cell belongs.

- *Row differences,* which selects cells whose contents are different from the comparison cell in each row.

- *Column differences,* which selects cells whose contents are different from the comparison cell in each column.

- *Precedents,* which selects cells that are either directly or indirectly referenced by the formula in the active cell.

- *Dependents,* which selects cells with formulas that refer either directly or indirectly to the active cell.

FIGURE 7.4

Find special types of data using the Go To Special dialog box.

Using the Validation Command

Excel's Validation command on the Data menu lets you restrict the type of data that can be entered in a cell or a range. You can use this feature to control accuracy when inputting data. For example, you can check that the data entered in selected cells is only whole numbers or decimals or dates. You can also set limits on the number of characters that can be entered in a cell or the values the data must fall within.

To restrict cell entries, select the cell or range you want to restrict, open the Data menu, and then choose Validation. The Data Validation dialog box appears (see Figure 7.5).

In the Allow drop-down list, choose the type of data to be permitted in the selected cells. Depending on the type you select, the Data box where you can enter minimum and maximum values the data must fall within may be activated. On the Input Message tab, you can enter a message that appears as a ScreenTip whenever the selected cells are activated. The message can let the user know the restrictions. On the Error Alert tab, you can choose an alert button and a message that displays when a user tries to enter an incorrect data type.

FIGURE 7.5

Set restrictions on data that can be entered.

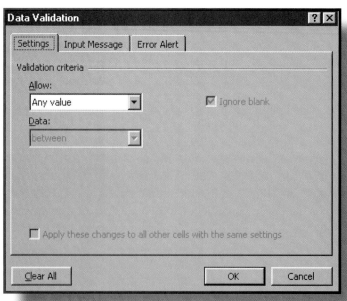

STEP-BY-STEP 7.2

1. Open the workbook **Step-by-Step 7-2 Validation.** Be sure cell **A1** is active.

2. To find all the cells in the worksheet that contain formulas, click the **Edit** menu, click the **Expand** button if needed, click **Go To,** and click **Special.**

3. In the Go To Special dialog box, click **Formulas** and then click **OK.** The range C9:H9 is selected, indicating those cells contain formulas.

4. To find all cells that contain references to the formula in C9, click **C9,** click the **Edit** menu, click **Go To,** and click **Special.** In the Go To dialog box, click **Precedents** and click **OK.** Notice C6:C8 is selected.

5. To use the Validation command, select **I6:I8,** click the **Data** menu, and click

Validation. Be sure the Settings tab is displayed. Click the **Allow** list drop-down button, click **Whole number,** click the **Data** drop-down button, click **greater than,** click in the Minimum text box and type **0** (zero). Click the **Input Message** tab, type **Round to the nearest dollar** in the Input message text box. Click the **Error Alert** tab, click the **Style** drop-down button, click **Warning,** and then click **OK.** Notice the message appears as a ScreenTip.

6. To test the validation feature, type **25550.50** and press the **Enter** key. A message box appears about the restrictions placed on the cell. Click **No** when asked to continue, and then type **25551** and press the **Enter** key.

7. Save and then close the workbook.

Protecting Data

Excel provides several options for restricting others from both accessing and editing your worksheets. You can also:

- Restrict others from opening a workbook.

- Allow others to open a workbook and change the contents, but prevent them from replacing the original file.

- Restrict others from changing all or some of the contents, organization, or display of a workbook.

- Restrict others from seeing selected sheets in an open workbook.

Using Passwords When Saving Workbooks

You can use passwords to apply different levels of protection to a workbook. Choose Save As on the File menu to open the Save As dialog box. Use the Tools drop-down button and then choose General Options to open the Save Options dialog box shown in Figure 7.6. There are three different password levels you can apply to a workbook:

 Hot Tips

Write down your passwords and keep them in a safe place so you can always check them.

- The *Password to open* option protects your workbook from unauthorized use by requiring a user to enter the correct password to open the workbook or access its data through links from other workbooks.

- The *Password to modify* option protects your workbook from changes by requiring the user to enter a password to save a file.

- The *Read-only recommended* option requires a user to use the Save As command and save the workbook with a new name to make changes. The original workbook remains intact.

FIGURE 7.6
Enter workbook passwords in the Save Options dialog box.

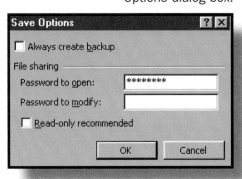

A password can contain up to 15 characters and can include letters, numbers, symbols, and spaces. Passwords are case sensitive. That means, for example, that *PASSWORD, password,* and *PaSsWoRd* are three different passwords.

You must be very careful when putting passwords on workbooks. *If you forget the password, you cannot open your workbook, remove protection from the workbook, or access data in your workbook.* You can remove a password *only if you can open and change the workbook.*

As you enter a password or confirm it, Excel displays asterisks, not the password itself. Always check the position of your fingers on the keyboard when entering passwords to make sure they are on the right keys. Excel displays a Confirm Password dialog box (see Figure 7.7) so you can enter your password a second time. Even when entering the password a second time, you have no way of knowing from the screen if you are actually typing what you think you are typing without checking the position of your fingers on the keyboard.

FIGURE 7.7
Notice the warning in the dialog box.

S TEP-BY-STEP ⟹ 7.3

1. Open the workbook **Step-by-Step 7-3 Passwords.**

2. To put a password on the file, click the **File** menu, click **Save As,** click the **Tools** button, and click **General Options** on the drop-down list. In the Password to open text box, type **password,** click **OK,** type **password** again in the Confirm Password dialog box, read the Caution statement, and click **OK.**

3. To save and close the file, click **Save,** and click the workbook's **Close** button.

4. To open the file again, click the **File** menu and click **Step-by-Step 7-3 Passwords** at the bottom of the menu. In the Password dialog box, type **password** and click **OK.**

148

5. To remove the password, click the **File** menu, click **Save As,** click the **Tools** button, and click **General Options.** The asterisks representing the password are selected. Press the **Delete** key, click **OK,** click **Save,** and respond **Yes** when asked to replace the existing file.

6. To close the file, click its **Close** button.

7. To reopen the file, click the **File** menu and click **Step-by-Step 7-3 Passwords.** Notice the file is no longer password protected.

8. To add a password that allows others to open the file but does not allow them to save changes to the file, click the **File** menu, click **Save As,** click the **Tools** button, and click **General Options.** In the **Password to modify** text box, type **PASSWORD,** click **OK,** type **PASSWORD** again, click **OK,** click **Save,** and respond **Yes** when asked to replace the existing file.

9. To close the file, click its **Close** button.

10. To open the file, click the **File** menu and click **Step-by-Step 7-3 Passwords.**

11. To open the file in read-only mode, click the **Read Only** button.

12. To enter data in cell C5, select **C5,** type **25000,** and press the **Enter** key.

13. To adjust the column width, double-click the right border of the column C heading.

14. To save the file with the change, click the **Save** button. Notice you cannot save the change to the original file because the file was opened in read-only mode. Click **OK.** In the Save As dialog box, type **Password Protection** as the File name and click **Save.**

Using the Protection Command on the Tools Menu

The Protection options on the Tools menu let you protect the structure and content of your workbooks, worksheets, and selected items on the worksheet.

Protecting Items on a Worksheet

When you learned about the Format Cells dialog box, you did not look at the Protection tab in that dialog box (see Figure 7.8). By default, the Locked option is always turned on in the Protection tab. This means that cells on the worksheet cannot be changed, moved, resized, or deleted. However, this option is only in effect if you apply the Protect Sheet option.

With the Locked option turned on, you can open the Tools menu, choose Protection, and then choose Protect Sheet. The Protect Sheet dialog box appears (see Figure 7.9). You can protect worksheet contents, objects, and scenarios as well as add a password.

If you want, for instance, to protect the worksheet except for cells where others must enter information, you can first unlock those cells and then apply protection to the worksheet.

 Hot Tips

You can use the Group feature to lock or unlock cells on more than one worksheet at a time. Excel, however, does not let you use the Protect Sheet option when sheets are grouped. You must first ungroup the sheets. Then you can apply the sheet protection separately to each sheet.

149

FIGURE 7.8
This option is only in effect if you apply the
Protect Sheet option.

FIGURE 7.9
Protect Sheet dialog box.

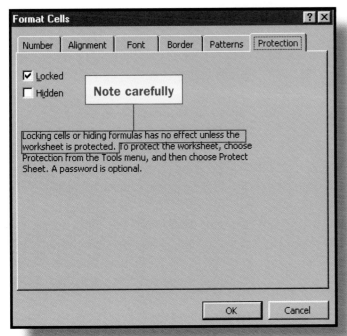

FIGURE 7.10
Protect a workbook's structure
and display options from
being changed.

Protecting a Workbook

Choose the Protect Workbook protection option on the Tools menu to display the Protect Workbook dialog box shown in Figure 7.10. Use this command to protect the workbook structure to ensure that sheets in the workbook cannot be deleted, unhidden, or renamed, and that sheets cannot be inserted. You can also protect workbook windows to ensure that the windows are always sized and positioned the same way when you open the workbook.

The Protect and Share Workbook protection option on the Tools menu provides protection for workbooks that are opened and changed by more than one user. You will learn about sharing workbooks next.

STEP-BY-STEP ⟹ 7.4

1. To unlock the cells in which you want to be able to insert data in all three sheets, click the **Kayak** tab, hold the **Shift** key and click the **JetSki** tab. Select **C5:H7,** click the **Format** menu, click **Cells,** click the **Protection** tab, click **Locked** to *turn off* the lock, and click **OK.**

2. To hide formulas, select **C8:H8,** click the **Format** menu, click **Cells,** click the **Protection** tab if needed, click **Locked** to turn off the lock, click **Hidden,** and click **OK.**

3. To ungroup the sheets because Excel will let you protect only one sheet at a time,

right-click any sheet tab and select **Ungroup Sheets.**

4. To protect the Kayak sheet, click its sheet tab, click the **Tools** menu, click **Protection,** click **Protect Sheet** and click **OK.** Repeat this procedure for the Windsurfer and JetSki sheets.

5. To try to enter a new employee name in cell B5 on the *Windsurfer* sheet, click **B5** and type any character. Respond **OK** to the message that locked cells cannot be changed.

6. To enter data in the unlocked cell C5, click

C5, type **50000,** and press the **Enter** key. Try to adjust column width to see the number (the sheet is protected).

7. To see if the formula in C8 is hidden, click **C8** and notice the formula is not displayed on the formula bar.

8. To remove protection from each of the three sheets, click the **Kayak** sheet tab, click **Tools,** click **Protection,** and click **Unprotect Sheet.** Repeat the procedure for the Windsurfer and JetSki sheets. Adjust the column width of Column C.

9. Save and then close the workbook.

Sharing Workbooks

The Share Workbook command on the Tools menu lets you specify that the workbook can be shared and how history and conflicts will be handled.

If you are working on a shared network resource, you can use the Share Workbook command on the Tools menu and select the *Allow changes by more than one user at the same time* option (see Figure 7.11). Users can then review and edit a workbook at the same time and see each other's changes.

IMPORTANT:

See your system administrator to find out how to give others access to workbooks on your hard disk.

The Advanced tab in the Share Workbook dialog box is where you designate how to track changes, update changes, and solve conflicting changes between users (see Figure 7.12).

Each person can be assigned to work on a different area on the worksheet. Two people, for instance, could be entering and changing figures while a third enters formulas. You can give each user the same access to the shared workbook or limit access by protecting the shared workbook.

FIGURE 7.11

The Editing tab in the Share Workbook dialog box is where you allow others to use a workbook at the same time.

FIGURE 7.12

Make tracking, updating, and resolving conflicts decisions on the Advanced tab in the Share Workbook dialog box.

There are some things you should know if you are going to share workbooks:

- When you edit a shared workbook, Excel uses the user name set on the General tab in the Options dialog box.

- Not all Excel commands are available when sharing workbooks.

- More than one user can add comments to a cell, and all of the comments appear in the comments display.

- You will see changes made by other users when you save a shared workbook.

- Excel displays a Resolve Conflicts dialog box if changes you are saving conflict with changes saved by another user.

- Each user can save personal display and print settings for a shared workbook.

You can display a list of all changes to the workbook, including the users who made the changes, data that was deleted or replaced, and information about conflicting changes.

Inserting Comments on a Worksheet

You can flag or call attention to data with cell comments. You can add a comment to a cell in a worksheet to explain an entry or to add more information about the data. To add a comment to a cell, activate the cell in which you want to enter the comment and choose Comment on the Insert menu. A cell comment text box appears on the screen (see Figure 7.13). Notice the name of the user from the User Information tab in the Options dialog box.

After you type your comment, click anywhere outside the comment box to close it. A small red triangle appears in the cell containing the comment. Position the pointer on the cell to display the comment. To display the comment on the screen instead of just the red comment indicator, choose Show Comment on the cell's shortcut menu.

FIGURE 7.13
Notice the cell comment text box.

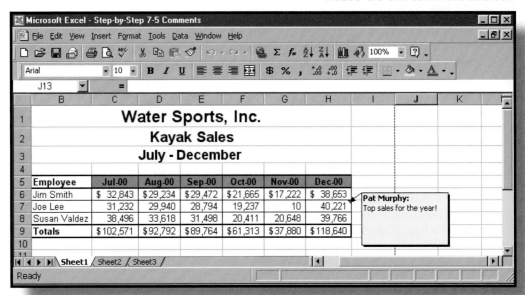

 **NOTE:**

On the Sheet tab in the Page Setup dialog box, you can choose to print all comments on a separate page at the end of the document, or as they are displayed on the sheet.

You can edit, delete, or choose to hide or display a comment by selecting commands on the cell's shortcut menu. To display the shortcut menu, right-click the cell containing the comment. You can also select the cell, open the Edit menu, choose Clear, and click Comment to delete a comment.

Inserting a Hyperlink to another Workbook

You have already inserted a hyperlink to a Web site. It is just as easy to insert a hyperlink that displays another Excel document.

 **NOTE:**

Remember the reader must have access to the hyperlink's destination to use the hyperlink.

When you click a hyperlink to display its destination object, Excel automatically displays the Web toolbar. You can use its Back and Forward buttons to move between the two workbooks.

153

1. Open the workbook **Step-by-Step 7-5 Comments.**

2. To allow the workbook to be shared, click the **Tools** menu, click **Share Workbook,** be sure the **Editing** tab is displayed, click the **Allow changes** box, click the **Advanced** tab, notice the settings, and click **OK.** When the warning message that the file will be saved appears, click **OK** again. Notice the file now has [Shared] after its name on the title bar.

3. To remove the workbook from shared status, click the **Tools** menu, click **Share Workbook,** be sure the **Editing** tab is displayed, click the **Allow changes...** box to clear it. When the message about losing history appears, click **OK.**

4. To add a cell comment, click **H7,** click the **Insert** menu, and click **Comment.** In the comment box, type **Top sales for the year!**

5. To close the comment box, click in a blank cell. You should see a red comment indicator in **H7.** To display the comment, position the pointer on the cell.

6. To display the comment rather than the comment indicator on the worksheet, right-click **H7** to display the shortcut menu. Then click **Show Comment.**

7. To print the worksheet with the comment displayed, click the **File** menu and click

Page Setup. Click the **Page** tab, click **Landscape.** Click the **Sheet** tab, click the **Comments** drop-down button and click **As displayed on sheet.** Click **Print Preview.** Click **Print.** Click **OK.**

8. To enter some text to use for the hyperlink, click **B12,** type **See Sales Summary file for all product sales,** and press the **Enter** key.

9. To display the Insert Hyperlink dialog box and choose a workbook file for the destination, click **B12** again, click the **Insert** menu, click **Hyperlink,** click the **File** button, be sure your folder is displayed, double-click the Sales Summary workbook file.

10. To set the Kayak sheet as the destination, click the **Bookmark** button, click **Kayak,** and click **OK.** Click **OK** again.

11. To go to the destination, click the hyperlink in cell **B12.** The Sales Summary workbook opens and the Kayak sheet appears.

12. To return to the original workbook, click the **Back** button on the Web toolbar.

13. To return to and close the destination workbook, click the **Forward** button on the Web toolbar, and click the Sales Summary **Close** button. Click **No** if you are asked to save changes.

14. Save and then close the workbook.

Using Templates

Excel comes with some predesigned workbook files—called **templates**—that you can use as a basis for building your own workbooks. Excel has templates for expense statements, invoices, and purchase orders. They are formatted to make data entry quick and easy.

154

IMPORTANT:

In addition to the templates Excel provides, you can create a workbook, enter the data for a template, and save the file as a template. Excel will display your template on the General tab in the New dialog box.

 Did You Know?

The Village Software® template is licensed by Microsoft. To learn more about Village Software and the products and services they offer, double-click the Village Software template on the Spreadsheet Solutions tab in the New dialog box.

In the next exercise, you will look at an invoice template to see how you might customize the template to work for you.

STEP-BY-STEP ▷ 7.6

1. To open the Expense Statement template, click the **File** menu, click **New,** click the **Spreadsheet Solutions** tab. Click the various template icons to preview them in the Preview window. Then, double-click **Expense Statement.**

2. To enable the macros, since we can assume Microsoft is a safe source, click **Enable Macros.** Notice the template and the comment indicators.

3. To display the Customize Your Invoice tab, click the **Customize** button. Notice you could customize the template for your organization.

4. To display comments about customizing the template, point to some of the red comment indicators.

5. Close the template without customizing it.

Using the Online Collaboration Feature

Because Excel and Microsoft NetMeeting are now integrated, you can share and exchange information with others at different sites in real time—just as if everyone were in the same room. To host a meeting, you can either schedule the meeting in advance with Microsoft Outlook or start an impromptu Microsoft Outlook meeting from within an Excel workbook. Just use the Online Collaboration command on the Tools menu.

As the host of an online meeting you are in control of the workbook even though the other participants can see the workbook. You can let them change the workbook by turning on collaboration. You can turn off collaboration at any time. You can ask participants to join a meeting already in progress.

If you are invited to participate in a meeting, you will get a message asking you to take part in an upcoming or ongoing online meeting at a specific time and date. When you accept a request to join a meeting, the Online Meeting toolbar and the workbook being shared appear on your screen.

Be sure to use the online collaboration feature if your situation requires working with others on workbooks.

Summary

You have now learned to create and run macros, use protection features, insert cell comments and hyperlinks to other Excel workbooks, share workbooks, and open workbooks that are based on Excel templates.

Try the exercises on the following pages to test how well you remember what you learned. Don't be afraid to go back and look up the answers, because that will help to reinforce what you learned.

LESSON 7 REVIEW QUESTIONS

TRUE / FALSE

Circle the T if the statement is true. Circle the F if it is false.

T F 1. You can assign a shortcut key to a macro.

T F 2. You can only create a macro to run in the current workbook.

T F 3. A password can contain 30 letters, numbers, symbols, and spaces.

T F 4. You cannot remove a password unless you know the password and are able to access the workbook.

T F 5. If you forget your password, Microsoft will help you access your workbook.

T F 6. You can use the Group feature when you are using the Protection command on the Tools menu to protect individual sheets.

T F 7. You can display a comment indicator or the comment on a worksheet.

T F 8. You can save a workbook as a template.

T F 9. When you open an Excel template to use as the basis for a new workbook, you should save it with a new file name immediately.

T F 10. The case you enter a password with makes no difference when reentering the password to access the file.

COMPLETION

Complete the following sentences by writing the correct word or words in the blanks provided.

1. A(n) _____ is a recording of a series of Excel commands.

2. You can use the _____ command on the _____ menu to record a macro.

3. You can use the _____ button to indicate you are finished recording a macro.

4. You use the _____ button in the _____ dialog box to enter a password for a workbook.

5. Use the _____ option in the Save Options dialog box to require a user to enter a password in order to save the file.

6. You can use the _____ option on the _____ tab in the Format Cells dialog box to lock and unlock individual cells on a sheet.

7. You can choose to save a workbook as a template in the _____ dialog box.

8. You click the _____ button on the _____ toolbar to display a comment on the worksheet instead of the comment indicator.

9. You position the pointer over the _____ to display a cell comment.

10. You click the _____ command on the _____ menu to share a workbook.

LESSON 7 PROJECTS

PROJECT 7A

To practice what you've learned in this lesson, complete the following project:

1. Open the workbook **Project 7-A.** Display the *Spreadsheets* sheet.

2. Create a macro that inserts a header on the worksheet and then prints the current worksheet:

   a. Name the macro **Header** and assign the shortcut key combination of **Ctrl + u.** Store the macro in the current workbook.

   b. Select **Page Setup** on the **File** menu. Click the **Header/Footer** tab. Click the **Header** drop-down list and select the **Prepared by [user name] X/XX/XX, Page 1** header. Click **OK.** Click the **Print** button, and then click the **Stop Recording** button.

Extra Challenges

Use Help to search for information on how to create a button that you can press to run a macro. Review and print the Help topic(s) you find.

3. Run the macro on the **Database** and then the **Word Processing** sheets.

4. Save the workbook. Then close the workbook.

PROJECT 7B

To practice what you've learned in this lesson, complete the following project:

1. Open the workbook **Project 7-B.**

2. In cell **E20,** insert the comment **5% discount given on orders of more than $500.** Be sure the comment is displayed on the sheet.

3. Insert a hyperlink in cell **D6:**

    a. Type **See Pricing Schedule file for discount prices** in cell D6, and press **Enter.**

    b. Click **D6** and then click the **Insert Hyperlink** button on the toolbar.

    c. In the Insert Hyperlink dialog box, click the **File** button under **Browse for** on the right side of the dialog box. Select the **Pricing Schedule** workbook file in the folder containing your practice files as the destination file. Click **OK** to close the Insert Hyperlink dialog box.

4. To go to the destination, click the hyperlink.

5. Close the Pricing Schedule workbook.

6. On the **Sheet** tab of the Page Setup dialog box, opt to print the cell comment as it is displayed on the sheet.

7. Preview the worksheet. When you are satisfied with the placement of inserted objects, print a copy of the worksheet and then close the workbook.

PROJECT 7C

SCANS

Open the Help menu, click Microsoft on the Web, and click Microsoft Office Home Page. Search for information on Village Software. This is a company that creates many of the templates available in Microsoft applications. Print any information concerning templates you might want to use to create a workbook. Be sure to disconnect.

CRITICAL THINKING ACTIVITY

SCANS

Use Excel's **Purchase Order** template to create a purchase order you can use. Customize the template for the sporting goods chain. Be sure to position your mouse pointer on the red comment indicators so you can see tips for customizing the template.

WORKING WITH DATABASE FEATURES

OBJECTIVES

When you complete this lesson, you will be able to:

- Design a database.
- Create the database.
- Add records to the database.
- Find, edit, and delete records.
- Sort and filter records.
- Use the Subtotals command.
- Create a pivot table.

⏱ **Estimated Time: 1½ hours**

Introduction

In this lesson you will learn to use the Excel database features. Excel's primary function is as a worksheet for calculating and analyzing numbers. If you need to track a large amount of information, a database application such as Microsoft's Access is the appropriate software application. However, Excel has features that let you create and manipulate simple lists or databases. You will learn how to use those features in this lesson.

 **IMPORTANT:**

Excel provides templates on the Spreadsheet Solutions tab in the New dialog box (Invoice and Purchase Order) that automate common tasks and can automatically copy the workbook data to a linked Access database.

Understanding Databases

A **database** is an organized collection of related information. A list of company employees, houses for sale, or names and addresses can be organized into a database. Excel refers to its databases as **lists.**

All the information about one person or thing in the list is called a **record.** A row in the list is a record. Each piece of information in a record is called a **field.** One piece of information, such as a person's last name is a field. Fields define the structure of a data list, whereas records are the data entered about one person or thing in the structure. Figure 8.1 identifies the parts of a data list.

FIGURE 8.1

You can see a worksheet with information that will be used for a database.

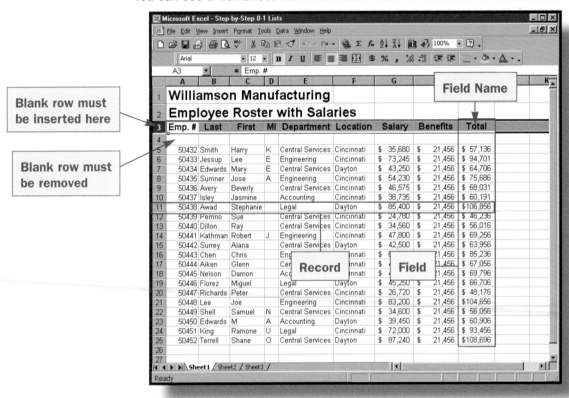

Designing a List

You can always add new fields and records to a data list. However, it is wise to determine the information you will need before you begin.

It's important to understand that when you create a list in Excel, you are actually setting up worksheet data so that you can use database features—such as sorting and searching. To take advantage of Excel's database capabilities, enter data in a list or set up existing data according to the following guidelines:

LIST SIZE AND LOCATION

■ The list must fit on one worksheet.

■ Don't put more than one list on a worksheet.

■ Leave at least one blank column and one blank row between a list and other data on the sheet (such as a title and subtitle).

1 6 0

■ Avoid storing other data to the left or right of the list.

■ In the list, all records must have the same number of fields, even if some are blank.

FIELD LABELS

■ Each field has a **field name,** or **field label,** which describes the field.

■ Enter field labels in the first row of a list. Field names must be on one row only.

■ Use different character formatting (font, alignment, border, capitalization, and so on) for the field names.

■ Use borders to insert lines below the labels to separate them from the data. Do not use blank rows or dashed lines.

RECORD AND FIELD CONTENTS

■ Use consistent formatting for all data located below the field names.

■ Delete any blank rows or columns in the data list.

■ Do not insert extra spaces at the beginning of a field. Spaces affect sorting and searching.

✓ **NOTE:**

It is wise to have a column with consecutive numbers in your database. That way you can always return the records to their original order. If you enter consecutive invoice or employee numbers, they will serve this purpose.

S TEP-BY-STEP ▷ 8.1

1. Open the workbook **Step-by-Step 8-1 Lists.**

2. To insert a row between the title rows and the field names to make the worksheet data conform to Excel's guidelines, click anywhere in row **3,** click the **Insert** menu, and then click **Rows.**

3. To delete the empty row between the field labels and the data, click anywhere in row **5,** click the **Edit** menu, click **Delete,** click Entire Row, and click **OK.**

4. Your data list is now in the range A4:I25.

Using a Data Form With Your List

An easy way to view and edit records in a list—especially a large list—is with a **data form.** A data form displays one record at a time.

To open a data form, select any cell in the data list and then choose Form on the Data menu. The data form with the same name as the worksheet appears and displays the first record in the list (see Figure 8.2).

The left side of the dialog box displays the column labels, or field names. Calculated values are not displayed in text boxes. Excel displays the fields in the same order in which they appear on the worksheet. To move from field to field, press the Tab key. To move back to a field, hold the Shift key and press the Tab key. You can edit data directly in the field text box, but you cannot edit formulas in a data form. Notice in Figure 8.2 that the Total field, a calculated value, does not appear in a text box.

FIGURE 8.2
A data form displays one record.

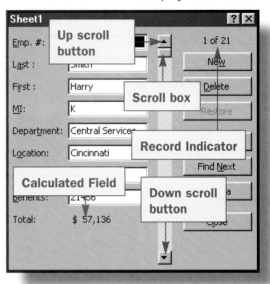

Displaying Records in the Data Form

You can use the Find Prev and the Find Next buttons to move to the previous or the next record, respectively. Or, you can use the scroll bar to move through the records. Table 8.1 lists techniques for moving quickly through records with the scroll bar.

TABLE 8.1
Moving through records

SCROLL BAR TECHNIQUES

TO MOVE TO THE	DO THIS
Same field in the next record	Click down scroll button
Same field in the previous record	Click up scroll button
Same field 10 records forward	Click below the scroll box
Same field 10 records back	Click above the scroll box
First record	Drag scroll box to top of scroll bar
Last record	Drag scroll box to bottom of scroll bar and then click the up scroll arrow

Adding and Deleting Records

In the right part of the dialog box, you see the record number indicator that tells you which record is displayed and how many records are in the list. To add a record to the database with the data form, click New and a blank data form appears in which you can enter data for one record.

To add a record directly on the worksheet, simply enter the data in the first empty row below the list. When adding records on the worksheet, you can quickly enter information that has already been entered in the column. *Right*-click the cell to display a shortcut menu. Choose Pick From List, and a drop-down list displays the entries already used in that field. You can then choose your entry from that list.

To delete a record from the list, either delete the row on the worksheet or display the record in the data form and click the Delete button. Excel deletes the record in the list and shifts all the rows below it up one row. You can cancel changes you make to a record by clicking Restore. You must click Restore, though, *before* you move to another record.

 **IMPORTANT:**

To ensure you can retrieve data meeting certain criteria, be sure you enter like data exactly the same way in each record. Don't spell out a word in one record and abbreviate it in another, for example.

Finding Records

You can find a record or subset of records with the Criteria button in the data form. When you click Criteria, a blank data form appears. Enter the data for which you are searching in the appropriate field text box. For example, if you want to find all employees in a certain department, type the department name (exactly as it is entered in the database) in the department field text box. Then, click Find Next. Keep clicking Find Next to find multiple occurrences of the data. You will hear a beep or see a message when all occurrences have been found.

Once you've found the records for which you are searching, click the Criteria button again, click Clear, and then click Form. If you don't clear the criteria, you will be able to access only the records meeting the criteria.

S TEP-BY-STEP ▷ 8.2

1. To display the data form, click any cell in the list, click the **Data** menu, and click **Form.**

2. To move to **record 11,** click in the scroll bar *below* the scroll box.

3. To move to **record 1,** click in the scroll bar *above* the scroll box.

4. To move to **record 3,** click the **Find Next** button twice.

5. To add a new record to the database, click the **New** button, type **50453**, press the **Tab** key, type **Nast**, press **Tab**, type **Jerry**, press **Tab** twice, type **Central Services**, press **Tab**, type **Cincinnati**, press **Tab**, type **45250**, press **Tab**, type **21456**, and press the **Enter** key.

6. To see the new record, click **Find Prev.** Notice the Total has been calculated for you.

7. To display the first record, drag the scroll box to the top of the scroll bar.

8. To find Damon Nelson's record, click **Criteria,** press the **Tab** key to move to the **Last** text box, type **Nelson,** and click **Find Next.** Nelson is record 14 of 22.

 **Hot Tips**

If you press the Enter key or an arrow key after entering data on a form, you will move to the next record and cannot use the restore feature.

(continued on next page)

9. To change Nelson's salary, select the amount in the **Salary** text box and type **51000.**

10. To return to the original salary, click the **Restore** button.

11. To clear the criteria you entered for Damon Nelson and redisplay the form with all the records in the list, click **Criteria,** click **Clear,** and click **Form.** Scroll to the first record in the list.

12. To find the records for all employees in Central Services, click the **Criteria** button, click the **Department** text box, type **Central Services,** and click **Find Next.** Click **Find Next** until you go through all the records of employees in Central Services. You should find 10 records.

13. To clear Central Services from the criteria, click the **Criteria** button, click **Clear,** and click **Form.**

14. To close the data form, click the **Close** command button.

15. To add another record to the data list, click cell **A27** and type **50454,** press the **Tab** key, type **Golden,** press **Tab,** type **Carol,** press **Tab** twice, type **L** and let Excel fill in *Legal* for you, press **Tab,** point to **F27** and click the *right* mouse button, click **Pick From List,** click **Cincinnati,** press **Tab,** type **84300,** press **Tab,** click **H26** and drag its fill handle to **H27.**

16. To add the formula to the Total field, click **I26** and drag its fill handle to **I27.**

17. Click the **Save** button on the toolbar to save the new record.

Sorting Data

Y̶ou can use the Sort command on the Data menu to organize data alphabetically, numerically, or chronologically (see Figure 8.3.). When you sort a database, Excel rearranges records according to the contents of up to three fields.

IMPORTANT:

Do not save a worksheet you have sorted unless you have a field such as an employee number that lets you easily put the records back in their original order.

FIGURE 8.3
You can designate three fields for a sort.

When you click any cell in the list and use the Sort command, Excel automatically selects your whole list and defaults to excluding the field labels in the first row from the sort.

You can specify whether you want the data sorted in ascending or descending order. When you choose Ascending order, numbers are sorted from 1 to 9, text is sorted from A to Z, and dates are sorted from earliest to latest. Descending order sorts numbers from 9 to 1, text from Z to A, and dates from latest to earliest.

You can use the Options button in the Sort dialog box to have Excel distinguish between uppercase and lowercase characters or to sort columns instead of rows.

Excel saves the options you select in the Sort dialog box until you change the options or sort another list.

If you need to sort a list by only a single field, you can select a cell in the field you want to sort by and click the Sort Ascending or Sort Descending button on the toolbar.

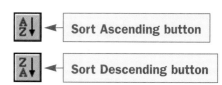

Hot Tips

If you do not like the result of a sort, use the Undo Sort command on the Edit menu immediately.

Sort Ascending button

Sort Descending button

STEP-BY-STEP ▷ 8.3

1. To open the Sort dialog box to sort the data list by Last name and then by First name, click a cell in column B in the list, click the **Data** menu and click **Sort**. Notice the *Last* field is already displayed in the Sort by text box.

2. To add another field to the sort, click the first **Then by** drop-down button, click **First,** be sure **Ascending** order is selected for both fields and **Header row** is selected, and then click **OK.** *Glenn Aiken* should be the first record. Notice the data is sorted alphabetically by the *Last* name field. Those records that have the same last name are sorted alphabetically by the *First* name field.

3. To sort the database by the **Department** field, click in a cell in the list in column **E,** and then click the **Sort Ascending** button on the toolbar. *M.A. Edwards* in the Accounting department should be the first record.

4. To sort the database by the Total field with the highest salary listed first, click any cell in the list in column **I** and then click the **Sort Descending** button.

5. To return the records to their original order (by Emp. # in ascending order), click any cell in the list in column **A** and then click the **Sort Ascending** button.

Filtering Records

You can use Excel's Filter feature when you want to find and work with a subset of records that meet certain criteria or a specified set of conditions. Excel displays only the records that contain a certain value or that meet a set of conditions. Excel has two types of filters: AutoFilter and Advanced.

Using AutoFilters

You can turn on the AutoFilter feature by opening the Data menu, choosing Filter, and then AutoFilter. When you use the AutoFilter command, Excel puts drop-down buttons directly on the field names. Just click a button to display a list of all the items in the column (see Figure 8.4). You can then select an item from the list so Excel finds all records in that field that meet that condition and temporarily hides the other records. To redisplay all the records, click the field's drop-down button and click All.

FIGURE 8.4

AutoFilter displays drop-down arrows on field names.

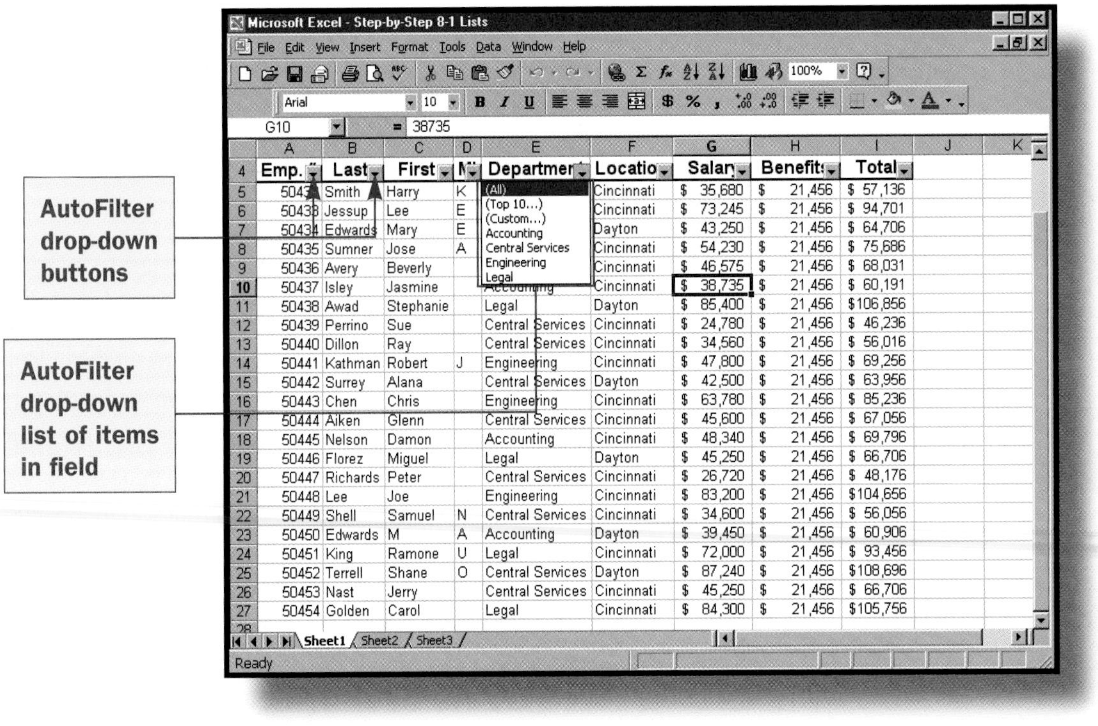

AutoFilter drop-down buttons

AutoFilter drop-down list of items in field

If you choose (Top 10) on an AutoFilter drop-down list, Excel displays the Top 10 AutoFilter dialog box. You can opt to find a specified number (it doesn't have to be 10!) of records at the top or at the bottom of the list.

If you choose (Custom) on an AutoFilter drop-down list, Excel displays the Custom AutoFilter dialog box (see Figure 8.5). In the text box under the field name (Department, in Figure 8.5), select a comparison operator. In the text box to the right, select or enter the value that you want the records in the selected field to match. Click the And button to find records that meet two sets of conditions. Click the Or button to find records that meet one condition or another.

You will learn more about entering conditions and specifying criteria in the next section.

Once you've found a subset of records, you can print, edit, sort, or use them to create a chart.

FIGURE 8.5
Notice the Custom AutoFilter dialog box.

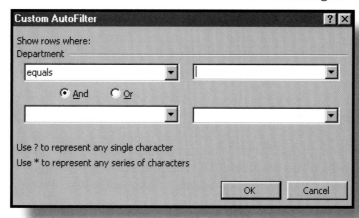

STEP-BY-STEP ▷ 8.4

1. To turn on AutoFilters, click a cell in the data list, click the **Data** menu, click **Filter,** and click **AutoFilter.**

2. To find those employees in the Engineering department, click the **Department** AutoFilter drop-down button, and click **Engineering.** You will find 5 records.

3. To redisplay all the records, click the drop-down button and Department, and click **(All).**

4. To find those employees with the top 5 salaries, click the **Salary** AutoFilter drop-down button and click **(Top 10).** In the Top

10 AutoFilter dialog box, be sure **Top** is selected, click the down button in the spin box to set **5** as the number of records, be sure **Items** is selected, and click **OK.**

5. To sort the records that you found, click cell **G6** and click the **Sort Descending** button.

6. Print the worksheet.

7. To reset the data list to its original order, click the **Data** menu, click **Filter,** and click **Show All.** Then click the **Data** menu again, click **Filter,** and click **AutoFilter.** Click **A5** and then click the **Sort Ascending** button.

Using Advanced Filters

With Advanced Filters, you can conduct more complex searches on your data. Running an advanced filter requires that you set up a criteria range. A **criteria range** specifies the fields you want to search and the criteria (or conditions) that records must meet.

You set up a criteria range in a blank range on the worksheet. A criteria range contains the labels of the field(s) you want to search in its first row, and the search criteria or conditions that the data must meet in the row(s) beneath the field name(s). It is better to simply copy the field name(s) from the list and paste the name(s) in the first row of the criteria range so you are sure they are exact duplicates. There must be at least one blank row between the criteria range and the list.

Types of Criteria

Before we discuss how to run an Advanced Filter, let's review some of the types of criteria you can enter in a criteria range.

- An *Exact value* criteria finds records that match a series of characters. When you use text as a criteria, Excel finds all items that begin with the specified text. For example, if you specify *Pat*, Excel finds *Patsy, Patrick,* and *Patricia.* To match only Pat, type the formula ="=Pat".

   You can use **wildcards** in your search criteria when you want to find records that share some of the same characters, or when you don't know exactly the values for which you're searching. For example, you might want to find all people in a database whose ZIP code begins with 452. You can use the question mark (?) and asterisk (*) wildcards to represent those characters of which you are unsure. The question mark (?) represents any one character in that position; the asterisk represents any number of characters in that position.

- *Comparison criteria* find records that contain a specified value that falls within a range. For example, you might want to find all records where an employee's salary is greater than $30,000. Table 8.2 lists the comparison operators you can use in a criteria.

TABLE 8.2

COMPARISON OPERATORS

OPERATOR	FINDS VALUES THAT ARE
=	Equal to specified value
>	Greater than specified value
<	Less than specified value
>=	Greater than or equal to specified value
<=	Less than or equal to specified value
<>	Not equal to specified value

- *Multiple comparison* criteria find records that meet more than one set of criteria or one set of criteria or another. For example, you might want to find all employees who make more than $30,000 *and* who are in the Engineering department (sometimes referred to as an AND search). Or, you might want to find all employees who make more than $30,000 *or* who are in the Engineering department (sometimes referred to as an OR search).

   Figure 8.6 illustrates the structure of a criteria range with basic comparison criteria entered and multiple comparison criteria. Notice that in an AND search, you enter the criteria in the same row; in an OR search, you enter the criteria in separate rows.

Concept Builders

You can use a field name more than once if you want to find all employees who work in Engineering and/or Central Services.

FIGURE 8.6
Examples of criteria ranges.

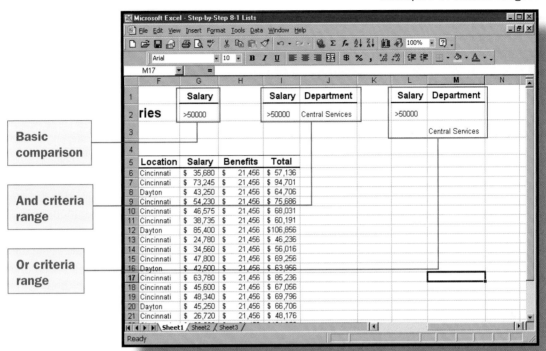

Basic comparison

And criteria range

Or criteria range

- *Computed criteria* display only records that meet computed criteria; for example, those records where the salary is greater than the average salary. You could enter a formula in a cell to calculate the average salary for all the records and then extract only those that exceed that average salary.

Hot Tips

When you enter column headings for criteria, it is better from the standpoint of accuracy to copy the headings than to reenter them.

Running an Advanced Filter

Once you've set up a criteria range, choose Filter on the Data menu and then choose Advanced Filter. The Advanced Filter dialog box appears (see Figure 8.7).

In the Action options, you can choose to Filter the list, in-place, meaning the records that meet the condition will be displayed. Or, you can choose to Copy to another location, which means that the records that meet the condition will be placed in a location you specify in the Copy to text box (option is grayed out until the Copy to another location option is selected).

In the List range text box, enter the range address of the data list (including the field names). You can click the Collapse Dialog button to return to the worksheet to select the range.

In the Criteria range text box, enter the address of the criteria range. Once again, you can click the Collapse Dialog button to select the range.

FIGURE 8.7
Advanced Filter dialog box.

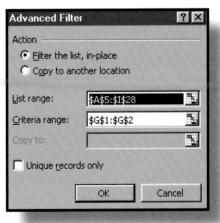

If you want to run another filter, you must clear the Criteria range (and the Copy to range, if there is one) by selecting it, opening the Edit menu, choosing Clear, and then choosing All. Redisplay all records by opening the Data menu, choosing Filter, and choosing Show All.

STEP-BY-STEP ⟹ 8.5

1. To prepare the worksheet for a criteria range, click anywhere in row **3**, click the **Insert** menu, and click **Rows.**

2. To set up criteria to find the employees whose salary is greater than $50,000, click **G5** and click the **Copy** button. Click **G1** and click the **Paste** button. Click **G2**, type **>50,000**, and press the **Enter** key.

3. To run the filter, click a cell in the data list, click the **Data** menu, click **Filter,** and click **Advanced Filter.** Be sure **Filter the list, in-place** is selected and the List range text box displays $A$5:$I$28. Click the **Criteria range** text box, type **G1:G2.** Click **OK.** You should find 8 records.

4. To redisplay all the records, click the **Data** menu, click **Filter,** and click **Show All.**

5. To set up criteria to find employees in the Central Services department who make

more than $50,000, click **E5**, click **Copy,** click **H1,** click **Paste,** and drag the right border of the column H heading to adjust the column width. Click **E6**, click **Copy,** click **H2,** click **Paste.** If the Office Clipboard appears, click its close button.

6. To run the filter, select a cell in the data list. Click the **Data** menu, click **Filter,** and click **Advanced Filter.** In the Advanced Filter dialog box, click **Copy to another location.** The **List range** text box should already display the range $A$5:$I$28. In the **Criteria range** text box, enter **G1:H2.** In the **Copy to** text box, type **A30.** Click **OK.** Scroll to row 30; you should find 1 record.

7. Print the worksheet.

8. To redisplay the original list, select A30:I31, click the **Edit** menu, click **Clear,** and click **All.**

Summarizing Data in a List

Once you've sorted data or filtered it into subgroups or categories, you can use the Subtotals command on the Data menu to calculate subtotal and grand total values for the selected field. You can see the Subtotal dialog box in Figure 8.8.

On the At each change in drop-down list, select the field that contains the groups or categories you want to subtotal. This will be the same field you sort by.

On the Use function drop-down list, select one of Excel's summary functions to subtotal the values. The functions available include Average, Sum, Min, and Max.

In the Add subtotal to list box, select the field or fields whose values you want to subtotal. The subtotal will be inserted just below the group in this field.

 INTERNET HTTP is the acronym for Hypertext Transfer Protocol, which controls the way the Web browser and the Web server communicate.

NOTE:

When you subtotal data, Excel automatically applies its Outline feature to your list. You will learn more about outlining in Lesson 9.

Turn on the Replace current subtotals option to replace any existing subtotals with a new summary. Deselect this option if you want to subtotal groups within a group of records.

Use the Page break between groups option to display each set of subtotaled records on a separate page. The Summary below data option inserts the subtotal below each group it summarizes.

Use the Remove All button to remove all subtotals from the current list.

Excel automatically inserts labels and totals rows and also outlines the list (see Figure 8.9). You will learn more about outlining in the next lesson.

FIGURE 8.8
Use the Subtotal dialog box to designate fields to subtotal.

FIGURE 8.9
Notice the subtotals Excel inserted.

	Emp. #	Last	First	MI	Department	Location	Salary	Benefits	Total
6	50437	Isley	Jasmine		Accounting	Cincinnati	$ 38,735	$ 21,456	$ 60,191
7	50445	Nelson	Damon		Accounting	Cincinnati	$ 48,340	$ 21,456	$ 69,796
8					**Accounting Average**		$ 43,538		
9	50432	Smith	Harry	K	Central Services	Cincinnati	$ 35,680	$ 21,456	$ 57,136
10	50436	Avery	Beverly		Central Services	Cincinnati	$ 46,575	$ 21,456	$ 68,031
11	50439	Perrino	Sue		Central Services	Cincinnati	$ 24,780	$ 21,456	$ 46,236
12	50440	Dillon	Ray		Central Services	Cincinnati	$ 34,560	$ 21,456	$ 56,016
13	50444	Aiken	Glenn		Central Services	Cincinnati	$ 45,600	$ 21,456	$ 67,056
14	50447	Richards	Peter		Central Services	Cincinnati	$ 26,720	$ 21,456	$ 48,176
15	50449	Shell	Samuel	N	Central Services	Cincinnati	$ 34,600	$ 21,456	$ 56,056
16	50453	Nast	Jerry		Central Services	Cincinnati	$ 45,250	$ 21,456	$ 66,706
17					**Central Services Average**		$ 36,721		
18	50433	Jessup	Lee	E	Engineering	Cincinnati	$ 73,245	$ 21,456	$ 94,701
19	50435	Sumner	Jose	A	Engineering	Cincinnati	$ 54,230	$ 21,456	$ 75,686
20	50441	Kathman	Robert	J	Engineering	Cincinnati	$ 47,800	$ 21,456	$ 69,256
21	50443	Chen	Chris		Engineering	Cincinnati	$ 63,780	$ 21,456	$ 85,236
22	50448	Lee	Joe		Engineering	Cincinnati	$ 83,200	$ 21,456	$104,656
23					**Engineering Average**		$ 64,451		
24	50451	King	Ramone	U	Legal	Cincinnati	$ 72,000	$ 21,456	$ 93,456
25	50454	Golden	Carol		Legal	Cincinnati	$ 84,300	$ 21,456	$105,756
26					**Legal Average**		$ 78,150		
27						**Cincinnati Average**	$ 50,553		
28	50450	Edwards	M	A	Accounting	Dayton	$ 39,450	$ 21,456	$ 60,906
29					**Accounting Average**		$ 39,450		
30	50434	Edwards	Mary	E	Central Services	Dayton	$ 43,250	$ 21,456	$ 64,706
31	50442	Surrey	Alana		Central Services	Dayton	$ 42,500	$ 21,456	$ 63,956
32	50452	Terrell	Shane	O	Central Services	Dayton	$ 87,240	$ 21,456	$108,696
33					**Central Services Average**		$ 57,663		
34	50438	Awad	Stephanie		Legal	Dayton	$ 85,400	$ 21,456	$106,856
35	50446	Florez	Miguel		Legal	Dayton	$ 45,250	$ 21,456	$ 66,706
36					**Legal Average**		$ 65,325		
37						**Dayton Average**	$ 57,182		

Sheet1 / Sheet2 / Sheet3 /

Ready

1. To clear the criteria range, select **G1:H2**, click the **Edit** menu, click **Clear,** and click **All.**

2. To group the records by the location and then by department at each location, select any cell in the list, click the **Data** menu, and click **Sort.** Click the **Sort by** drop-down button and click **Location.** Click the **Then by** drop-down button and click **Department.** Be sure **Ascending** order is selected for both and click **OK.**

3. To find the average salary paid at the Cincinnati office and the Dayton office, be sure a cell in the list is selected, click the **Data** menu, and click **Subtotals.** Click the **At each change in** drop-down button and click **Location**; click the **Use function** drop-down button, click **Average**; click **Salary** in the **Add subtotal to** list (if any other fields are checked, deselect them); and be sure the **Replace current subtotals** and **Summary below data** options are checked. Click **OK.**

4. To see the subtotals, scroll through the list and notice that Excel has inserted a Cincinnati Average, Dayton Average, and Grand Average. Double-click the right border of the column F heading to adjust column width.

5. To find the average salary paid in each department at each location, be sure a cell in the data list is active, click the **Data** menu, and click **Subtotals.** Click the **At each change in** drop-down button, click **Department;** click the **Use function** drop-down button, click **Average;** click **Salary** in the **Add subtotal to** list box; and click to deselect the **Replace current subtotals** check box. Click **OK.**

6. To see the subtotals, scroll through the data list and notice that a department average has been inserted and another Grand Average for the departments has been added. The Grand Averages will be the same because Excel summarizes all the values in the Salary field, not the subtotals. Don't worry about the outline markings you see around the worksheet. You will learn more about outlining in the next lesson.

7. Print the worksheet. Save and close the workbook.

Creating a Pivot Table

You can use a pivot table to display and analyze summary information about existing Excel data. A **pivot table** is an interactive tool that lets you summarize or cross-tabulate large amounts of data. For example, you might want to create a pivot table to display summary information showing the total salaries and benefits for individual company locations and for each of the departments at each location. You can rotate the rows and columns in a pivot table to see different summaries of the source data, to filter the data by displaying different pages, or to display details for areas of interest.

To create a pivot table, activate any cell in the data list, open the Data menu and then select PivotTable and PivotChart Report. The PivotTable and PivotChart Wizard opens to walk you through the steps for creating either a pivot table or a pivot chart.

The sheet displayed in Figure 8.10 was created with the PivotTable and PivotChart Wizard.

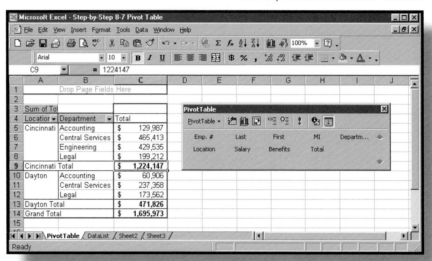

 **NOTE:**

When source data changes, you can use the Refresh Data command on the Data menu or click the Refresh Data button on the PivotTable toolbar to refresh or update data in a pivot table.

STEP-BY-STEP ▷ 8.7

1. Open the workbook **Step-by-Step 8-7 Pivot Table.**

2. To display the PivotTable and PivotChart Wizard, click any cell in the list, click the **Data** menu, and click **PivotTable and PivotChart Report.**

3. To create the pivot table from the data list, be sure **Microsoft Excel list or database** and **PivotTable** options are selected, and click **Next.**

4. To accept the data range *$A$4:$I$27*, click **Next.**

5. To place the pivot table on its own worksheet, click the **New worksheet** option.

6. To display the Layout dialog box, click the **Layout** button.

7. To show the Location field as a row, drag the **Location** button on the right side of the Layout dialog box to the **Row** area of the diagram in the center of the dialog box.

8. To show the Department field as a row, drag and drop the **Department** button to the **Row** area and drop it under **Location.**

9. To add the Total field to the Data area, drag the **Total** button to the **Data** area of the diagram.

10. To close the Layout dialog box, click **OK.**

(continued on next page)

11. To display the pivot table, click **Finish.** Excel displays the pivot table on a new sheet. The PivotTable toolbar appears on the sheet.

12. To bold the totals, click **C9,** hold the **Ctrl** key and click **C13** and **C14,** and click the **Bold** button.

13. To format for currency, select **C5:C14,** click the **Currency Style** button, and then click the **Decrease Decimal** button twice.

14. To rename the sheet containing the table, double-click its sheet tab, type **PivotTable** and press the **Enter** key.

15. Save the workbook as **Pivot Table,** print a copy of the PivotTable sheet, and then close the workbook.

Hot Tips

Remember you can drag a toolbar to a new location.

Summary

You have now learned to set up worksheet data so that it can be sorted, filtered, and subtotaled. You also learned how to use a pivot table to display data.

Try the exercises on the following pages to test how well you remember what you learned. Don't be afraid to go back and look up the answers, because that will help to reinforce what you learned.

LESSON 8 REVIEW QUESTIONS

TRUE / FALSE

Circle the T if the statement is true. Circle the F if it is false.

T F 1. Excel is well suited to maintaining large and complex databases.

T F 2. Each piece of information about an employee in an employee data list is a field.

T F 3. You can always add new fields to a data list.

T F 4. You can easily keep several different data lists on one sheet.

T F 5. You should always have one field with some kind of consecutive numbers so you can sort by that field to return records to their original order.

T F 6. You can separate the field labels from the data list with dashed lines.

T F 7. You should not insert extra spaces at the beginning of a cell because they affect sorting and searching.

T F 8. You cannot edit records on a data form.

T F 9. You cannot edit computed fields on a data form because they are the results of formulas.

T F 10. You can use the Sort command to organize data alphabetically, numerically, or chronologically.

COMPLETION

Complete the following sentences by writing the correct word or words in the blanks provided.

1. You can use the _____ button when you need to sort a list by only a single field in ascending order.

2. If you do not like the result of a sort, use the _____ command on the Edit menu.

3. When you click any cell in the list and use the _____ command to sort data, Excel automatically selects your whole list.

4. All the information about one person or thing in a data list is called a(n) _____.

5. You can use the _____ command on the Data menu to summarize data in a list.

6. You can use _____ to find text values that share some characters but are not exactly alike.

7. You can use _____ operators to display records that fall within certain limits.

8. When you use the _____ type of filter, Excel displays drop-down arrows directly on the field labels.

9. When you use the _____ type of filter, you must create a criteria range on your worksheet.

10. To save a subset of a list, use the _____ command and give the workbook a new name.

LESSON 8 PROJECTS

PROJECT 8A

To practice what you've learned in this lesson, complete the following project:

1. Open the workbook **Project 8-A.**

2. Set up the spreadsheet data in list format so that it can be sorted and filtered.

3. Sort the list in ascending order by the **Salesperson** field. *Ahawk* should be the first record.

4. Sort the list first by **Region** and then by **Salesperson,** both in ascending order. *Arick* should be the first record.

5. Sort the list first by **Region** in ascending order, and then by **Total** in descending order. *Nassium* should be the first record.

6. Run an AutoFilter on the **Total** field that finds the **Top 10** values in the field. Sort the records you find in descending order.

7. Print a copy of the active sheet. Save the workbook as **Sort & Filter Review.**

8. Redisplay all the records and turn off AutoFilter.

9. Run an Advanced Filter that finds all the salespersons who earned commissions of $50,000 or more. Copy the records you find to cell **A28.** Sort the filtered records in descending order by the **Commission Paid** field.

10. Print the active sheet. Then save and close the workbook.

PROJECT 8B

To practice what you've learned in this lesson, complete the following project:

1. Open the workbook **Project 8-B.**

2. Sort the data list by the **Region** field in ascending order and then by the **Total** field in descending order.

3. Insert a **Sum** subtotal in the **Total** field that summarizes values by region.

Extra Challenges

Use Help to find information on refreshing data in a pivot table. Review and print the Help topic(s) you find.

4. Insert an **Average** subtotal in the **Total** field that finds the average Total sales by region. Make sure you do *not* replace the current subtotals.

5. Format the cells containing the region averages and totals so they stand out.

6. Print the active sheet. Save and then close the workbook.

PROJECT 8C

Open a new workbook, display the Web toolbar, and click the Search the Web button. Use a search engine to find a database of ZIP codes. Select a major city in your home state and copy the ZIP codes to a worksheet or print them from the Web site. Don't forget to disconnect when you are finished.

CRITICAL THINKING ACTIVITY

SCANS

Create a data list for at least 25 of your friends, classmates, or acquaintances. Enter their first and last names (and middle names if you know them), street addresses, cities, states, postal codes, area codes, and telephone numbers. Format the data and set it up as a list. Sort the list by area code. Sort the list by postal code. Save the workbook as **Critical Thinking Activity 8,** print the sheet, and close the workbook.

EXPLORING EXCEL'S DATA ANALYSIS AND OTHER TOOLS

OBJECTIVES

When you complete this lesson, you will be able to:

■ Create and work with a worksheet outline.

■ Use the Goal Seek feature.

■ Build a data table.

■ Create Scenarios.

■ Use Solver.

■ Use the Text to Columns command.

⏱ **Estimated Time: 1½ hours**

Introduction

Excel has various tools you can use for analyzing data and generating forecasts. In this lesson you will learn how to use Excel's Goal Seek, Scenario Manager, Solver, and data table features. Each of these features has many options not covered in this book. Remember how easy it is to use the Help feature when you need more information about using a feature.

Creating a Worksheet Outline

As you learned in the last lesson, Excel's outlining feature kicks in when you insert subtotals in worksheet data. An outline lets you hide or display as much detail as you want. For example, if you only want subtotal and grand total amounts to show on the worksheet, you can temporarily hide the rest of the data by clicking an outline symbol.

If outline symbols are not displayed on a worksheet, open the Data menu, choose Group and Outline, and then choose Auto Outline. To remove the outline symbols, open the Data menu, choose Group and Outline, and then choose Clear Outline.

 **NOTE:**

You can use the Outline feature only when your worksheet contains detailed data such as that from the Subtotals or Consolidate commands.

 **Hot Tips**

If your outline has four levels, you can hide the fourth by clicking the row or column level symbol 3. To hide all details, click the first level symbol 1.

Outline symbols appear to the left of the row numbers if you have summarized rows of data, above the column letters if you have summarized columns of data, or both if you've summarized rows and columns of data. Figure 9.1 identifies outline symbols on the worksheet.

You can click the Hide Detail symbol to temporarily remove detail data, which is the data used to generate a subtotal or consolidation. Use the Show Detail symbol to redisplay detail data. You can also use the row or column level symbols to show or hide a specific level of an outline. To show a specific level, click the row or column level symbol identifying the level. To hide a specific level, click the symbol preceding the row or column level you want to hide.

FIGURE 9.1
Outlining worksheet data.

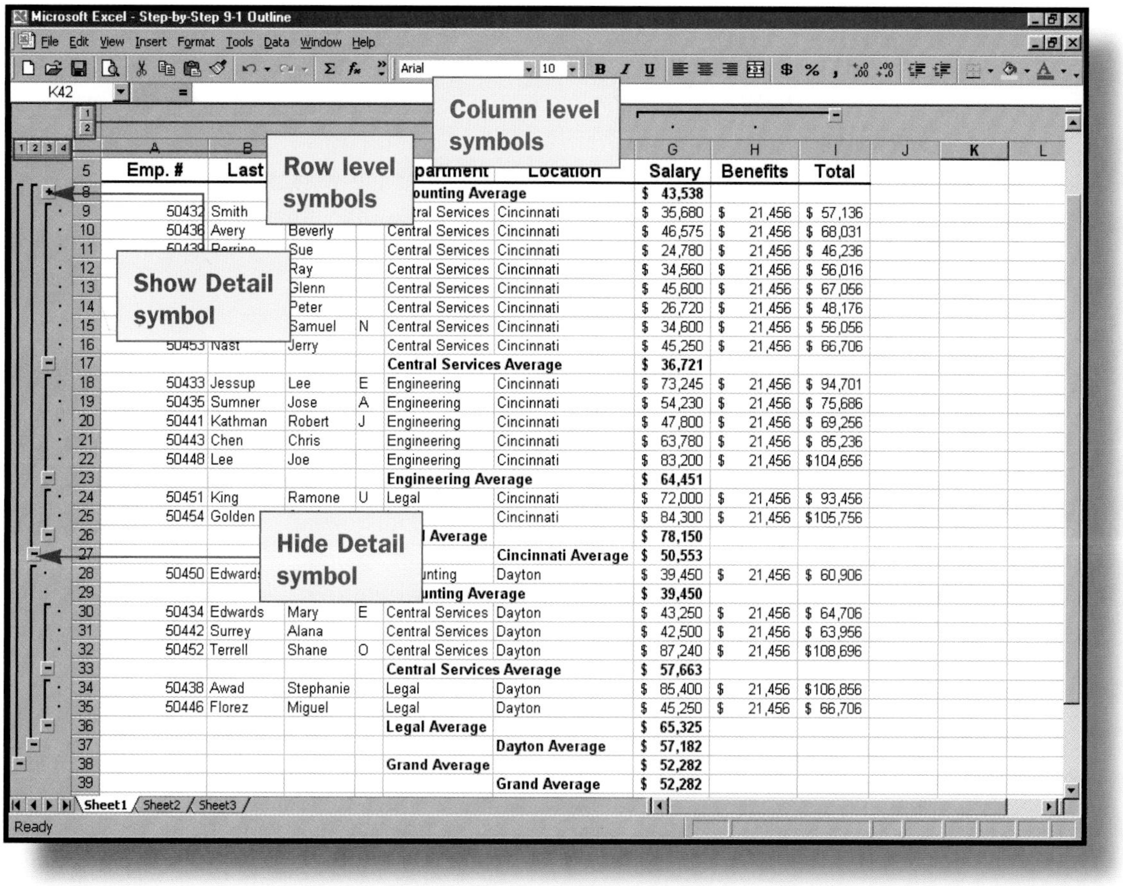

STEP-BY-STEP ▷ 9.1

1. Open the workbook **Step-by-Step 9-1 Outline.**

2. To display the outline symbols, click the **Data** menu, click **Group and Outline,** and click **Auto Outline.**

3. To hide the Accounting detail data in the Cincinnati location, click the **Hide Detail** symbol for **Accounting Average** in row **8.** Notice the symbol changes to the **Show Detail** symbol.

(continued on next page)

4. To redisplay the Accounting detail data in the Cincinnati location, click the **Accounting Average Show Detail** symbol.

5. To hide the detail data in columns **G** and **H,** click the **Hide Detail** symbol in column **I.** Redisplay the data by clicking the **Show Detail** symbol in column **I.**

6. To hide all the detail data and show only the subtotals, click the **row level 3** symbol. (You will notice that the record for M.A. Edwards is not hidden with the rest of the detail data. That's because it's the only record in the Accounting Average subtotal group for the Dayton location.)

7. To hide the M.A. Edwards row and the Department Grand Average, click the row **28 heading,** click the **Format** menu, click **Row,** and click **Hide.** Then click row **38** and hide it using the same procedure.

8. To hide empty columns, select columns **A, B, C,** and **D,** click the **Format** menu, click **Column,** and click **Hide.** Then select columns **H** and **I,** click the **Format** menu, select **Column,** and click **Hide.**

9. Print the worksheet. Then close the workbook without saving it.

Using Goal Seek

When you know the result you want a formula to return but not the input value needed to produce the result, use Excel's Goal Seek command on the Tools menu. Goal Seek prompts you to adjust the value of one cell to generate the desired result in another cell. You can see a worksheet set up to return the monthly payment on a $75,000 mortgage in Figure 9.2. The formula for the Goal Seek is in the Monthly Payment cell.

FIGURE 9.2
The price in the worksheet is not a formula.

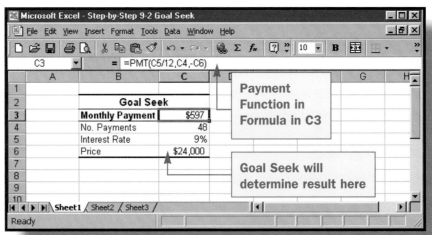

You could use that worksheet and the Goal Seek command to find out how much you could pay for a car if you could afford to pay $400 per month.

To display the Goal Seek dialog box (see Figure 9.3), open the Tools menu and choose Goal Seek.

Enter the address of the cell that contains the formula you want to solve in the Set cell text box. In the To value text box, type the amount you can pay. In the By changing cell text box, enter the address of the cell whose value can be adjusted to achieve the desired result. The Goal Seek Status dialog box appears indicating the solution if one is found.

FIGURE 9.3
Adjust values to find a known result in the Goal Seek dialog box.

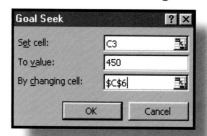

STEP-BY-STEP ▷ 9.2

1. Open the workbook **Step-by-Step 9-2 Goal Seek.**

2. To display the Goal Seek dialog box, click the **Tools** menu, and click **Goal Seek.**

3. To determine how much you can afford to pay for a new car if you can afford $450 a month for 48 months at 9% interest, type **C3** (the cell containing the formula) in the **Set cell** text box.

4. To enter the known result, type **450** in the **To value** text box.

5. To reference the cell whose value you want to change (monthly payment) to achieve the desired result, press the **Tab** key and click **C6** to enter it in the **By changing cell** text box. Click **OK.**

6. To close the Goal Seek Status dialog box, click **OK.** According to Goal Seek, your monthly payment of $450 enables you to buy an $18,083 car.

7. Print a copy of the sheet.

Using a Data Table

You can use a data table to see how changing specific values in formulas affects the results of those formulas. Use a data table as a shortcut for calculating multiple variations and displaying the results of all the calculations together on the worksheet.

You can enter different values either for one variable or for two variables. For example, you might want to figure out the monthly payment on a new car using varying interest rates, where the interest rate represents the one variable; or you might want to figure out the monthly payment using varying interest rates *and* varying loan amounts.

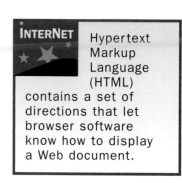
INTERNET Hypertext Markup Language (HTML) contains a set of directions that let browser software know how to display a Web document.

To set up a data table:

■ Enter the formula whose values you want to change in a blank cell.

■ For a one-variable table, enter the input values (those values you want to substitute for the variable value in the formula) in consecutive cells directly below the formula cell, *or* directly to the right of the formula cell. For a two-variable table, enter one set of input values below the formula cell *and* the other to the right of the formula cell.

■ Select the range containing the formula and the input values.

■ Open the *Data* menu and then choose *Table*. The Table dialog box is displayed in Figure 9.4.

If you set up input values directly to the right of the formula cell, type the address of the cell containing the variable value in the Row input cell text box. If you set up input values directly below the formula cell, type the address of the cell containing the variable value in the Column input cell text box. If you set up a two-variable table, type the addresses of both cells containing the variable values.

You will now create a data table to see how monthly payments for a new car will change with varying interest rates and varying number of payments.

FIGURE 9.4
Notice the data table containing various numbers of payments and percentage rates.

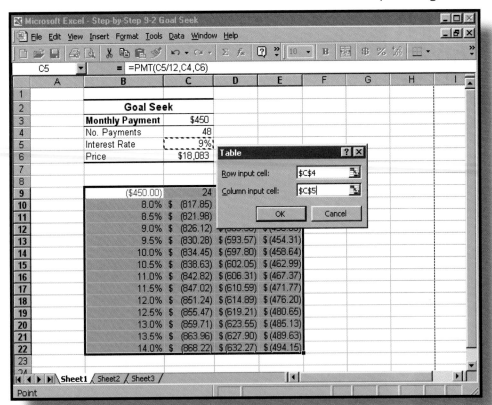

STEP-BY-STEP ▷ 9.3

1. To place the formula in the first cell of the data table, click **B9**, type **=PMT(C5/12,C4,–C6),** and press the **Enter** key.

2. To enter input values representing varying interest rates, be sure cell **B10** is the active cell, type **.08,** press the **Enter** key. type **.085,** press the **Enter** key. type **.09,** and press the **Enter** key.

3. To format the data as percentages with one decimal place, select **B10:B11,** click the **Percent Style** button, and then click the **Increase Decimal** button.

4. To fill the data to 14.0% in cell **B21,** be sure the range **B10:B11** is still selected, drag the fill handle to cell **B21.**

5. To enter input values representing a varying number of payments, click cell **C9,** type **24,** press the **Tab** key, type **36,** press **Tab,** type **48,** and press the **Enter** key.

6. To indicate input cells, select the range **B9:E21,** click the **Data** menu, and click **Table.**

7. To reference the input cell for the row of input values, type **C4** in the **Row input cell** text box.

8. To reference the input cell for the column of input values, type **C5** in the **Column input cell** text box. Click **OK.** Excel instantly calculates the monthly payments based on varying interest rates and a varying number of payments.

9. To format the data table, select the range **C10:E21** and click the **Currency** button.

10. Print the worksheet and then close the workbook without saving changes.

Using Scenarios

You can use the Scenarios command to create and save sets of input values that produce different results. Scenarios are often used in developing budgets where the annual income or revenues are not certain. For instance, you can set up scenarios that determine the most likely, best-case, and worst-case scenarios.

IMPORTANT:

You must name and save the initial values in your worksheet as a scenario if you want to be able to restore those values.

To display the Scenario Manager dialog box, open the Tools menu and then choose Scenarios (see Figure 9.5).

FIGURE 9.5
Notice the three scenarios and the worst case appears on the worksheet.

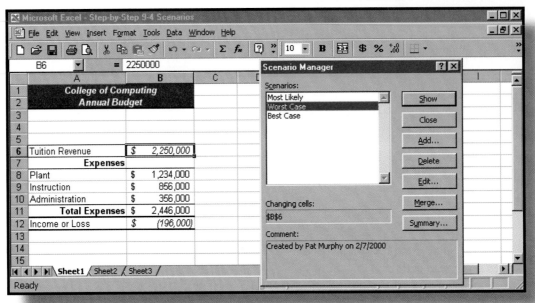

Use the Add button in the Scenario Manager dialog box to display the Add Scenario dialog box (see Figure 9.6). Enter a name for each scenario in the Scenario name text box. Type the address of the cell or cells that contain the value or values you want to change. In the Scenario Values dialog box, enter the value you want to substitute in the text box.

To review each scenario, click the scenario name in the Scenario Manager dialog box and then click Show. If you want to display the scenarios on a worksheet in the workbook, click the Summary button in the Scenario Manager dialog box. In the Scenario Summary dialog box, determine if you want to create a Scenario summary or a Scenario PivotTable. Excel places the scenarios on a new sheet in the workbook.

FIGURE 9.6
You can see the Add Scenario dialog box.

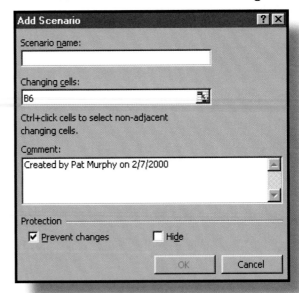

S TEP-BY-STEP ⟹ 9.4

1. Open **Step-by-Step 9-4 Scenarios.** Annual budget figures for the College of Computing are displayed on the worksheet, and the tuition revenue is the unknown amount.

2. To set up scenarios, click **B6** as the changing cell, click the **Tools** menu, and click **Scenarios.** In the Scenario Manager dialog box, click **Add.**

3. To set up the current values as the most-likely scenario, type **Most Likely** as the Scenario name, and click **OK.** In the Scenario Values dialog box, leave the initial value as is and click **OK.**

4. To add a worst-case scenario, click the **Add** button, type **Worst Case,** notice B6 is still entered in the **Changing cells** text box, and click **OK.** In the Scenario Values dialog box, type **2,250,000** (which represents the predicted low Tuition Revenue figure), and click **OK.**

5. To add a best-case scenario, click the **Add** button, type **Best Case,** notice B6 is still the changing cell, and click **OK.** In the Scenario Values dialog box, type **2,750,000** (which represents the predicted high Tuition Revenue figure), and click **OK.**

6. To display the worst-case scenario, click **Worst Case** in the Scenario Manager dialog box and click **Show.** Notice the negative value in cell B12.

7. To display the best case scenario, click **Best Case** and click **Show.** Again, notice the result in cell B12.

8. To redisplay the current values, click **Most Likely** in the Scenario Manager Dialog box and click **Show.**

9. To summarize the scenarios on a separate worksheet, click **Summary.** In the Scenario Summary dialog box, make sure **Scenario summary** is selected and click **OK.** The scenarios are summarized on a new Scenario Summary worksheet that Excel inserts at the beginning of the workbook.

10. Print the summary worksheet.

11. To return to the original worksheet, click **Sheet1.**

12. Save the workbook.

Using Solver

You can use the Solver command to find the optimum value for a cell by adjusting the values of several related or referenced cells. For example, you might want to determine how you can adjust expense figures in various categories in order to achieve a zero loss.

To use Solver:

■ Click the Tools menu and then click Solver. The Solver Parameters dialog box appears, as shown in Figure 9.7.

■ In the Set Target Cell text box, enter the cell that will display the optimum value. The cell must contain a formula.

■ In the Equal To options, select Max if you want the optimum value to be as large as possible; click Min if you want it to be as small as possible; or click Value of and enter the optimum value in the text box to set the value yourself.

■ In the By Changing Cells text box, type the address of each cell whose value can be changed in order to achieve the optimum result. If there is more than one cell and they are not adjacent, separate each address with a comma.

If you want to apply constraints to any of the data used by Solver, add them in the Subject to the Constraints text box, which will display the Add Constraint dialog box (see Figure 9.8).

FIGURE 9.7
You can see the Solver Parameters dialog box.

FIGURE 9.8
Notice the Add Constraint dialog box.

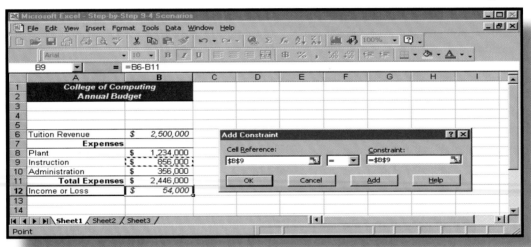

You can choose to keep the Solver's solution on the worksheet or to restore the original values. If you want to save the solution as a scenario, click the Save Scenario button and type a scenario name. You can then review the scenario in the Scenario Manager, as you did in the preceding section.

S TEP-BY-STEP 9.5

1. To alter the College of Computing's expenses so that you can achieve an optimum Income or Loss of 0, click the **Sheet1** tab, click **B12,** click the **Tools** menu, and click **Solver.**

2. To set the optimum value for cell B12, click **Value of** in the Equal to options and be sure **0** is entered in the text box.

3. To designate the cells whose values can be adjusted to achieve the optimum result, click the **By Changing Cells** box and type **B8,B10** (indicating that the Plant and Administration expenses can be adjusted).

4. To enter a constraint that prohibits the Instruction expense from being changed, click in the **Subject to the Constraints** box, click **Add,** type **B9,** click the **Operator** drop-down button, click **=,** click the Constraint box, type **B9** again in the **Constraint** box, and click **OK.**

5. To solve the budget problem, click the **Solve** button. The Solver Results dialog box displays and the solution is automatically cal-

culated on the worksheet data. Notice Excel solved the budget surplus by increasing the Plant and Administration expenses.

6. To save the Solver solution as another scenario, click **Save Scenario,** enter **Break Even** as the Scenario Name, click **OK.** To return the original values to the worksheet, click the **Restore Original Values** option and click **OK.**

7. To display the Break Even scenario, click the **Tools** menu, click **Scenarios,** click **Break Even,** click **Show,** and click **Close.**

8. Print the worksheet. Save and then close the workbook.

Converting Text to Columns

If you copy data into Excel from another application, you may find several columns of data condensed into one column. Use the Text to Columns command on the Data menu to start the Convert Text to Columns Wizard. The Wizard walks you through the steps necessary to parse the data—distribute text from one column to a number of columns.

You can, for instance, select a column containing first and last names and separate the names into two columns (see Figure 9.9).

FIGURE 9.9
The names in Column A are distributed into two columns.

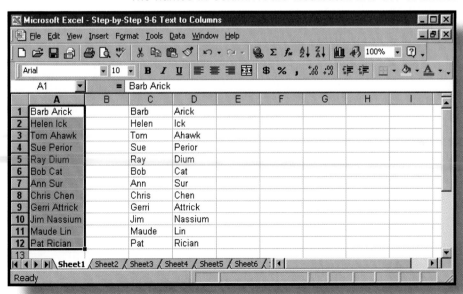

1. Open **Step-by-Step 9-6 Text to Column.**

2. To parse the data in the cells with the Convert Text to Columns Wizard, select **A1:A12,** click the **Data** menu, and click **Text to Columns.**

3. To specify that your data is delimited, be sure the **Delimited** option is selected and then click **Next.**

4. To specify the delimiters, click the **Space**

option to select it and click any other options that have a check mark to deselect them. Then click **Next.**

5. To accept the General data format and display the columns beginning in C1, select the **Destination** text box, type **C1,** and click **Finish.**

6. Save and close the worksheet.

Using the Auditing Feature

Use the Auditing command on the Tools menu or the tracer buttons on the Auditing toolbar to display the precedents, dependents, and data flow path for a cell. The auditing features are very helpful when you need to trace problems on your worksheets.

You can see the Auditing toolbar and a tracer arrow in Figure 9.10.

Six of the buttons on the Auditing toolbar provide you with an easy way to use tracers for troubleshooting on your worksheet. The toolbar also has a New Comment, a Circle Invalid Data, and a Clear Validation Circles button.

The precedent, dependent, and error tracers track data flow by drawing arrows that connect the active cell with related cells on the worksheet (see Figure 9.10). The arrows always point toward the formula.

You can only trace one cell at a time, but tracer arrows for all cells you trace remain on the screen until you click the Remove All Arrows button or edit a formula or change the structure of the worksheet.

FIGURE 9.10
The Auditing toolbar.

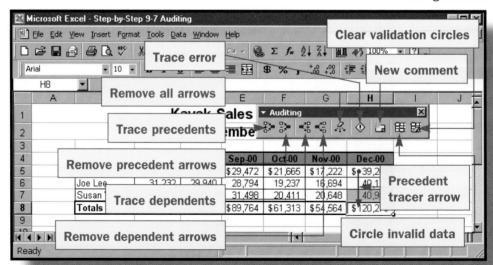

You can use the Auditing command's Trace Error option or the Trace Error button on the toolbar to find an error that might be the cause of error values on your worksheet. The Trace Error command works only when the active cell contains an error. Error values in a chain produce red arrows.

STEP-BY-STEP ▷ 9.7

1. Open **Step-by-Step 9-7 Auditing** workbook.

2. To find all precedents for H8, click **H8,** click the **Tools** menu, click **Auditing,** and click **Trace Precedents.**

3. To display the Auditing toolbar, click the **Tools** menu, click **Auditing** and click **Show Auditing Toolbar.**

4. To find all dependents for G6, click **G6,** click the **Trace Dependents** button on the Auditing toolbar.

5. To remove the tracer arrows, click the **Remove All Arrows** button.

6. To close the Auditing toolbar, click its **Close** button.

7. Close the file without saving.

Summary

You have now learned how to create a worksheet outline, and how to conduct different types of analysis on data using Goal Seek, data tables, Scenarios, and Solver. You have also learned to change text to columns and to use the Auditing feature. Be sure to use the Excel Help system to get more information about features you reviewed in this lesson.

Try the exercises on the following pages to test how well you remember what you learned. Don't be afraid to go back and look up the answers, because that will help to reinforce what you learned.

LESSON 9 REVIEW QUESTIONS

TRUE / FALSE

Circle the T if the statement is true. Circle the F if it is false.

T F 1. Outline symbols appear to the left of the row numbers if you have summarized columns of data.

T F 2. When you click the Hide Detail outline symbols, you permanently remove the detail data.

T F 3. To hide a specific level in an outline, click the symbol preceding the row or column level you want to hide.

T F 4. You can move a dialog box by dragging it by its title bar to another location.

T F 5. For a one-variable data table, enter the input values in consecutive cells directly below and to the left of the formula cell, or directly above and to the right of the formula cell.

T F 6. Scenarios are useful when you want to develop best- and worst-case outcomes.

T F 7. The only way to display a scenario on the worksheet is by clicking it in the Scenario Manager dialog box and then clicking Show.

T F 8. Goal Seek prompts you to adjust the value of one cell to generate the desired result in another cell.

T F 9. You can use the Solver command on the Data menu to summarize large amounts of data from many sources.

T F 10. You can save a Solver solution as a data table.

COMPLETION

Complete the following sentences by writing the correct word or words in the blanks provided.

1. To remove the outline symbols from a worksheet, select the Data menu, click _____, and then click _____.

2. Outline symbols appear to the left of the row numbers if you have summarized _____ of data, and above the column letters if you have summarized _____ of data.

3. When you know the result you want a formula to return but not the input value, use the _____ tool.

4. You can use a(n) _____ to see how changing specific values in formulas affects the results of those formulas.

5. To create a data table, select the formula cell and input values on the worksheet and then click _____ on the _____ menu.

6. For a one-variable data table, enter the input values in consecutive cells directly _____ the formula cell, or directly to the right of the formula cell.

7. Use the _____ command to create and save sets of input values that produce different results.

8. To review each scenario, click the scenario name in the Scenario Manager dialog box and then click _____.

9. You can use the _____ tool when you want to find the optimum value for a cell by adjusting the values of several cells.

10. To start Solver, select it on the _____ menu.

LESSON 9 PROJECTS

PROJECT 9A

To practice what you've learned in this lesson, complete the following project:

1. Open the workbook **Project 9-A.**

2. Display the outline symbols on the subtotaled data.

3. Hide everything but the **Grand Average** and **Grand Total** rows.

4. Redisplay all the data.

5. Hide the detail data for all the regions except the **South,** which represents the largest total sales.

6. Hide the detail data for the **South** region and for the **JetSkis, Kayaks,** and **Windsurfers** columns.

7. Select the range **A1:A2** and move it to **B1:B2.**

8. Temporarily hide column **A.** Make any formatting adjustments you feel are necessary.

9. Print the worksheet. Save and then close the workbook.

PROJECT 9B

To practice what you've learned in this lesson, complete the following project:

SCANS

1. Open the workbook **Project 9-B.**

2. Find the monthly payment for a **$15,400** loan at **7** percent interest for **five** years. (Remember *term* refers to the number of months, not the number of years).

3. Use **Goal Seek** to figure out how much you can reduce the number of payments you make on the loan (term) by increasing your monthly payment to **$425.** Round the result to the nearest whole number.

4. Save the workbook as **Analysis Review** and print a copy of the sheet.

5. Create three scenarios for the data that show how your monthly payment will change when the loan amount is changed:

   a. Name the first scenario **Current,** reference cell **D5** as the changing cell, and make sure **15400** is the value to be entered in the changing cell.

   b. Name the second scenario **Small Loan,** reference **D5** as the changing cell, and enter **10000** as the value in the changing cell.

   c. Name the third scenario **Big Loan,** reference **D5** as the changing cell, and enter **16000** as the value in the changing cell.

   d. Show each of the scenarios on the sheet. Leave the **Big Loan** scenario displayed and create a **Scenario Summary** sheet that shows all three scenarios.

Extra Challenges

Use Help to search for information on Excel's outlining feature. Review and print the Help topic(s) you find.

6. Print a copy of the **Scenario Summary** sheet.

7. On **Sheet1,** use **Solver** to figure out what interest rate and term you must have in order to achieve an optimum monthly payment of **$400.** Save the Solver solution as a scenario named **Optimum.** Select to restore the original values to the worksheet.

8. Show the **Optimum** scenario on the worksheet, decrease the decimals for the interest rate amount, and then print a copy of the sheet.

9. **Save** and then close the workbook.

PROJECT 9C

Open a blank workbook to determine the future value of a savings account that pays at a constant 3% annual interest rate in which you deposit $50 per month for 10 years. *Hint:* Use the **FV** (Future Value) function in the financial category and use a monthly interest rate.

CRITICAL THINKING ACTIVITY

SCANS

Open the workbook **Critical Thinking Activity 9.** Copy the data to another range on the worksheet and change the loan amount to **$25,000** and change the term to **five** years. Create scenarios on the original loan data that show the current data and the change in payments when the interest rate is at **7** percent and **10** percent. Summarize the scenarios on a Scenario Summary sheet.

See what the difference is in the payment with a **15 year** loan. Again, you should create a scenario using the current loan data and another using the 15-year loan amount. Save the scenarios to a second Scenario Summary sheet.

Print, save, and then close the workbook.

Good luck and enjoy Excel!